"Although there have been a number of attempts recently to combine Buddhism and Marxism, this is the first full length systematic demonstration of how these two perspectives are complementary and can mutually supplement each other to guide the political praxis that would create a more humane world. The author skilfully inserts elements of anarchism in order to challenge the top-down political thinking that has all too often infected Marxism and presents a powerful argument for the necessity of building a bottom-up revolutionary movement that would pre-figure a post-capitalist society. Overall, the author draws on an impressive range of philosophical, psychological, and political resources to show how effective social political action requires a fundamental shift in our way of seeing and of being in the world."

Karsten J. Struhl, *New School for Public Engagement, New York, USA*

CAPITALISM—ITS NATURE AND ITS REPLACEMENT

In this third decade of the 21st century, deep problems plague our world. Many people lack adequate nutrition, health care, and education because—while there is enough wealth for everyone to meet these basic needs—most of it is tightly controlled by precious few. Global warming causes droughts, floods, rising sea levels, and soon the forced migrations of millions of people. In this book, philosopher Graham Priest explains why we find ourselves in this situation, defines the nature of the problems we face, and explains how we might solve and move beyond our current state. The first part of this book draws on Buddhist philosophy, Marx' analysis of capitalism, and their complementary role in explaining our present crisis and the events that led us here. In the second part of the book, Priest turns to the much harder question of how one might go about creating a more rational and humane world. Here, he draws again on Buddhist and Marxist ideas as well as some key aspects of anarchist thought. His discussion of the need for bottom-up control of production, power, ideology, and an emerging awareness of our interdependence is a must-read for anyone who cares about the future of the planet and our latent capacity to care for each other.

Key Features

- Explains the necessary elements of Marxist, Buddhist, and anarchist thought—no background knowledge of political theory or Buddhism is necessary
- Shows how Buddhist and Marxist notions of persons are complementary
- Convincingly shows capitalism's role in creating current socio-economic problems
- Provides an analysis of the corrosiveness of top-down power structures and why they should be eliminated in a post-capitalist state
- Discusses capitalism's role in war, environmental degradation, and race and gender-based oppression.

Graham Priest is Distinguished Professor of Philosophy at the City University of New York Graduate Center. His books include *In Contradiction* (1987, 2006), *Beyond the Limits of Thought* (1995, 2002), *Introduction to Non-classical Logic* (2001, 2008), *Towards Non-being* (2005, 2016), *Doubt Truth to Be a Liar* (2006), *One* (2014), and *The Fifth Corner of Four* (2018).

CAPITALISM—ITS NATURE AND ITS REPLACEMENT

Buddhist and Marxist Insights

Graham Priest

Routledge
Taylor & Francis Group

NEW YORK AND LONDON

First published 2022
by Routledge
605 Third Avenue, New York, NY 10158

and by Routledge
2 Park Square, Milton Park, Abingdon, Oxon, OX14 4RN

Routledge is an imprint of the Taylor & Francis Group, an informa business

© 2022 Graham Priest

Library of Congress Cataloging-in-Publication Data
A catalog record for this book has been requested

ISBN: 978-1-032-04911-3 (hbk)
ISBN: 978-1-032-04910-6 (pbk)
ISBN: 978-1-003-19514-6 (ebk)

DOI: 10.4324/9781003195146

Typeset in Bembo
by Apex CoVantage, LLC

*In solidarity with all those who strive genuinely to
make the world a better place for all*

CONTENTS

Die Philosophen haben die Welt nur verschieden interpretiert; es kommt aber darauf an, sie zu verändern.

Marx, 11th Thesis on Feuerbach

PROLOGUE

I finished writing *One*[1] in 2013. The last two chapters were about Buddhist ethics, and the very last section of the second of these (15.10, 'Matters Socio-political') was about the socio-political implications of the ethics. It was clear to me that the ethics undergirds a trenchant critique of the sort of societies that most now live in. It was also clear to me that a major cause of much of the present unhappy state of affairs is capitalism, and especially its structural requirement which produces the agglomeration of capital, so that fewer and fewer come to own more and more.[2] But beyond that, I found myself able to make only a few very sketchy comments concerning how one might move the world to a better place.

The matter is one I have wrestled with constantly since I finished *One*. It is an exceptionally hard subject. For a start, it depends on empirical questions concerning, for example, human psychology, social structures, their dynamics, and the interaction between individuals and social structures. Such issues are not going to be settled in the philosopher's armchair (or by the simplistic and worthless pontifications of the apologists of capitalism). But worse than this, societies are not closed systems, in the sense that one can sometimes deal with in physics. Even if how a society runs in itself has been sorted out, each society is subject to exogenous factors—such as those of its history, international affairs, and the environment—the effects of which are, to a very large extent, unforeseeable. Compared with this, the problems of logic and even metaphysics are simple—and god (any

---

1. Priest (2014).
2. If one had any doubts about capitalism producing such lopsidedness, it has since been demonstrated with cold, hard facts by orthodox economists such as Piketty (2013) and Stiglitz (2019).

one you like) knows, these can be hard enough. Still, for better or for worse, this book contains the results of my reflections.

The book has two parts. The first thing needed if the world is to be moved in a more rational and humane socio-economic direction is an understanding of the hows and the whys of it now. Providing this is the aim of the first part of the book. The analysis draws essentially on ideas from two philosophical traditions: those of Buddhism and Marxism. I discuss the relevant aspects of those two philosophies, and how they can be seen as providing complementary parts of the understanding required. And let me make it clear straight away that the Buddhist ideas in play here are philosophical ones, not religious ones. Buddhism as a religion is not on the agenda of the book.

In the second part of the book I turn to the much harder question of what is to be done in the light of this analysis. This part of the book is much more tentative; indeed, I think it must be so, for appropriate action is always going to depend on what we learn as we go along—both our successes and our failures. The discussion in this part of the book draws on the ideas articulated in the first half of the book, but also on a number of ideas from anarchist philosophy. It will take us into various inter-related issues concerning, amongst other things, ideology, education, power, and the human psyche.

Many matters in the book involve complex empirical questions concerning economics, psychology, race, and other matters on which there are substantial literatures. I wish I had had the time to master all of it before writing the book. However, I don't have the luxury of a decade or two to spend in the Reading Room of the British Museum—or whatever the contemporary equivalent of this is. I hope the reader will forgive me if there are parts of the discussion which might have been more authoritative. I trust that what I do say on these matters is at least not too far off the mark. As will be clear, I have learned much from the thought of others. In many parts of the book I have made use of (sometimes extensive) quotation. I have done so in order to allow others to speak in their own voices. (Italics in all quotations are original.)

And now, to head off any misconceptions, let me make it plain what the book is *not*. This is not a book about Marxism or Buddhism (or anarchism). For those who want introductions to those areas, or scholarly analyses of them, there are plenty to choose from. Nor am I attempting to defend these traditions as such. Indeed, there are parts of the various traditions that I do not endorse, as will become clear.

Nor is the aim of the book to show that these traditions are compatible. Clearly, there are tensions, if not flat-out incompatibilities, between aspects of the three traditions—and even *within* each of the three traditions themselves. I appeal to the ideas I do, not because of their provenances, but because I think that they are true. (And yes, I don't have any problem with the notion of truth. The Earth is not flat; the human species has evolved; and Donald Trump was corrupt.

Anyone who thinks otherwise is sadly benighted.) Indeed, I do not just explain the relevant ideas, I argue for them.

Neither is this a book of scholarship. I think that the interpretations of the parts of the various thinkers and philosophical traditions I offer are correct, but I have not tried to mount detailed defences of this. If people wish to tell me that this is not an accurate account of Marxism or Buddhism or whatever, I don't care. This is a book of socio-political philosophy, not of the history of philosophy. Indeed, though there are footnotes with references, so that those who wish may follow up aspects of the discussion, I have tried to resist the temptation (in as much as an academic can!) of going off down scholarly rabbit holes. Scholarly discussions of historical traditions or thinkers are not only irrelevant, they would detract from the main aim of the book.

That aim is to help move the world in a better direction, if only a little. This involves seeing that capitalism is a major factor in so many of the unsatisfactory aspects of our contemporary world, and of seeing how it might be dismantled. Of course, removing capitalism will not remove all of the unsatisfactory aspects of our contemporary world. But the aim of the book is not the Quixotic one of designing a utopia—though capitalism is not unconnected with other major problems the world faces, such as those concerning the environment, racism, and war, as we shall see.

I have now been thinking about these ideas for several years. In the process I have discussed them with many friends and colleagues.[3] I have greatly benefitted from thoughts, criticism, and suggestions from many people in the process. I warmly thank them all. In the the first half of 2020 I taught courses based on a draft manuscript of the book at the CUNY Graduate Center and the University of Melbourne. I received much thoughtful feedback from those taking the courses, which improved many aspects of the book. I owe my students a special thanks. The same comment applies to Niko Strobach, Martin Pleitz (especially), and their students. At the start of 2021, Niko and Martin taught a course at the University of Münster using the manuscript. This was followed by a two-day (online) workshop at which many aspects of the book were discussed. A special thanks goes to my old friend, Jay Garfield, who gave me his written comments—perceptive as ever—on an earlier draft of the book; and to two referees for Routledge, who, I learned later were Terry Gibbs and Karsten Struhl. A warm thank you also goes to Andy Beck, the Routledge editor with whom I worked, for his friendly and professional advice, and to the rest of the Routledge team involved in the production of the book. Finally, the book owes a great deal to my partner, Anna Malavisi. Not only have our many discussions and her thoughtful comments made this a better book, her encouragement has helped me to persevere when it all seemed too hard.

---

3. I have given talks based on some of the the ideas at venues in New York, Bonn, Bethlehem (PA), Havana, Singapore, Melbourne, and Kolkata.

Many times I have felt the problems with which the book deals to be completely intractable; but I have been motivated to pursue them because of their immense import—well beyond the cloistered concerns of academe. They deal with things that concern us all deeply: our living conditions and what these do to/for us and those around us. I am well aware that the book is still a rather inadequate essay on the matters at hand. I wish I had more to offer. But such as I presently have, this book offers it. If nothing else, I hope that it will make those who read it reflect, discuss, and, with others, push the project forward in thought and deed.

The first book I wrote, *In Contradiction*,[4] bore the dedication:

> To the end of exploitation and oppression in all its forms and wherever it may be.

Readers of the book would, however, have found nothing much relevant to the dedication. I hope that readers of this book will find otherwise.

Graham Priest
New York, NY
May 2021

---

4. Priest (1987).

PART I

Right View

As far as social economic theory goes, I am a Marxist.

Tenzin Gyatso, His Holiness the 14th Dalai Lama[1]

1. https://www.watch?v=D/watch?v=DhvlnC-oKEw

DOI: 10.4324/9781003195146-1

1

PROLEGOMENON TO PART I

1.1 Introduction

It is clear that the world at the start of the 21st century has many problematic aspects. The majority of its wealth is in the hands of a small minority of people and corporations ("the 1%"). A large part of the world's peoples lack adequate nutrition, health care, and education, whilst there is enough wealth in the world for all to have these things. Global warming is causing erratic weather patterns, droughts and floods, rising sea levels, and—soon—mass migration. Clearly, the world could be a much better socio-economic place, and we should act to make it so.

If one is to act effectively in some situation, one must understand that situation, its features, the causal factors operating, and so on. If one does not, there is a good chance that one's action will have no positive effect. Thus, exorcism of demons is not a good way of curing mental illness; and if one designs small microchips using classical electro-dynamics rather than quantum electro-dynamics, they will not work. Even worse than producing no effect, one may produce negative ones. Thus, think, for example, of practices in the history of medicine which were aimed at curing a person but which actually, because of medical ignorance, injured them. Or, closer to home, if one does not understand the mentality of some bully or dictator, one may attempt acts of appeasement for self-protection, whereas, in reality, such acts merely encourage the bully/dictator to further acts.

The aim of this book is to promote action aimed at moving the world in the direction of a more humane and less irrational one.[1] It is therefore necessary to

---

1. The term *irrational*, here, has no heavy-duty theoretical sense. It just means manifestly stupid when you think about things.

DOI: 10.4324/9781003195146-2

understand the present situation. That is the function of this part of the book. It provides an analysis of the social/economic/political situation in which we find ourselves in the first part of the 21st century.[2]

1.2 Buddhist and Marxist Philosophies

The analysis I shall provide has two mainsprings: aspects of Buddhist philosophy and aspects of Marxist philosophy.

Buddhism and Marxism may seem unlikely bedfellows. The first originated 2500 years ago in an Asian and largely agricultural society. The second originated less than 200 years ago, in a European and developing industrial society. And *prima facie*, their concerns are quite different. The aim of the first is the attainment of *nirvāṇa*; the aim of the second is political revolution. These are obviously different goals.

But the two philosophies have at least this much in common: both say that life, as we find it, is unsatisfactory; both explain aspects of why this is so; and both offer the hope of making it better. In fact, they have a lot more in common than this. Waistell puts matters as follows:[3]

> Both philosophies are based on questions of how we can be reconciled with ourselves and each other; both recognise the depth of human suffering and offer liberation from it; both critically analyse existence and seek radical change; both seek to transform consciousness, ending alienation and selfish individualism; both recognise that thought is not enough to end alienation and suffering—practice is also necessary; and both emphasize causality—it is necessary to eliminate the causes of suffering.

More on all of these matters in due course.[4]

Perhaps just as important as what these traditions have in common is what they do *not* have in common. There are a number of matters about which the one does not say much and the other does. In this way, the two may be taken to complement each other.

Thus, for example, there is obviously a strong connection between ethics and political philosophy. Ethics has implications for the kind of society in which we live—or in which we should live; and the kind of society in which we live is very often a crucible for ethical decisions.

Buddhism has always been strong on ethics and its rationale: its core principles go back to the very foundation of the subject. There are remarks of a

2. This part of the book started life as Priest (2018a).
3. Waistell (2014), pp. 202 f. He attributes the thought to Shields (2013).
4. I note that mine will hardly be the first attempt to put together ethical and political views from different times and places. Notably, Liberation Theology, as developed largely in Latin America, melds Catholicism and Marxism. Personally, I find this conjunction less felicitous.

political nature in some of the canonical texts, such as the *Aṅguttara* and *Dīgha Nikāyas*, and Nāgārjuna's *Ratnāvalī*;[5] and over the last 50 or so years, there have been Buddhist thinkers such as Thich Nhat Hanh and other members of the "Engaged Buddhist Movement", such as Sulak Sivaraksa and Bikkhu Bodhi, who have been concerned with ending wars and establishing more compassionate societies.[6] However, generally speaking, Buddhism has had relatively little to say about socio-political philosophy. It has clearly put more emphasis on private practice than public practice. Its major emphasis has been on how individuals can change themselves.

By contrast, Marxism has always been strong on political philosophy and, in particular, the nature of capitalism and its unsatisfactory consequences; but it has always been weak on a systematic ethics. Marx and Engels combine suggestions that ethics is part of the superstructure, and so relative, with a moral condemnation of capitalism whose tone is anything but relative. Perhaps the closest we get to a systematic account of ethics is in Marx' *Paris Manuscripts* of 1844. The young Marx operates with a notion of human flourishing based on a certain understanding of human nature ("species being"). Whether or not he gave up these ideas is a moot point, but the notion largely disappears from his later writings—those which contain his detailed analysis of capitalism.

Turning to matters metaphysical, it might well appear that Buddhism and Marxism have different, and quite incompatible, views.[7] On closer inspection, however, there is much more commonality than one might expect. Both have similar views on what it is to be a person, and both are much concerned with human interdependence. Yet even here, Buddhism and Marxism provide different, and complementary, aspects of these matters. When it comes to personal identity, Buddhism stresses the role of conceptualisation and self-conceptualisation; Marxism, on the other hand, stresses the essentially social nature of persons. Concerning interdependence, Marx stresses the social interconnectedness of people and the false and ideological nature of social atomism. Buddhism says little of this, but locates matters in a much more general picture of the interdependent nature of all things, and of our failure to understand this.

In a nutshell, then, Buddhist philosophy provides a *general* account of the human condition: the place of people in the kind of world in which we live. By contrast, Marxist philosophy provides a *specific* account of the human social condition, and in particular, of the human social condition in a capitalist political economy.

5. For a discussion of some of these, see Bodhi (2012).
6. See, e.g., Queen (1995), King (2005), Bodhi (2009). In this context, the life and thought of the anarcho-socialist Zen Buddhist priest Uchiyama Gudō (1874–1911), executed for criticism of, and alleged conspiracy against, the Meiji state, deserves to be better known. See Victoria (2006), ch. 3.
7. I refer here to what one might call the core aspects of Buddhist metaphysics. Different schools of Buddhism articulate these in radically different ways.

Thus, aspects of Marxist and Buddhist philosophy can each provide something the other lacks. These may be combined to form a more comprehensive picture. In this part of the book we will see how.[8]

1.3 *Nota Bene*

To forestall some misunderstandings about what is going on here, let me make certain things clear about how I am (and am not) proceeding.

First, historically, Buddhism and Marxism both have a substantial diversity of forms. There are striking differences between, for example, Theravāda Buddhism, Tibetan Buddhism, Pure Land Buddhism, and Chan (Zen) Buddhism.[9] Similarly, there are striking differences between the Marxisms of Lenin, Gramsci, Althusser, and G. A. Cohen.[10] I will not be endorsing any one school of Buddhist or Marxist thought. What I will be endorsing are quite generic views, held in most of the different traditions of each kind.

Indeed, even within these generic views, it is only certain parts of Marxist and Buddhist thought on which I will be drawing. In fact, there are parts of both with which I disagree, as will become clear in due course. Which views I am endorsing I will explain—and not only explain: I will defend them and argue that they are correct.

And if someone wishes to tell me that without the other parts, it's not Buddhism or Marxism, this is a matter of indifference to me. I attach no importance to the labels. They are there to acknowledge the sources of the ideas.

1.4 The Structure of Part I

A more detailed account of the structure of Part I of the book is as follows. I shall not assume that the reader knows much about either Buddhist or Marxist philosophy. So in Chapter 2 I shall explain and defend those parts of Buddhist philosophy on which I wish to draw. In Chapter 3, I will do the same for Marxist philosophy.

Behind much socio-political philosophy is an understanding of what a person is. Those with but a passing acquaintance with Marxist and Buddhist philosophies might well have the impression that they have a radically distinct understanding. As I have already said, they do not—though each may put

---

8. Sympathetic discussions of the connections between Buddhism and Marxism can also be found in Brien (2004), Slott (2011), Struhl (2017), Waistell (2014), Gibbs (2017), and, in its own way, Loy (2008)—though it is not explicitly thematised in this way. Karsten Struhl and I, in particular, have been discussing these matters for some years now, and we find ourselves very much on the same page about most points.

9. For an outline of the different Buddhisms, see Mitchell (2002).

10. For an outline of the different Marxisms, see McLellan (2007).

emphasis on different matters, and so complement the other. In Chapter 4 I will explain and defend this account of what it is to be a person.

In Chapter 5, I will draw a number of the threads of the previous chapters together to provide a much more general picture of how the aspects of Buddhist and Marxist thought I have endorsed complement each other. What will emerge from this synthesis is the general analysis of the present social/economic/political situation sought.

Chapter 6 draws the general conclusion that we need to move to a post-capitalist society, and so lays the ground for the discussion of Part II of the book.

1.5 Conclusion

The analysis of the world that will emerge from the discussion in this part of the book is obviously a synthetic one. But it does not simply cobble together two independent things. There is a genuine synergy between them, each amplifying and enhancing the other. Moreover, in any genuine synthesis of this kind, the whole is greater than the sum of its parts. What will emerge then, I hope, is a highly distinctive—and correct—analysis of the contemporary human socio-economic situation.

2

SOME ELEMENTS OF
BUDDHIST PHILOSOPHY

2.1 Introduction

In this chapter I will lay out and defend the first mainspring of the analysis: certain elements of Buddhist philosophy.

A little history may provide a useful context. According to the standard history,[1] the Buddha (enlightened, awakened one), Siddhārtha Gautama (6th or 5th century BCE), experienced enlightenment (awakening) in Bodh Gaya (north-east India). The Four Noble Truths (*Chatvari-arya-satyani*) form the content of this first teaching after that, at Sarnath.[2] This is recorded in a number of early sūtras, such as the *Dharmachakrapravartana Sūtra* (The Setting in Motion of the Wheel of the Dharma Sūtra).[3] The Four Noble Truths provide an analysis of what one might call the human condition, its nature, and its prospects. After this initial teaching, the Buddha continued to teach and develop these ideas, and other ethical and metaphysical matters related to them—though his concern was always a thoroughly practical one: how to eliminate the *duḥkha* from people's lives. (What *duḥkha* is, we will come to shortly.) Buddhist philosophy continued to develop all of these themes and many others after the Buddha's death. Indeed, in the next 2,000 years many quite different schools of Buddhist thought developed in India, China, and other parts of

1. See Siderits (2019).
2. 'Noble' in this context, means something like 'worthy of respect'.
3. http://www.thebuddhacenter.org/buddhism/sutras/the-dhammacakkappavattasutta/.

DOI: 10.4324/9781003195146-3

South and East Asia. In what follows, I will mention some of these schools; but, for the most part, their differences will not concern us.[4]

In the first part of the chapter, we will look at the Four Noble Truths themselves. We will then move on to look at the crucial notion of compassion. In the final part of the chapter, we will look at a number of further issues, including the important notion of interdependence. What will emerge from all this is a general account of the world, and how one should live in it.[5]

2.2   The Four Noble Truths

So, to start with, the Four Noble Truths. For shorthand, I will call these 1NT, 2NT, 3NT, and 4NT. They are in the form of a medical evaluation: illness, cause, prognosis, cure. Let us take them in order.[6]

2.2.1   First Noble Truth: Duḥkha

The 1NT is to the effect that life is standardly characterised by *duḥkha* (Pāli: *dukkha*).[7] The usual translation of this term is *suffering*. This certainly captures something of what is at issue, but the Sanskrit word has much richer resonances, which include: suffering, pain, discontent, unsatisfactoriness, unhappiness, sorrow, affliction, anxiety, dissatisfaction, discomfort, anguish, stress, misery, frustration, and—one might add in the present context—sense of alienation. I will leave the word untranslated.

The thought behind the 1NT is that everyone experiences unpleasant pain (physical and mental), illness, old age, and infirmity (if they are lucky enough to live that long); they suffer unhappy life experiences, such as a marriage break-up, the death of a child, the pain of not getting a job wanted, the loss of a job, a treasured possession, or even of a body part; they may well be the subject of natural disasters, such as floods and earthquakes, or human disasters such as wars, car crashes, stock markets collapsing; and so on.

Of course, it is clear that good things happen in life too: partners and children give us joy and happiness; we sometimes get something we really want; we experience the beauty of a sunset or an opera. But if one considers carefully, it is clear that these things normally come with an edge. When one is in a state that makes one happy, at the back of one's mind there is usually the insecurity of losing it. (Think of jealousy, or rivalry at work.) Moreover, if and when we do lose it,

---

4. For a very brief introduction to the development of Buddhist philosophy, see Priest (2014), pp. xxiii–xxvii.
5. This chapter draws on Priest (2014), chs. 14, 15, and Priest (2017).
6. For further explanation and discussion of the Four Noble Truths, see Carpenter (2014), ch. 1, and Siderits (2007), ch. 2.
7. Note that Indian Buddhist texts are written in two languages, the scholarly Sanskrit, and the vernacular Pāli. I will stick to the Sanskrit.

there is the chagrin and pain of loss. And more than often, we find that what we really wanted does not live up to our expectations, or satisfy us in the way that we thought it would.

Such is the 1NT; and it would seem to be a plain statement of an empirical fact. I don't know anybody whose life has not been thus—and I live a relatively privileged life in an affluent country, not subject to ravages of famine, civil war, or the diktats of some religious power group. I wager that you don't know anyone who has escaped the 1NT either.

2.2.2 The Second Noble Truth: Tṛṣna

Let us turn to the 2NT. This is that there is a cause of *duḥkha*: *tṛṣna* (pronounced 'trishna'). Literally, the word means something like *thirst*. It is often translated as *craving*; but again, I shall leave the word untranslated. The thought behind the 2NT is that *duḥkha* is caused by the affective attitude that we bring to bear on the slings and arrows of (sometimes not so) outrageous fortune. We have a natural attitude of aversion to the things that we do not want to happen, or want to go away; and we have a natural attitude of attachment to the things we do want to happen, or want to continue.

Of course, life is complex, and events are never monocausal. Many things conspire to produce an effect. Events that cause *duḥkha* can be brought about by viral infections, icy roads, the declaration of war by someone in power, a government cutting medical benefits, and so on. But such things are not, at least for the most part, under our control. It makes sense, then, to single out the one thing that is: our own mental attitude to what happens to ourselves and those we care about.

The 2NT is perhaps not as obvious as the 1NT. But think about it for a moment. Suppose something happens that causes you *duḥkha*. Suppose, for example, that you lose your job. Was your attachment to the job one of the causal factors involved? Yes, of course. Suppose that you didn't like your job, or just that you didn't care one way or the other: you'd be just as happy doing something else with your time. Would you have been upset by being made redundant? Of course not. Or take another possible cause of *duḥkha*: your neighbour has a habit of playing Wagner—or rap, or atonal music—not to your taste. Is your aversion to this one of the causal factors involved? Of course. If you liked this kind of music, or really didn't mind it one way or the other, would you be upset? No. In fact, it's almost a truism to say that the subjective effect that things have on us is determined by our affective attitude.

This is not to say that it is easy to change these affective attitudes. They appear to be deeply ingrained in us, and are highly resistant to change. Why so? Buddhist philosophy attempts no explanation of this. Given what we now know, it is plausible that these attitudes are deeply ingrained in us for evolutionary reasons. Creatures with these attitudes are more likely to survive and pass on their genes.[8] However, whatever the reason, this takes us to the 3NT and 4NT.

2.2.3   The Third and Fourth Noble Truths

The 3NT is that one can get rid of *duḥkha* by getting rid of *tṛṣṇa*. This is a simple corollary of the 2NT: get rid of the cause, and you get rid of the effect. As such, there is not a lot to say about it. One might well have doubts that getting rid of *tṛṣṇa* is achievable. A religious Buddhist might answer that we know it to be achievable, since the Buddha achieved it. This was the state of *nirvāṇa*, which means something like *extinction*. Note that this does not mean extinction of the person. The Buddha, after all, is supposed to have achieved it while alive. Rather, the extinction is the extinction of *duḥkha*.

But even if one believes that the Buddha himself did not achieve this, even if one believes that *nirvāṇa* is not (fully) attainable, this does not mean that it is not something that one should aim at. Moral ideals may well not be fully obtainable in practice. They are, after all, *ideals*. But the more they can be achieved, the better it is. So, in this case, the more that one can get rid of *tṛṣṇa*, the less *duḥkha* one will experience. And that is a good thing.

So let us move to the 4NT. Because of the 1NT, Buddhism is sometimes portrayed as a pessimistic philosophy. This is quite misleading. For a start, it does not deny that there are times of joy and happiness in life. And it certainly does not advocate eliminating or downplaying these things. However, it is undoubtedly a philosophy of realism. It urges us to face up to the hard facts of life. Sticking your head in the sand, like the proverbial ostrich, is not a very sensible recipe for happiness.

More importantly, the outlook of Buddhism on life is not one of pessimism but one of optimism. It tells you that you can do something about *duḥkha*. That's the 4NT. This says that you can, indeed, get rid of it, or at least mitigate it. You have to work at it, certainly, but there are things you can do. Thus, the 4NT enunciates something called the Eightfold Noble Path. This comprises eight practices you can engage in to change your outlook on the events of life. They are what Foucault (1988) calls a technology of the self—though for reasons that we will come to in due course, they might better be called a technology of the person. Standardly, the eight are broken up into three groups, and are as follows:

Wisdom:

[1] right view
[2] right intention

---

8. See Wright (2017), esp. ch. 6.

Action:

[3] right speech
[4] right action
[5] right livelihood

Mental state:

[6] right effort
[7] right mindfulness
[8] right concentration

Note that these practices are not meant to be successive; they are meant to be carried out in parallel. Nor do they rule out other practices which may be effective for this end. Perhaps certain kinds of political activity, say those of solidarity, could be of this kind. Still, let us look more closely at these.

2.2.3.1   Right View

Item [1] is *right view*. This is, perhaps, the most fundamental of the bunch. If you don't understand what you are dealing with, you are most unlikely to be able to do anything effective about it. And what is the right view? Well, of course, part of it makes up the Four Noble Truths themselves. But there is more to it than this. For aspects of the Noble Truths depend on general factors concerning the nature of the world in which we live, and how we are wont to misunderstand this. I will come back to the matter later in the chapter.

Let us move to item [2] of the Eightfold Noble Path. We can take item [6] at the same time. These can be dealt with quickly. Item [2] says that if you want to change things (including yourself) you have to intend to do this. Matters are complex enough that you can't just leave it and hope that it will happen by accident. Moreover, intending is not enough—as anyone who has tried to give up smoking or keep some other New Year's resolution knows. Weakness of the will (*akrasia*) all too easily kicks in. *Tṛṣṇa*, and the factors underlying this, are deeply engrained into our psyche. They are not simply going to pack their bags at the end of the week and go home.

Again, this all seems obvious enough.

2.2.3.2   Right Action

Let us now turn to the second group of practices, [3]-[5]. These are what any Western philosopher would regard as ethical. It is fairly standard to distinguish between the ethical and the non-ethical; but from the point of view of the Noble Path, there isn't really much difference between [3]-[5] and the others. They are all practices whose point is to change the agent in such a way as to eliminate, or at least lessen, their *tṛṣṇa*.⁹

Item [3] is right speech. Wrong speech is lying, deceitful, abusive, or hurtful in other ways. Right speech is truthful, kind, considerate. Of course, these things can conflict. To take a very extreme case: someone asks you as they are on their deathbed whether you think they have lived a good life. Honesty would have you answer no; but you also know that this would be extremely hurtful. Assuming that you have no way to avoid answering, [5] would counsel you in different directions. Of course, it is well known that moral desiderata can conflict, and Buddhist ethics is hardly an exception to this. One must choose the speech act which seems, all things considered, the best. I am inclined to think that in the present case, this would be to lie, but this is a matter of judgement. We will return to the matter of ethical conflicts in due course.

Item [5] is right livelihood. The standard examples of wrong livelihood are things like selling armaments, slaughtering animals, living by the slave trade. What these all have in common is that they are livelihoods which cause suffering. The 21st century has provided many more examples of such, of which the Buddha could have had no idea (not that the others are not still with us): making advertisements which create *duḥkha*-making desires in people; profiteering by financial scams (illegal *and* legal); killing innocent people by operating drone strikes—to name but a few.

Item [4] is right action. In an obvious sense, this includes the other two, since earning a livelihood and speech are clearly actions of some kind. Standard Buddhist examples of wrong actions are stealing from someone, physically injuring someone, sexually abusing someone. Right actions include those that are considerate, compassionate, helpful, thoughtful.

There is nothing terribly special about these ethical principles ([3]-[5]). What they enjoin is common to most ethical codes, be they religious or secular. But one might well ask why a Buddhist should endorse such things.

---

9. For that reason, it is somewhat dubious that Buddhist ethics fits into the standard taxonomy of Western ethical views (virtue ethics, deontology, consequentialism), though it has elements of all these things—and of others. Some have argued that it is a species of virtue ethics (Keown (2001)) or of consequentialism (Goodman (2009)). I am inclined to agree with Garfield (2015), ch. 9, that it is *sui generis*. This issue of metaethics is, however, of no concern here.

The same is true of other metaethical issues. Metaethics is a second-order debate about the ontological, semantic, and epistemic status of moral statements and properties—such as being good. Such debates have played an important role in Western philosophy. They have played virtually no role in Buddhist philosophy. Indeed, Buddhist ethics has got on happily without them for over 2,000 years. This is because many first-order ethical issues are independent of metaethical issues. And, moreover, it is often easier to reach agreement on first-order issues than second-order issues. Thus, it is easier to reach agreement that suffering is not good, and that people want to avoid it, than to reach agreement about what 'good' means. For the purpose of this book, metaethical issues are of no significance.

First, ask: what holds all these ethical injunctions together? The answer is not difficult to see. What is enjoined are those actions which are considerate to others—human and animal: all things that can suffer pain, 'sentient creatures', as Buddhism describes them. What is disenjoined are those actions that are hurtful and harmful to others. In other words, one should act out of compassion, not malice or indifference. Why is this a good thing?

There are two parts to the answer. The first is for the effect that such acts, and the dispositions which develop as a result of systematically engaging in them, have on the agent. They are a way of eliminating self-centredness and selfishness. This is prime territory for attachment, and the *duḥkha* this causes. We all find ourselves—perhaps for evolutionary reasons—with a strong desire to put ourselves and our own interests first. We experience *duḥkha* when we do not get our way, or are thwarted by the actions of others. And, usually, when we do get our way, we are just motivated to want more of it. Both things are evident in the behaviour of small children and bullies. But the perhaps sad truth is that such desires do not disappear in most normal adults. Socialisation just teaches us to control the urges. Notwithstanding some altruistic acts towards those whom we love, what each of us naturally values most, in the last instance, is themself. The acts which put others first are a way of mitigating this disposition.

That is one reason for such acts, and it concerns the actor. There is a quite different reason, which concerns those acted upon. Compassion for others is a virtue in itself. This will hardly be clear from what I have said so far, but it is so important that I will set the matter aside for the moment, and come back to it at greater length later in this chapter.

2.2.3.3   Mindfulness and Concentration

Let us turn to the last two items in the Eightfold Path, [7] and [8], mindfulness and concentration. What these two things mean will be less clear than the other cases of the Path.

Let us start with mindfulness. The Sanskrit, here, is *smṛti* (pronounced *smriti*), and it means the ability to hold something (not necessarily actually present) in mind, allowing one to contemplate it and so to take certain things to heart. (Etymologically, it is close to the notion of remembering.)[10] A particular aspect of this (closer to the sense in which the term is currently used outside Buddhist circles) is *samprajaña*, which means something like *awareness* or *alertness*, particularly with respect to what one's mind and body are doing. Let us stick with that for the present. We will come back to the more general notion in a later chapter.

One should be aware of what one's body is doing. It might be thought that one is of course aware of what one's body is doing. This, however, is not the case, as

---

10. See Dreyfus (2013). This has only a very tenuous connection—if any—with the contemporary fashion for "mindfulness training".

anyone knows who has walked behind someone engrossed in their cell phone. Next, and harder, is to be aware of what one's mind is doing. We should be aware of our thoughts and beliefs, the emotions we experience, the effects that someone else is having on us. Third, one should be aware of the *effects* of what one's body and mind are doing. These have an effect on oneself. What we do with our bodies—eating, smoking, exercising—has a major effect on our physical and mental capacities. And of course, what it is we feel and think has an enormous effect on the way we are disposed to behave. Perhaps even more importantly, these things have an effect on others. Evidently the position of one's body can affect the comfort or discomfort of others. Even more evidently, what we think and feel affects others, via the actions that these mental states engender.

Now, how is one going to control all of these things if one is unaware of them? We are all familiar with people who hurt others, physically or mentally, not because they are ill-willed, but simply because they are oblivious to the effects on others of what they are doing—from the person who talks in your face to the person who makes hurtful (perhaps racist or sexist) remarks without realising it. In other words, mindfulness in this sense is required to realise effectively other steps of the Path, especially [3]-[5].

Of course, one's body and mind are doing innumerable things all the time. There is no way that one can be aware of all of these; but one can at least be aware of the important things. Not that that is easy either. Perforce, we all run on autopilot a lot of the time. Mindfulness requires effort.

Finally, concentration. This is the ability to focus one's attention on a single thing—one-pointed attention, as it is sometimes put. The ability to concentrate is essential to the success of any complex activity. If one fails to concentrate, one may lose track of one's methods, values, and goals, lose discipline, and behave in ways that are counterproductive. In this sense, right concentration is an aspect of right effort.

However, in Buddhist philosophy, right concentration is most frequently cited in the context of meditative practices. There are many such practices, and many of these proceed by such one-pointed attention. Moreover, meditative practices are not restricted to the familiar cushion-sitting. They can be performed whilst moving, and when doing other things. Many Zen Buddhist masters have noted that virtually any practice can be meditative if done with the right concentration—even mundane things, such as walking and cooking.[11] Indeed, some Zen Buddhist masters, such as Hakuin (1686–1769), held sitting meditation to be somewhat useless.[12] Meditation will play little role in the rest of this book, but let me make a couple of comments on it here.[13]

---

11. See, e.g., Hanh and Ann Huong (2019), Wright (2005).
12. See Kasulis (1981), p. 111.
13. For a thoughtful discussion of meditation, see Goodman (2013).

Why might one take meditation to be important? It is often claimed by Buddhists that such meditative practices are important for the effects that they have on people: they make people calmer, more peaceful, less egotistical, less stressed and frustrated. In short, they dissipate the effects of *tṛṣṇa*. This may well be true, though whether or not it is so is an empirical matter. Impressionistic judgements may carry some weight, but such judgements are notoriously prone to error and bias. If the claim is to stand up, it is of a kind that can be established only by systematic scientific investigation. Such investigation is still, as far as I am aware, in its infancy.[14]

However, there is another, less speculative reason why meditation is important. Deep, one-pointed concentration has a very distinctive phenomenology. No doubt this is familiar to skilled meditators, but it is also familiar to skillful musicians, martial artists, sports people, and others whose effective action is achieved by being "in the zone", or by having *mushin* (no mind), to give it its Japanese Buddhist expression. In such experiences, any sense of self disappears; there is no longer a duality between the person acting and the things being acted upon. Conceptual thought drops away, and nothing remains but things happening.

Most of us are not, of course, accomplished musicians, martial artists, rock climbers, and so on. But I suspect that most experienced drivers of motorbikes and cars are familiar with what I am describing. Driving requires, of course, intense concentration, as anyone who has learned to drive a motorbike or car will remember; but sometimes, particularly in long-distance driving, the sense that one is doing the driving just drops away. There is no person driving the car; there is no car; there is just a thought-less process of driving happening.[15]

As Dōgen Kigen (1200–1253), the Japanese Zen teacher and philosopher, put it in his essay *Genjō kōan* (The Issue at Hand):[16]

> To model yourself after the way of the Buddhas is to model yourself after yourself. To model yourself after yourself is to forget yourself. To forget yourself is to be authenticated by all things. To be authenticated by all things is to effect the molting of body-mind, both yours and others'.

The mind and body drop away. There is just "something happening".

And why is this important? Here I will have to anticipate the discussion of the self again. A person does not have a self; that is, does not have a part which is constant and defines the person as that very person. We all, however, have an illusion of self. (This fact does not stop one studying it, as Dōgen says should be

---

14. For some relevant discussion, see Sedlmeier *et al.* (2012), Van Dam *et al.* (2018), Eberth *et al.* (2019).
15. For a light-hearted look at the matter, see Priest (2006).
16. Quoted in (and translated by) Kasulis (1981), p. 87.

done. One can, of course, study an illusion.) In the experience I have just described, the illusion of self drops away. Now, *believing* (rationally) that one does not have a self is one thing, but *experiencing* reality without the illusion is a quite different matter. And it is exactly that which the experience in question gives.

So, we are back with a central aspect of [1], right view, but with "knowledge by acquaintance", and not merely "knowledge by description". Now, knowledge by description is often quite sufficient for most things one wishes to do; but I think it fair to say that knowledge by acquaintance is usually more powerful.

2.2.4   The Zeroth Noble Truth

What I said so far assumes, of course, that *duḥkha* is bad. This is not explicit in the Four Noble Truths, but it is certainly presupposed by them. (I sometimes think of this as the Zeroth Noble Truth.) And it seems a very reasonable presupposition: I certainly don't know anyone who likes the experience of *duḥkha*. The experience is, in itself, bad.

But, it might be suggested, *duḥkha* can be good because of what it brings about. What might such things be? A lame answer is that it is good because it motivates one to act in such a way as to get rid of it. This is like saying that hospitals are good; so illness is good because it makes hospitals possible. That puts the cart before the horse. Hospitals are good precisely because of their effect on illness. This does not justify illness. In the same way, the Noble Path is good precisely because it mitigates *duḥkha*. This does not justify *duḥkha*.

A better suggestion is that *duḥkha* can motivate one to achieve other good things. Thus, for example, an athlete, to achieve their goal, must undertake training exercises to strengthen muscles, increase stamina, and so forth. And such exercises can often be painful. However, one should not think that pain is necessarily suffering. Suffering is a matter of the attitude one brings to bear on the pain. Most athletes take on such exercises happily and gladly. This is not *duḥkha*. Of course, most pain is not like this. Pain does normally cause suffering; sports training is a rather special case. But the point remains: pain is not necessarily *duḥkha*. It becomes so when a certain attitude is brought to bear on it. It can hardly be denied that this attitude is a very natural one, and very hard to shake, especially when the pain is connected with illness. Still, that is a different matter.

Perhaps, then, it might be suggested that the experience of *duḥkha* is good since it makes one more compassionate. Well, the 1NT reassures(?) us that we are not likely to lose such motivation any time soon. But in any case, once one has taken Buddhist ethics to heart, one can be motivated simply by the ethics itself. (In at least some branches of Buddhism, it is held that there are some people—

bodhisattvas—who are so far along the Buddhist path that they no longer experience *duḥkha*; they act, however, simply out of compassion for others.)

Perhaps—a final thought—it might be suggested that *duḥkha* is good because it is "character-building". That is, the fact that one has experienced it and worked through it makes one a more resilient, stronger person. Again, the 1NT assures us that such character-building is going to be with us for a long time. But in any case, there are many things one can do which require one to persevere, overcome obstacles, and so forth, and so may be "character building", which do not require *duḥkha*. Eliminating *tṛṣṇa*, as I have already observed, is no easy matter. And working for the well-being of others out of a sense of compassion can be anything but easy: it can require dedication, hard work, self-sacrifice.

So much for the possible goodness of *duḥkha*. A distinct, but closely related thought is that *tṛṣṇa* is good, and that this justifies at least some of the *duḥkha* it produces.

Prima facie, the thought that *tṛṣṇa* can be an intrinsic good is much more plausible than the thought that *duḥkha* can be. Without it, it might be thought, life would be bland and boring. However, this is a simple mistake. Life without *tṛṣṇa* is not life on constant Valium, or after a lobotomy. It is quite consistent with throwing oneself into life, and experiencing its joys—including, I note, the joy of acting compassionately. It is just not compatible with being attached to such things. Indeed, arguably these things may occasion more joy without the *tṛṣṇa*: one does not have, at the back of one's mind, the nagging and joy-decreasing thought that they may or will come to an end. Buddhist thought does not free one *from* life; it frees one *for* life.

It might be suggested that there are some good and joyful things in life such that *tṛṣṇa*, in the form of attachment, is an intrinsic part of them. The most obvious example where this is plausible is in the case of the love of a child or a partner. How could it be love if one does not want to possess and/or be possessed? Now, I have no wish to deny that love and attachment do frequently go together. I do not think that attachment is a necessary component of love, though. One can care for someone, seek the best for them, enjoy being with them, and so on, without being possessive. Indeed, I note that possessiveness is often damaging to a loving relationship. Merely think of jealously, controlling parents, and so on. The relationship can be better without these features.

And if one holds that attachment *is* intrinsic to love, then it is yet the case that there is something like love. This is the caring, the mutual enjoyment, the warmth and affection, but without the possessiveness. Call this love*, if you like; and we are better off without love, but with love*.

So let us turn to the possibility that *tṛṣṇa* is good, not intrinsically, but because of what it brings about. It can motivate one to experience the joys of life, achieve goals—such as acting compassionately—and so on.

We are now in much the same territory as with the similar claim for *duḥkha*. First, one does not need *tṛṣṇa* to motivate one to engage in the joys of life. That they are joyful is quite sufficient. But, it might be said, some of the joys of life cannot be achieved without hard work; and attachment to a goal can help one achieve this. Thus, obtaining a philosophy degree, winning a national sports competition, writing a piece of music, and being compassionate might be examples of such. These require hard work and effort, and usually a number of setbacks along the way. However, one can be motivated to act towards such goals simply because one believes that they are worth achieving. And, strange as it may seem, this does not require attachment to those ends: it needs only a decision that these ends are worth working for. (And one might call this a desire, if one wishes, though normally the term is used for this *plus* the emotional loading which goes with it, for the blend of the cognitive and the affective. In some Buddhist writings, the term *aspiration* is used for the cognitive component.)

Moreover, the setbacks one may receive along the way are actually easier to deal with without the *tṛṣṇa*. One does not get discouraged. One simply picks oneself up and carries on. Of course, if and when one does achieve the goal, one should not be attached to that either. One can simply experience the joy of the moment, knowing full well that it will pass in due course. Non-attachment, it must be remembered, most certainly does not mean not caring. It means not being emotionally derailed when things go wrong (or right). Action is much more effective without attachment, both in the short term and the long term. In the short term, action and planning are all more effective without emotional overload. In the long term, engagement is easier to maintain when not blown off course by the gusts of attachment.

The bottom line of all this discussion is that neither *duḥkha* nor *tṛṣṇa* is good in and of itself. Moreover, neither is necessary because of the good things to which it can lead. Such things can be achieved without them. Indeed, if anything, *duḥkha* and *tṛṣṇa* may merely serve to get in the way of these ends.

2.3 Compassion and Other Virtues

2.3.1 Compassion

So much for the Four (or Five) Noble Truths. Let us now turn to the topic, centrally important for the book, of compassion.[17]

If we left a discussion of ethical matters at this point, it would be seriously misleading. For all I have said so far, Buddhist ethics is about an agent working to eliminate, or at least mitigate, their own *duḥkha*—though a compassionate attitude may be one strategy to achieve this. Of course, in acting this way,

17. Of course, compassion is an important virtue in the ethics of many other religions, such as Christianity and Islam. However, the Buddhist insistence on compassion is distinctive, in that it is not something done for a more important reason: the service of God. None the less, the importance I place on compassion in this book should find a resonance with adherents of those religions.

one should not be attached to the result. That would be entirely self-defeating. As I have already noted, there is nothing contradictory about working for an end without being attached to it. Still, should we not be concerned with the *duḥkha* of others for its own sake?

Buddhist philosophy is unanimous about the answer. We should. An important Buddhist virtue—indeed, the *central* virtue of later Indian Buddhism—is *karuṇā*. The standard translation for this is *compassion*, though better, I think, is *care*.[18] For a start, compassion sounds rather passive (suffering-with). *Karuṇā* is actively working for the well-being of others. *Care* picks up this feature. Second, it doesn't make sense to talk of being compassionate for oneself. But one can care for oneself and for others. *Karuṇā* is an attitude with respect to *all* creatures which can suffer.

So one should care for oneself *and* for others. Why one should care for oneself is clear; it is simply a matter of prudence; but why should one care for others? Why should we be as concerned to eliminate, or at least mitigate, the *duḥkha* of others too? We have already seen part of the answer. It is an element of care for oneself. But this hardly gets to the root of the matter.

Why should I get rid of *duḥkha* in general? Because *duḥkha* is a bad thing, and bad things should be eliminated, just because they are bad. In the same way, oppression, say racial or patriarchal, is bad in itself, and should be eliminated. And it matters not one whit that I, who say this, am a white male. In other words, you don't have to have a reason to act compassionately, being compassionate is *itself* a reason to act.

The point can be seen as made by the Buddhist ethicist Śāntideva (traditionally dated as 685–763), in his *Bodhisattvacharyāvatāra* (A Guide to the Bodhisattva's Way of Life[19]). He says:[20]

> To begin with one should thus diligently foster [the thought of] the sameness of others and oneself. All are equally subject to suffering and happiness, and should be protected just like myself.
>
> Just as the body, with its multiplicity of forms due to the differences of hands, etc., should be protected as one whole, in the same way all different beings, being alike with respect to suffering and happiness, should be treated as one.

18. Thanks to Amber Carpenter for this translation. Despite this, I will stick to 'compassion' for the most part in what follows. Indeed, in a moment, I will even stretch the ambit of the word slightly.

19. A *bodhisattva* is someone who has determined to help all others achieve enlightenment. On Śāntideva, see Goodman (2016).

20. VIII: 90–96. Translation by Siderits and Goodman (2015). There is an issue about how, exactly, to interpret this text, which we need not go into here. See Garfield, Jenkins, and Priest (2015). The argument for compassion I endorse in what follows is called there the *rationality reading*. See that paper for further discussion of the argument. See also Garfield (2015), pp. 310–4.

> While my suffering does not harm the bodies of others, it is indeed still suffering, which is hard to bear due to my self-love.
>
> So while others' pain is not felt by me myself, still that pain is difficult to bear for the one whose pain it is, due to [that person's] self-love.
>
> I should prevent the suffering of others, because it is suffering, like my own suffering. I should also be benevolent to others, because these are beings, just as I am myself a being.
>
> Since I and others are exactly alike in desiring happiness, what is so special about me that justifies striving after only my own happiness?
>
> Since fear and suffering are unwanted by both me and others, what is so special about me such that I protect this and not that?

There is nothing special about some *duḥkha*, simply because it is mine. Morality is not self-interest. In the same way, suppose that a parent divides a cake in two, and gives half to each of their two children. One then says 'I want both halves'. This is just irrelevant to the parent's actions. The kid just doesn't get it.

2.3.2   Interlude: Social Atomism (for the First Time)

How could this even be a move in the ethical game? There is an answer, though it will take us into deeper waters. There is a certain view concerning the nature of individuals and the society which they constitute. Each person is a self-sufficient metaphysical atom, fully formed with desires and interests, completely independent of all others. People come together and make an agreement to abide by a set of rules, and to have them enforced if necessary. Some of these may be against an individual's proper interests; but, overall, they benefit from the security of the rules. This is social contract theory.

If one looks at things this way, then it is natural to view everything from the perspective of self-interest, and thus for a person to care about the elimination of their own *duḥkha* to the exclusion of others looks quite rational. To illustrate the view, Marlin quotes Diderot's 18th-century *Encyclopédie* as saying:[21]

> The citizens have rights, rights that are sacred for the very body of society: the citizens exist independently of society; they form its necessary elements; and they only enter it in order to put themselves, with their rights, under the protection of those laws to which they sacrifice their liberty.

He then draws the appropriate socio-economic consequences:

> From a libertarian point of view, it makes no sense to ask how to maximize the size of the economic pie for society as a whole. … No one is—or should

21. Marglin (2008), p. 61.

be—concerned with anything more than his or her slice, and an individual will not agree to participate in society unless by doing so his or her slice is enlarged. And society's only legitimate role is to ensure that whatever rules of the game have been accepted by the players are in fact followed.

For the most part, those who espoused social contract theory (e.g., Hobbes, Locke, Rousseau) did not regard the situation before the contract as an historical reality. It was simply a conceptual framework aimed at justifying a certain set of social relations. Moreover, it is no coincidence that social contract theory arose in Europe just when capitalism was hitting its strides. For it was exactly capitalist social relations that it legitimated.

But the social contract is not just a myth; it is a fairy tale. The metaphysical account of what it is to be a person, and the social relations in which they are embedded, is completely false. Sayers puts the matter as follows:[22]

> We are inherently and essentially social beings. We develop our natures ... only by participating in society ... Sociality is inscribed in our very biology.

And as Marx himself put it in the *Grundrisse*:[23]

> The human being is in the most literal sense a *zoon politicon* not merely a gregarious animal, but an animal which can individuate itself only in the midst of society. Production by an isolated individual outside society ... is as much of an absurdity as is the development of language without individuals living together and talking to each other.

This is an important matter, and I will come back to it in more detail in due course.

2.3.3   Back to Compassion

Let us return to the subject of compassion. This is certainly not the only Buddhist ethical virtue. Śāntideva himself lists a whole suite of others, including generosity, concentration, persistence (effort), and patience. These are obviously aspects of the 4NT or other things conducive to the aims this is meant to achieve.

Another important suite falls under the rubric of the *Brahma Vihāras*. Literally, this means something like 'the abodes of Brahma' (Brahma is an aspect of the Hindu godhead, Brahman), but it concerns four very important ethical virtues, which are:

22. Sayers (1998), p. 7.
23. Nicolaus (1973), p. 84.

- *Maitri*: loving kindness, goodwill
- *Karuṇā*: care, compassion
- *Muditā*: empathetic joy, joy at the happiness of others
- *Upekṣā* (Pāli: *upekkhā*): equanimity, peace of mind.

As the name suggests, these attitudes are not specifically Buddhist, and they play a role in Indian ethical thinking more generally. However, they are alluded to in a number of the Buddhist *sūtras*, and their importance for Buddhist ethics is stressed, perhaps most famously, by Buddhaghosa (fl. ca. 5th century CE).[24]

Karuṇā we have already met: it is an attitude directed towards the suffering of others. *Matrī* is the wishing well to others for their own sake. (Etymologically, the word is closely connected with friendship.) Though these two things are different, they are clearly closely related. They might both be captured under the rubric of benevolence/beneficence. In the rest of the book, I will use 'compassion' for this nest of attitudes generally.

Muditā is obviously an excellent attitude to have if one is trying to eliminate self-centredness and promote the well-being of others.

Upekṣā might seem to be of a rather different kind from the others, but is, in fact, closely connected with them. One Buddhist thinker puts the matter as follows:[25]

> The real meaning of upekkha is equanimity, not indifference in the sense of unconcern for others. As a spiritual virtue, upekkha means equanimity in the face of the fluctuations of worldly fortune. It is evenness of mind, unshakeable freedom of mind, a state of inner equipoise that cannot be upset by gain and loss, honor and dishonor, praise and blame, pleasure and pain. Upekkha is freedom from all points of self-reference; it is indifference only to the demands of the ego-self with its craving for pleasure and position, not to the well-being of one's fellow human beings. True equanimity is the pinnacle of the four social attitudes that the Buddhist texts call the 'divine abodes': boundless loving-kindness, compassion, altruistic joy, and equanimity. The last does not override and negate the preceding three, but perfects and consummates them.

We will come back to *upekṣā* a little later in the chapter.

Whilst we are on the subject of compassion, let me make a final point about the material causes of suffering. As I have observed, a plurality of things will normally conspire to produce *duḥkha*. Many of these will be material circumstances, such as illness, war, being made redundant, and so on. It might be thought that an implication of what I have said is that one does not have to

24. See Keown (2003), p. 41. On Buddhaghosa, see p. 43.
25. Bodhi (1998).

worry about getting rid of this sort of thing; one just has to work on people's *tṛṣṇa*. Nothing could be further from the truth.

To see the absurdity of this, suppose that someone comes to a Buddhist and says, 'I am in poverty. My children are starving and constantly sick'. The last thing the Buddhist is going to say is, 'Don't worry about it. Just teach them to meditate'. Why?

For a start, the sorts of activities that are involved in working on *tṛṣṇa* are hardly likely to be available if one is living in a war zone, worrying about where the next meal for one's children is coming from, or is being constantly harassed because of one's race or gender. Of course one should try to eliminate these things too.

More importantly, exactly the same logic that enjoins getting rid of *tṛṣṇa* enjoins getting rid of the material causes of *duḥkha* too. If *duḥkha* is bad, and it can be gotten rid of, or lessened, by attacking some cause, then, *ceteris paribus*, one should attack that cause—whatever that cause is. It may be the case that getting rid of *tṛṣṇa* is ultimately the most robust way of getting rid of *duḥkha*, but that is irrelevant to the point.

As I have already noted, many of the material causes of *duḥkha* are not under an individual's control; but sometimes they are. For example, many people can ensure that their children are inoculated against disease and that they are healthily nourished. Perhaps more importantly, many of these things, though not under the control of any one individual, are under our collective control. No group of people can control a tsunami, and things such as the outbreak of new diseases like AIDS/HIV. But collectively, we can control declarations of war, the support of exploitative multi-nationals, international aid, and so on.

2.4 Interdependence

In what remains of this chapter, let us look at a number of other important issues some of a more metaphysical nature, starting with the crucial notion of interdependence.

Let us go back to the topic of Right View. As I said, the Four Noble Truths are part of this, but only part. According to Buddhist philosophy, we are prone to misunderstand the nature of the world in which we live. Indeed, Buddhism often claims that there are three things which poison our life (*kleśas*): attachment, aversion, and ignorance (*avidyā*)—or sometimes, delusion or confusion (*moha*), since this is not merely a matter of not knowing something, but of having a false (and damaging) view. The first two of these we have already met as the poles of *tṛṣṇa*; we now meet the third.

We are disposed to misunderstand ourselves and the world in which we live in a number of fundamental ways. First of all, we take it that there is permanency (at least relative permanency) in life. We get the job we want, and we assume that it will last indefinitely; we marry the one we love, and we assume that the relationship will last forever; we live in good health, and assume that it will continue; we live in peace, and assume that this will not be disturbed by war. The fact is, however, that we live in a world of impermanence (*anitya*). Everything comes into existence when causes and conditions are ripe, is maintained in existence for a while, and then goes out of existence when causes and conditions so determine. If we do not face up to this fact, then, of course, when the things we treasure disappear, the result is *duḥkha*.

Anitya is a simple empirical claim. Presumably the Buddha and his cohort believed it purely on the basis of their experience of the world. (This is hardly the sort of thing one can prove *a priori*.) Modern science has, however, reinforced the point for theoretical reasons. The Third Law of Thermodynamics (that entropy tends to a maximum) assures us that every structured system (be it a painting, a person, or a planet) will go out of existence as the structure comes apart. Moreover (and relatedly), the cosmos itself is expanding. Either it will start to contract, and will go out of existence in the mirror image of the big bang—the big crunch; or it will continue expanding indefinitely until the density of matter becomes so close to zero as makes no difference.

Actually, I doubt that people *really* believe in permanence. Most thoughtful people know that things will not last forever. They simply repress the thought, until its consequences become painfully obvious. For this reason, rather than talking about ignorance, a better term might be *illusion*. For illusions can be maintained when one knows that they are false. (Things in a mirror still look as though they are in front of you, even when you know they are behind you).

The second way in which we misunderstand things concerns us, ourselves. *Anitya* assures us that there is nothing permanent to be possessed. *Anātman* assures us that there is nothing permanent to do the possessing. We all normally think of ourselves as possessing a self (*ātman*), in a certain sense—something that gives us permanency—at least relative permanency. We do not. This matter is so important that I will set it aside for the present and devote a whole chapter to it later.

The third way in which we are prone to misunderstand the world concerns *pratītyasamutpāda*—dependent arising, interdependence: everything physical or mental is located in a network of causes and effects. According to this, every state of affairs, be it physical or mental, is brought about by an array of causes which work together to produce it; and every state of affairs has, in conjunction with others, an array of effects. This is perhaps not something that most people would find surprising. Our failure to understand it is occasioned by the fact that we do not think the matter through systematically.

Thus, to take one small example. Suppose that I go and have a coffee in a local coffee shop in Manhattan. The coffee was grown on a bush in a country far away. The energy to grow the bush came, ultimately, from the sun. The water needed came from rainfall and local streams. The berries were picked by local labour (being paid much less than I earn). The coffee was transported by ships belonging to yet another country, most of whose sailors (who are paid, again, much less than I earn) being from a third country. The ship's engines are powered by coal mined and sold in yet a fourth country. The coffee was bought by distributors in New York, roasted, and distributed to the chain of shops they run, subject to a whole bunch of laws passed by both federal and state legislators. The coffee is sold to me by those who work there, most of whom do this as a part-time job, as they study or pursue a professional career. My purchase helps to keep them employed, so to achieve their goals. Often I have a friendly chat with them. This (I hope!) helps to put them in a good mood, and so to enjoy the day. They will then be friendly to other customers, which helps to put them in a good mood; and so on.

Or another: I decided to write this book because I find the socio-economic world in which we live a very sorry place. I learned about this by reading books and newspapers, written by others, and listening to international broadcasters, such as the BBC. When it is finished, I will send it to a publisher, who may be in another country, and who will consult referees from anywhere in the world. It will go into print on paper made from trees produced by our natural environment. But most people (now) will probably read it online. To do this, they depend on networked computers developed by generations of computer scientists, and satellites circling the Earth developed, again, by generations of engineers. All of this, of course, uses energy, which heats the Earth, and so changes its ecosystem. The book will be read by some people (I hope!), and they will either disagree with it or agree with it. If they disagree with it, they will probably think me some sort of misguided ideologue; if they agree with it then, maybe, it will change some of the things they think and do. This will have an effect on those with whom they come in contact. And so on.

These are the barest details of some of the chains of cause and effect of those two events. Once one starts to think about the matter, the causal connections ramify indefinitely. And so it is for all other events. Yet, one hardly ever thinks about these things. When one does so, it becomes clear that we are deeply entangled with the natural world, our social environment, and people all over the world. The world is a causally highly complex place, and we are deeply interdependent beings.[26]

Different schools of Buddhism build on this picture in various ways. According to Madhyamaka, this interdependence determines not only *that* something happens, but the very nature (*identity*) of what it is that happens.

---

26. Indeed, as Callicot (2010), p. 404, puts it, organisms may be thought of as 'knots in the web of life, or temporary formations or perturbations in complex flow patterns'. More on the nature of those organisms which are persons in Chapter 4.

According to Huayan, the dependence is universalised. Everything depends on *everything* else. These are profound views, and I will say a little more about some of them in Chapter 4. For the present, they need not concern us.[27] Simple interdependence of the kind I have indicated is quite enough for present purposes.[28]

Sometimes in Buddhist writings,[29] the interdependence I have noted is taken, in itself, to have the moral consequence that we should look after the well-being of others. It does not. Interdependence of the kind I have noted is a purely descriptive matter; and notoriously, as Hume noted,[30] it is impossible to wring out any substantial *ought* from a purely descriptive *is*. To see this, note that the slave and the slave owner are tightly interdependent. The slave owner depends on the labour of the slave to deliver them wealth, and the slave depends on the slave owner for whatever they need to live. Nothing moral follows from this. It is perfectly compatible with these facts that the slave owner is morally permitted to exploit the slave to their death (as many slave owners do and did).[31]

To get moral conclusions out, moral premises need to be put in. Thus, in the case of the slave owner, we need the further premise that to use the slave in this way is to abuse them. In the Buddhist case concerning interdependence, the extra moral premise is the one at the root of the Four Noble Truths: that *duḥkha* is a bad thing, and ought to be extirpated.

What follows from this moral premise and interdependence is that in considering how to act compassionately, we need to bear in mind that our actions have effects on *all* the things on which we interdepend. And this will be, as near as makes no difference, all people, present and future—as well as to other creatures that can suffer.[32] Garfield puts the matter as follows:[33]

> To cultivate care in this sense is to recognize both the omnipresence of suffering and our interconnectedness through the web of dependent

---

27. The matters are discussed in detail in Priest (2018b). For Madhyamaka, see ch. 4; for Huayan, see ch. 8. I note that these metaphysical considerations deliver yet other reasons for compassion. See Priest (2014), 15.3, 15.4.

28. Note that there is nothing in this picture which entails that people do not have free will—whatever, indeed, that means. Indeed, an understanding of cause and effect is a necessary component of choosing effectively. Though one may certainly have more compassion for someone who hurts others when one understands what led them to this, it does not follow from the truth of *pratītyasamutpāda* that people cannot do other than they do. (On the general matter of free will, see O'Connor (2018). On Buddhist aspects of the matter, see Repetti (2017).)

29. E.g., King (2005), p. 160.

30. *Treatise on Human Nature*, Selby-Bigge (1978), bk. 3, pt. 1, sect. 1.

31. See, further, Priest (2014), ch. 15.

32. One of the people who has most stressed this aspect of interdependence is Thich Nhat Hanh. Indeed, the Buddhist order he founded is called the *Order of Interbeing*. See, e.g., Hanh (1987), esp. ch. 6.

33. Garfield (2015), p. 289.

origination: it is to recognize that one cannot solve even the problem of one's own suffering without caring for that of others as well, given our essentially social nature and the claims that nature ensures we make upon one another.

Moreover, as Garfield notes, my well-being cannot be separated from that of others, nor theirs from mine. Clearly, I cannot help others to flourish if I, myself, am not flourishing (for example, if I am starving or depressed). Conversely, I cannot flourish if (at least many) others around me do not: being a social animal, I depend on what they do for me, and how they do it. Thus, flourishing is a collective process. Morality is often seen as a zero-sum game. My rights are your duties, and vice versa. This is already to model morality on capitalism, where, if the buyer makes a profit, the seller makes a loss, and vice versa. Buddhist morality is quite the opposite. Moral action is a win/win situation.

2.5 *Karma* and *Upekṣā*

On an entirely different matter: a few sections ago, I discussed meditation. That is one thing that is associated with Buddhism in popular thought. Another thing that is so associated is rebirth. The association is certainly justified. It is a standard view in many forms of Buddhism, such as Theravāda Buddhism and Tibetan Buddhisms. The view fades in importance in a number of Chinese Buddhisms, and especially in Chan (Zen, in Japanese), where the focus of importance is the present; rebirth becomes entirely irrelevant to this. However, as far as I know, no Chan Buddhist ever explicitly repudiated the view (other than in the process of repudiating all views). Let me say a few words here about the doctrine.

According to this, when one dies, one will be reborn, and this process will continue until and unless one achieves enlightenment. This is the round of *saṃsāra*. How to understand what rebirth means when there is no self (*ātman*) to be reborn is a ticklish question. In this respect, Hindus, who also believe in rebirth, but who endorse the existence of an *ātman*, have a much easier time. In Buddhism, since there is no *ātman*, an account of personal identity must be given in terms of a certain kind of causal continuity. This may be true, of course, even of personal identity in this life. Western accounts of personal identity in terms of certain causal continuities (such as those of Locke) are well known.[34]

But it is easy enough to see what sorts of causal continuity are relevant in this life: those concerning body and mind. However, it is much less clear what sorts of causal continuity are applicable *across* rebirths. Continuity

34. See, e.g., Olson (2019).

of body is clearly ruled out and, at least for most of us, there is no continuity of mind.

I leave the question of whether an account of personal identity across births can be made philosophically respectable for those who subscribe to rebirth. For me, this is not an issue, since I do not believe in it. There is little argument for rebirth in canonical Buddhist texts. The view is simply taken over from the context of Indian thought circa the middle of the first millennium BCE. The Buddhists rejected some of the standard ideas of the period, such as the existence of a self and of a godhead; but this one, they retained. At any rate, I know of no canonical attempts to justify the truth of the view.

And the reason I do not subscribe to the view is that I see no kind of justification at all for it. There certainly could be. For example, someone born in 2017 might appear to remember something that had occurred in 1900, and which was unknown to anybody else. And perhaps the veridicality of this apparent memory could be independently verified. For example, the person could remember hiding a box with certain contents in a certain place; the box might then be found. But as far as I know, there is no respectable scientific evidence of such things.

Of course, this does not show that the view is false. But, as Hume noted, a rational person apportions their belief according to the evidence.[35] In particular, then, it would certainly be foolish to try to justify any view on the basis that it followed from one for which there is no evidence.

This raises the question of *karma*. Literally, *karma* means *action*; and the doctrine of *karma* is to the effect that actions have consequences, both for the actor and for those acted upon. In particular, in those forms of Buddhism for which rebirth is important, the effects of one's actions determine the sort of rebirth one has in the next. The good actions lead to a rebirth in a fortunate state; bad actions lead to a rebirth in an unfortunate state. Indeed, if the *karma* is bad enough, this can lead to a rebirth in a particularly unfortunate state—say, as a (non-human) animal.

If one rejects rebirth, one must also reject this. This does not mean that one must reject the notion of *karma* for this life, however. Indeed, one should not. It is a simple fact about human relations that if you go round being kind and thoughtful to people, they are more likely to be kind and thoughtful to you. And if you go around being unpleasant to others, they are more likely to be unpleasant to you. Moreover, if you make a practice of being kind and compassionate, you will turn yourself into a kinder, more compassionate person. Whereas if you go around being unpleasant to people, you will become an unpleasant person. As Aristotle noted, we train ourselves into our virtues and vices.[36] This is all just plain (and, for the most part, common-sense) empirical psychology—an aspect of *pratītyasamutpāda*.

35. *Enquiry Concerning Human Understanding*, Section 10, Part 1. Selby Bigge (1902), p. 110.
36. *Nichomachean Ethics*, Book 2, Ch. 1.

But if I cannot accept the view of rebirth, or those aspects of *karma* associated with it, why do I raise the matter? For a simple reason. The aim of Buddhism—at least as far as I have described matters till now—is the elimination of *duḥkha*. If that were the sole aim, there would be an easy way to achieve it: commit suicide. And it would be an act of compassion to someone else to kill them.

If someone accepts the doctrine of rebirth, there is a ready reply: that will not help you (or them); you (or they) are going to have to come back and do it again (and again, and again) till you (or they) get it right.

Without endorsing rebirth, this reply is not possible. Buddhist ethics cannot be simply about the elimination of a negative. It must be about the accentuation of a positive. What is that positive? The answer is to be found in the discussion of the *Brahma Vihāras*, and is *upekṣā*, peace of mind: a state of equanimity, brought about by the elimination of *tṛṣṇa*.[37] And it is hardly contentious that peace of mind is a good thing. We experience this sometimes, and we know that it is so.

Let me stress that peace of mind does not simply mean a withdrawal from life, sitting inertly on a cushion. Peace of mind is quite compatible with engaging in the joys of life. Indeed, the joys of life will be more joyful if one does not have one's peace of mind disturbed by troubling thoughts about what the pain one has been experiencing means, or what one's kids are doing. And as we saw in 2.3, this peace of mind does not mean ignoring others. If peace of mind is a good, it is a good for everyone, and one should act in such a way as to help others to bring this about.[38]

2.6 *Phronesis* and *Upāya*

Finally, let us turn to the question of determining how to act.

For a start, deciding what should be done is no *a priori* matter, to be decided from the philosopher's armchair. We are dealing with issues that involve matters psychological, sociological, and economic. These empirical matters are complex, and need to be taken into account as best one can.

Moreover, even where we can be pretty sure of the results of our actions, it may not be obvious what should be done. Just because of *pratītyasamutpāda*, the effects of actions are complex, and often some effects may be good and some may be bad. Thus, for example, a doctor may have to choose between giving a blood transfusion to a child, without which the child will probably

---

37. One can find a notion in the same ballpark in Hellenistic philosophies, such as Stoicism and Epicurianism. In Greek it was called *ataraxia*; in Latin it was called *tranqullitas*. See Irwin (1989), chs. 8, 9.
38. Peace of mind is discussed further in Priest (2014), 14.4.

die, and respecting the wishes of the child's parents. Or one may have to decide whether to vote for a political party which will implement some good things, such as universal health care, but which will do some bad things, such as support the sale and manufacture of armaments. In each case, one has to make an overall judgement. And this will have to be done on a case-by-case basis.[39] In every case, however, the guiding principle should be that of compassion, that is, the elimination of *duḥkha*, and its replacement with *upekṣā*.

The complexity of matters should not induce a general skepticism, however. In many situations matters are perfectly clear. Thus, if, next time I am in a class I pull out a gun and shoot one of my students who has not handed in an assignment, to make sure the others do so next time, this is clearly not an overall compassionate act. I think that many things about the current socio-economic situation are equally clear; but that is a matter for later chapters.

The virtue of making judgements of the appropriate ethical kind is called by Aristotle *phronesis*—practical wisdom.[40] In Buddhist philosophy, it is an aspect of *upāya*—skillful means. *Upāya* plays a significant role in a number of areas of Buddhist philosophy, especially epistemology, hermeneutics, and ethics.[41] Here we need be concerned only with the last of these. As we have just seen, ethical skill includes knowing what to do in the particular context in which one finds oneself—and one cannot simply apply hard and fast rules. Thus, in the *Lotus Sūtra* (*Saddharma Puṇḍarīka Sūtra*, an early Mahāyāna text, possibly 1st or 2nd century CE) there is a well known (analogical) story, told by the Buddha, about a father whose house is on fire.[42] He tries to call his children to come out, but they are too engrossed in playing with their toys. The father calls them, saying—falsely—that there are even better toys outside. They come running, and their lives are saved. The action is endorsed, even though it violates the ethical precept not to lie.

Exercising the virtue of *phronesis, upāya*, is, then, a kind of skill. A core aspect of skill finds particular articulation in the Buddhist Zen tradition. Skill is at its highest when the dispositions to act are spontaneous.[43] One does not need to apply rules. (Indeed, applying rules may not give the right result.) One just acts—or reacts. The action is smooth and effortless. Clearly, if one can do this, it is the most effective way to exercise a virtue. (This does not mean, though, that skill *never* involves thinking. In very complex matters, thought may well be necessary. But if one

---

39. So Buddhist ethics is a certain kind of moral particularism, on which, see Dancy (2017).
40. *Nichomachean Ethics*, Book 6, Chs. 5, 7.
41. On these and other matters, see Garfield and Priest (2020).
42. Watson (1993), pp. 56–7.
43. Zen, like most Chinese Buddhisms was heavily influenced by Daoism, and such spontaneity is the Buddhist version of Daoist *wuwei*, literally non-action. This most certainly does not mean not acting. It means acting in a way that is natural and unforced. See, e.g., §9.4 of Hansen (2007).

thinks, this thinking, too, at its best, is smooth and effortless—skillful thinking, as one might put it.)

2.7 Conclusion

What I have done in this chapter is to outline and defend certain of the core aspects of Buddhist philosophy. The key to this is the elimination, or at least mitigation, of *duḥkha*—that of oneself and others. As we have seen, a central aspect of this is working on oneself, working on one's *tṛṣṇa*, to make oneself a more peaceful person. Another is developing an understanding of the inter-connectedness of things, and so helping others to do the same; that is, making oneself a more compassionate person. A third is the development of appropriate ethical skills.

So much for the Buddhist ideas to be deployed in what follows. In the next chapter I will turn to the other mainspring of our analysis: the understanding of how a capitalist political economy functions, as provided by Marx.

3

SOME ELEMENTS OF MARXIST PHILOSOPHY

3.1 Introduction

In this chapter, we turn to the second mainspring of our analysis: some aspects of Marx' philosophy and, in particular, his analysis of the socio-economic structure of capitalism.

Again, some historical background may help to orient the discussion.[1] Karl Marx (1818–1883) wrote a great deal throughout his life—though he seemed to have a problem finishing anything off! In his younger writings he was much concerned with human nature (species being) and alienation. His sights then became fixed on historical materialism: the view that the economic base of society determines the superstructure of human thought, culture, and law, which sits atop it. With his years of study in the British Museum, he then became engrossed in the economic nitty-gritty of how a capitalist economy functions. Scattered through his work are comments on the end of capitalism, and what should come after it. And throughout his life, he combined his economic and philosophical writing with political activism, aimed at bringing about the end of capitalism.

It is Marx' writings on political economy which are, it seems to me, by far the most substantial and enduring part of his work. It is important to note that the sort of economics in which Marx was engaged is different from contemporary economics, which focusses on the study and manipulation of economic quantities, such as interest rates, prices, GDP, and so forth. Marx was certainly interested in such things, but, like most of his near contemporaries writing on similar

---

1. For a general overview of Marx, his life, and his work, see Wolff (2017).

DOI: 10.4324/9781003195146-4

matters, such as Smith and Ricardo, he was much concerned with the nature of the society which generates these numbers. One cannot divorce the economic quantities from the social and political institutions which produce them. This is why it is appropriate to call his work *political economy*, and not just *economics*.

As with any great thinker, Marx' ideas were taken up and developed in a number of different ways. And as might be expected when these ideas are embedded in political movements, there has been fierce disagreement about how to interpret a number of Marx' ideas. Quite different interpretations were put forward by thinkers such as Lenin, Luxemburg, Gramsci, Lukács, Marcuse, Althusser—to name but a few of many,[2] and many political leaders and groups have appropriated his name. So some 130 years after his death, it is perhaps less clear than ever what, exactly, Marxism is.

In what follows, I intend to ignore most of these matters. What I wish to focus on is Marx' analysis of the way a capitalist political economy works, how it functions, and the kind of society in which it is embedded. This is explained at greatest length in *Capital*, especially Volume 1,[3] but there is also much valuable discussion in Marx' *Grundrisse*,[4] a set of notes that Marx wrote for himself in 1857–1858, but which were not published until 1939. These two works alone comprise nearly 2,000 printed pages, so it goes without saying that I cannot attempt a review and discussion of the whole wealth of their contents. In what follows, I will explain and defend what I take to be the core ideas of Marx' analysis of capitalist political economy.[5]

In the first half of the chapter I will explain Marx' analysis. In the second half we will turn to its defence.

3.2 Capital

First, then, Marx' analysis.

The exact details of how capitalism is implemented vary from place to place and time to time, depending on differences of national and regional history and culture.[6] A tee shirt and pair of jeans can come in a multitude of different colours and styles; but in the end, they are still just a tee shirt and a pair of jeans. In the same way, whatever its local differences, the basics of capitalism are the same everywhere.

The main player in a capitalist socio-economic formation is capital itself. Capital comprises machines, buildings, land, people (or, strictly speaking,

---

2. On these matters, see McLellan (2007).
3. *Das Kapital. Kritik der Politischen Ökonomie*, Vol. 1, 1867. Vols. 2 (1885) and 3 (1894) were published posthumously by Marx' lifetime collaborator, Friedrich Engels (1820–1895), though much of these were written before Vol. 1.
4. *Grundrisse der Kritik der Politischen Ökonomie* (Outlines of a Critique of Political Economy).
5. For lengthier exegeses, one might start with Robinson (1942) and Mandel (1976).
6. For a simple overview, see Fulcher (2015).

their ability to work, that is, their labour power), food, money, information—anything that can be bought and sold. It is important to understand, though, that these objects are capital only because they exist and function in a particular way. That is, they are embedded in a certain network of social relations of production, exchange, and consumption. If people went out of existence, these things would no longer be capital; they would simply be bits of metal, earth, or paper. (So to attribute properties to capital is really to attribute properties to those relations. To suppose that it is the objects themselves that have these properties is what Marx calls fetishism.)[7] And the distinctive feature of these social relations, and so of capital itself, is simply the production of more capital. That is, capital just is wealth in search of more wealth. As Marx puts it in *Grundrisse*:[8]

> as representative of the general form of wealth—money—capital is the endless and limitless drive to go beyond its limiting barrier. Every boundary ... is and has to be a barrier ... for it. Else it would cease to be capital—money as self-reproductive. ... Capital as such creates a specific surplus value because it cannot create an infinite one all at once; but it is the constant movement to create more of the same.

Or as Mandel puts it more pithily:[9]

> Capital is ... by definition, value looking for accretion, for surplus value.

How does it do this? It is a cyclical process, but let us break into the cycle where we have a quantity of capital in the form of money. This is used to produce commodities, that is, things to be bought and sold. In the process, capital is used up—money is spent on the purchase of raw materials, on machines that depreciate, on labour that is expended. So one may think of the money as being transformed into a bunch of commodities. These are then sold, turning the commodities back into money, completing the cycle. But more money is returned than was laid out. That, indeed, was the whole point of the exercise. In other words, a capitalist society is a commodity society, that is, one in which things are produced not to be used, but to be *sold*.

But why does the initial pot of money *increase* in the process? Why doesn't it remain the same, or even decrease? The quick answer is that the commodities may be sold for more than was used to produce them. Hence, one can make a

---

7. As Marx says: 'The mysterious character of the commodity-form consists therefore simply in the fact that the commodity reflects the social characteristics of men's own labour as objective characteristics of the products of labour themselves. ... I call this the fetishism which attaches itself to the product of labour' (Fowkes, 1976), pp. 164 f.).
8. Nicholas (1973), p. 334.
9. Mandel (1976), p. 60.

profit. This is true enough, but hardly gets to the root of the matter. No doubt a quantity of capital can increase by "buying cheap and selling dear". But sale/ purchase is a zero-sum game. Commodities—say, farm produce and money— are simply exchanged in the process. If the seller increases the value of their capital in this way, the buyer decreases the value of theirs, and vice versa. This is, hence, no way for the totality of capital in a whole economy to increase.

The increase of this cannot be in the exchange phase of the cycle. So where is it? The answer is that it is in the production phase. There is something in the very process of the production of a commodity which means that it is worth more than the capital expended to make it. What is this? According to Marx, it is the human work expended. Thus, take a very simple example. A farmer works during the year. In that time, they can grow enough food to feed them- selves and their family. That is, they have produced enough of the commodity (food) to reproduce their labour power—the thing that was consumed in the process of farming. But the totality of what their labour has produced is more than this (unless it is simple subsistence farming). Hence their labour has created *more* value than was expended to produce it, that is, *surplus value*. Marx held that labour power was the *sole* commodity that has the ability to produce surplus value. That might be contested, but it cannot be contested that labour power is a highly significant source of surplus value, and, moreover, that its deployment is entirely necessary for a capitalist economy.

Why so? Because the extra value created in production must be realised in exchange. That means that there must be people to buy the goods; that means that they must have money; that means that capital has to employ them. For, on the other side of the ledger in a capitalist structure, most people possess very little capital other than their labour power. Indeed, in the early years of Euro- pean capitalism, steps were taken to ensure that people in this category had nothing else, by driving them off the land.[10] It is true that in many contempo- rary capitalist countries, some people may have a house, some money in a bank account, and in a pension fund. But few of these have enough to live off these things; and in any case, this is a small part of the world's working population. Hence, most people must sell their labour power to capital (or, in legal terms, those who control it), resort to crime, or, in the last instance, die. The need for employment means that capital can then exploit this position of weakness, and appropriate the surplus value that people produce. Hence it grows. In simple terms: the capitalist can sell the commodities produced by the work for more than they pay for the work.

The expropriation of the value produced by labour over and above what is required to reproduce the labour-power is transparent in a feudal economy, where peasants worked on their own land for, say, four days a week, producing

10. See, e.g., E. P. Thompson's classic (1991).

enough for themselves to live. For two days a week, they then worked on the lord's land, the result of their production going to him. The expropriation works in exactly the same way in a capitalist economy, though the mechanism of appropriation is hidden by the more opaque process involved.

Those who know their Marx will have observed that I have said nothing about the labour theory of value, which has been taken to be central to Marxian economics, but which has also been the target of much criticism. This is because nothing I have said depends on this. According to the labour theory of value, the value of a commodity is the summation of all the work that has gone into producing it.[11] It is hence an account of *quantity*. However, it is not necessary to subscribe to the labour theory of value to understand that labour produces surplus value—in other words to understand the *quality* of the relationship between labour and value.

3.3   Many Capitals

Capitalism came into existence (gradually), when numerous quantities of capital, in the form of money, came into existence, through a process of war, trading, robbery, expropriation, and so on. (This started in Europe in the late Middle Ages. Marx calls the process one of *primitive accumulation*.) Thus, the total social capital was in the form of a number of independent quantities of capital, each of which was driven by the imperative of the nature of capital: growth. The fragmentation of capital in this way is not a necessary feature of capitalism. Capitalism is quite compatible with all capital being owned by one party, perhaps the state—monopoly capitalism. Indeed, as we shall see in a moment, the unification of capitals into a single quantity is perhaps the natural long-term outcome of its inner dynamics. However, the fragmentation of capital into independent quantities is a feature of capitalism as it has been, and as it continues to be.

Since each quantity is driven by growth, this inevitably brings it into conflict with other quantities, in the same way that the different kinds of flora in an ecosystem will compete with each other for natural resources (light, nutrition, etc.). Hence, we have competition.

Competition manifests itself in a number of ways. The first is in the phase of selling. Suppose that corporations *A* and *B* make apples. The amount of money you can make depends on the number of apples you can sell: the more you sell, the more money you make. So each of *A* and *B* will try to get purchasers to purchase their apples, as opposed to their rival's.

One way to do this is to make apples more cheaply than the rival. This, in turn, can be done in several different ways. The first is to pay the workers employed as little as possible, other things being equal. The agents of capital will, then, pay their workers as little as they can get away with. Of course, if

11. On the labour theory of value, see Bottomore (1983), pp. 564 ff.

a rival can offer higher wages, and still produce the apples more cheaply, they are liable to lose their workforce. So competition for labour power also puts constraints on what these agents do. However, it remains the case that each apple manufacturer is trying to minimise labour costs.

In general, then, capital—those who own or manage it, and those politicians who look after the interests of those who do—will resist anything that makes this harder. Individual employees, in general, have very limited bargaining power; they have much greater power if they act collectively. It is unsurprising, then, that unionisation, that is, forming a group with collective bargaining power, has been resisted and attacked ever since the first unions were formed in the 19th century. This was so then, and is still so now, as we have seen in the "neo-liberal" attacks on unionism by Thatcher, Reagan, Howard (in the UK, the US, and Australia, respectively), their successors, and fellow travellers.

The second thing one can do to produce more cheaply is to reduce the amount of human labour required if one can find a machine which will do the job for less. Hence, the history of capitalism has witnessed vast numbers of workers losing their jobs to mechanisation—and now to computers and artificial intelligence. Those who would wish to reverse this process are bound to be unsuccessful. If a manufacturer maintains jobs for a workforce, when a competitor can use machines and make a cheaper product, they will be unable to sell their products, and so go out of business (serious negative growth!).

Another way to try to capture more of the market, and to get people to buy what you are producing quite generally, is by advertising. People must be made to want to buy what you are selling. They may not really need it, and there may be very little difference between your product and those of your competitors. But if you can induce a *desire* in consumers for your product with appropriate advertising, you can achieve your aim. This can be, and increasingly is, done by deploying psychological techniques, which simply manipulate people's minds: their emotions and beliefs.

These, then, are some of the consequences of competition aimed at maximising market share. A second way to achieve growth at the expense of a competitor is even more direct: take it over! Thus, if I am a large corporate retailer of apples, and a little local grocery store opens up also selling apples, I can simply buy them out (or, alternatively, sell apples much more cheaply for a while, thus driving them out of business). Hence we see a law of capitalist dynamics: big capitals eat smaller capitals. Thus, there is a tendency for quantities of capitals to become fewer and fewer, but larger and larger. In an era where one cannot read, see, or listen to the news for very long without hearing discussions of corporate takeovers, the point needs little illustration.

In this context, I think it is worth quoting the opening paragraph of Mandel's introduction to the Penguin edition of *Capital*:[12]

12. Mandel (1976), p. 11.

When Volume 1 of *Capital* was published, capital industry, though predominant in a few Western European countries, still appeared as an isolated island encircled by a sea of independent farmers and handcraftsmen which covered the whole world, including the greater part of even Europe. What Marx's *Capital* explained, however, was above all the ruthless and irresistible impulse to growth which characterizes production for private profit and the predominant use of profit for capital accumulation. Since Marx wrote, capitalist technology and industry have indeed spread all over the world. As they have done so, moreover, not only have material wealth and the possibilities for freeing mankind definitively from the burden of meaningless, repetitive and mechanical work increased, but so too has the polarization of society between fewer and fewer owners of capital and more and more workers of hand and brain, forced to sell their labour power to these owners. The concentration of wealth and power in a small number of giant industrial and financial corporations has brought with it an increasingly universal struggle between Capital and Labour.

This was written in 1976. Mandel died in 1995. Had he lived to the present, he would have been able to underline his point about the international concentration of wealth with appeal to multinational corporations, like banks (such as Citibank and HSBC); media companies (such as 21st Century Fox, taken over largely by Disney in 2018, and Time Warner, taken over by AT&T in 2018); technology manufacturers (such as Apple and Samsung); and IT companies (such as Facebook and Google, or its parent body, Alphabet Inc).

3.4   The Effects of Capitalism on People

Such, then, is the nature of capital and the capitalist socio-economic system in which it is located. Capital exists simply to make more capital. In the process, people are employed, but the capital does not function for them but for self-enlargement. Capital is not used for the benefit of people; people are manipulated, used, and abused for the benefit of capital.

Starting with the most obvious, and moving to the perhaps less obvious, these uses and abuses, together with their consequences, include the following:

[1] As noted, one way to make as much profit as possible is to pay workers as little as possible. If someone owns no significant capital, they must work for someone else. They have no choice. Capital can therefore take advantage of this position of weakness. In other words, it can exploit them.[13] Capital can keep them in a position of relative poverty (relative, that is, to the *actual* value their labour produces).

13. 'Exploitation' has a technical sense in Marxist economics. I use it in the more familiar sense.

[2] One way to keep people in this position of weakness is to have a pool of unemployed. Capital then no longer needs any particular person. They can be dispensed with, and their job filled by one of the unemployed. Hence, capitalism maintains a "reserve pool" of unemployed. That is, we have structural unemployment. Unemployment leads to impoverishment, not in a relative sense, but in an absolute sense of living below the poverty level.[14] Such poverty, naturally, leads to illness, crime, turning to drugs (including daytime television and social media), and numerous other social problems. Moreover, under capitalism, there is always the threat of losing one's job (because the business goes bust, or because one can be replaced by a cheaper, younger person or a machine). Insecurity produces a raft of psychological problems of its own.[15]

[3] Another way to maximise profit is to produce commodities as efficiently, and so as cheaply, as possible. A major way of achieving this is with the division of labour. Someone employed by capital will then spend their whole time doing essentially one thing. Such a practice ensures that one aspect of a person's abilities becomes highly developed, whilst the others atrophy. As a person, then, they become deformed.

[4] Again as noted, a quantity of capital must try to get people to buy its products, rather than those of a competitor. To do so, it uses the techniques of advertising (thought manipulation) to create desires, most of which are entirely spurious. People are made to desire things for which there is no rational ground. They are manipulated to form a consumer society. Capitalist production for the sake of production therefore produces its mirror image: consumption for the sake of consumption.[16]

[5] Moreover, capital can allow its workers no say in the way a business is run. For they would then do things that would damage profit (by requiring better working conditions and wages, greater health and safety conditions, etc.). Since they have no say in this central aspect of their life, they become alienated from it. Work is not life-affirming; it is nothing more than necessary to live.

[6] The social relations of capitalism involve those who own/manage capital and those who are simply employed by it. Naturally, those in the first class are a

---

14. It is important to distinguish between poverty and a low level of material affluence. The two are not the same. Thus, Schweickart (2011), p. 112: 'It is important to distinguish between "living in poverty" from "being poor". The people of Cuba, for example, are poor. The per capita income of Cuba is but a fraction of that of the United States (one-fifth, according to the CIA Fact Book), yet there is little malnourishment or homelessness in Cuba, and everyone has access to basic health care. The striking result: infant mortality and life expectancy in Cuba are nearly identical to what they are in the United States. The people of Cuba are poor, but they do not live in poverty'.

15. On the connection between job insecurity, unemployment, and mental health, see, further, Fisher (2012).

16. As Bookchin (2004), p. 5, puts it.

lot richer than those in the second. Hence we have large inequalities of wealth, and so social inequality. In a capitalist "democratic" structure, money means power. Hence we have political inequality as well. A majority of people are disempowered, relative to the few who have wealth. These will use their power, of course, to further the interests of the capital that they own/manage. The state, therefore, does not function in the interest of people but of capital. Thus, in contemporary "liberal democracies"—or better, "capital dictatorships"—the democracy is a facade.

[7] Of course, it is not in the interest of capital that people should understand how the system works, which is not to their benefit. If they did, there would be significant pressure to change it. Capitalism therefore produces an ideology which deceives people and covers this over. People are led to believe that capitalism is natural, in their best interests, and so forth. The ideology is imposed on people's thinking by advertising, the mass media, statements made by politicians and "captains of industry", and so on. People are therefore made and kept deceived.

[8] Capital acts in its own self-interest. To justify this, its ideology says that this is perfectly fine: indeed, the "rational man" of capitalist economics is a person who maximises their own goods, never mind the needs of others. That is, it legitimises selfishness. Those influenced by the ideology (most of us) take the point: it's fine to be selfish. Hence, the knock-on effect of the economic relations is behaviour that is humanly and socially dysfunctional.[17]

[9] Finally, capitalism requires constant growth, and this is leading to environmental destruction and ecological change which seriously and negatively impact on people, especially on those who are less affluent. This impact is already a reality, though the matter is most serious for future generations. There is a lot more to be said about this topic, but rather than having an extended interlude to discuss the matter here, I have reserved it for an appendix.

It might be thought that, though capitalism has these negative consequences for the majority of people—those who are merely employed by capital—at least it does not have these effects on the few (the globally *very* few) who own or manage it. They are, after all, richer. However, this would be a shortsighted view. The latter are in the thrall of capital no less than the former.

They may be richer, and so less likely to go hungry or commit common crime—though their very position, and the ideology of maximisation, opens them to temptations to white-collar crime and shady dealings not open to most people. There is, moreover, a much greater tendency amongst this class for people's personalities to be deformed by greed and a disregard for the humanity of others, simply because these capacities are exercised on a daily basis. They become used to treating people as cyphers, not humans.

---

17. Marglin (2008), p. 2: '[the capitalist market is a system that] not only regulates itself, but regulates [us] ourselves, a process that shapes and forms people whose relationships with one another are circumscribed and reduced by the market'.

The requirement to make a profit also exploits their labour. They are likely to work extraordinarily long hours, to the detriment of their personal and family life. And though they have more control over their working tenure than most people, in the last instance they are just as much hostage to the requirements of capital, to being fired if they do not make enough profit, or to being disposed of if their company goes bankrupt or is taken over.

Moreover, they cannot isolate themselves from the society in which they live. The kind of society in which they live produces crime, migration, climate change, and so on. These things affect everyone—if some more than others.

Perhaps people in this situation would say that these things are of no importance—at least as long as they are succeeding in their enterprises. But, if so, this tells us something about their values: those enshrined in the ideology of capitalism. And such people are just as much subject to this as everyone else—perhaps more so, since they are actively involved in its propagation.

3.5 The Global South

The effects of capitalism which I have just enumerated are all present in "advanced capitalist" countries. However, they are present in a much more extreme form in the global South, where capitalism has run rife, wreaking havoc on both the environment and the lives of millions of people. The nature and extent of this is documented by Leech (2012)—writing from the perspective of someone who spent many years as an investigative journalist in Latin America—who summarises matters as follows:[18]

> [the] structure of global capitalism, whilst providing impressive opportunities for wealth generation, ensures that most of the wealth generated remains in the hands of a small minority. ... [The capitalist structures] contribute to the death of millions of people around the world annually.

The imbalance between the global North and the global South which Leech notes is illustrated by a few simple statistics. As reported in a recent UNICEF report,[19] $8 billion is spent annually in the US on cosmetics; it would require only $6 billion to ensure that all children in the global South receive a basic education. Europeans spend $11 billion a year on ice cream; it would require only $9 billion to ensure safe drinking water and adequate sanitation for everyone in the global South.[20] The relative values of cosmetics versus education, or ice cream versus sanitation, hardly needs belabouring.

18. Leech (2012), pp. 3 f.
19. UNICEF (2004). Quoted in Gibbs (2017), p. 67.
20. I'm not suggesting that affluent consumers intend these effects. For the most part, people just don't know these things. I will return to the questions of ignorance and education later in the book.

Nor is this disparity an "accident". This is the way that capitalism works. Leech again:[21]

> Such a degree of global inequality is not simply an unintended consequence of capitalism; it is an essential component of the capitalist system. After all, from the perspective of capital, there are hundreds of millions of dollars in profits to be made selling cosmetics, ice cream, and pet food to North Americans and Europeans, whereas there is no viable market for education and health care in the global South, where the majority of recipients simply cannot afford to pay for them. Furthermore, decisions which prioritize the production of luxuries for consumers in the global North over essentials for people in the global South are not simply callous choices; they are perfectly 'rational' decisions made according to the logic of capital.

It is the nature of capital to produce more capital, and it will do whatever does this most productively.

Making a similar point earlier in the book, Leech describes the matter (as have some Engaged Buddhist thinkers) as 'structural violence':[22]

> capital's internal logic forces it to expand to every corner of the globe, and the resulting inequality and deprivation of basic needs for billions of people are inherent components of capitalism. These inequalities in wealth and power constitute a form of structural violence that targets large sectors of the world's population, particularly those living in the global South, because it necessarily deprives them of their fundamental needs.

The term 'violence' is indeed appropriate, since death and suffering are inflicted; and the term 'structural' is appropriate because this is not simply one person inflicting violence on another; the violence is inherent in the very system. As Gibbs summarises matters:[23]

> structural violence manifests itself in many ways, but its common theme is the deprivation of peoples' basic needs as a result of existing social structures. The basic needs include food, healthcare and other resources essential for achieving a healthy existence and the fullest human development possible. Such inequality is rooted in the oppression of one group by another.

21. Leech (2012), p. 82.
22. Leech (2012), p. 5.
23. Gibbs (2017), p. 62.

And as she notes, such violence may well be more insidious than individual violence, just because no individual perpetrates it.

Leech goes so far as to claim that this is a form of genocide:[24]

> [w]hile more than 10 million people die annually as a result of capitalism's structural genocide, hundreds of millions more survive on a non-living wage or no wage at all, a lack of basic housing, hunger, sickness and many other social injustices. Furthermore, the structural violence perpetrated against these people often results in them also being victimized by direct physical violence in the forms of criminal aggression, state repression, social cleansing and even suicide. At the core of this structural genocide is an inequality in power and wealth that ensures that interests of capital are prioritized over those of the majority of human beings and of nature.

Now, I would not go so far as to call the matter 'genocide', since at least as normally understood, genocide is intentional, and the intention of capital is not to kill people, but to make a profit. The killing might be said to be an unintended side effect. However, this "collateral damage" is mind-numbingly obvious to any educated, thoughtful person. So whether the effect is one of commission or omission, the moral culpability is the same.[25]

3.6 Critiques of Marx' Theory

So far in this chapter, I have done nothing but explain Marx' analysis of capital, and some of the consequences of the socio-economic relations in which this is embedded. Of course, many people are likely to object to Marx' analysis of capitalist political economy. In this section I will defend it against some of the more obvious objections.

I think it unlikely that people will deny that an essential part of a capitalist economy is capital growth. That is pretty obvious. We see this in a small way in the fact that the whole nature of the position of a CEO of a corporation is to make as much profit as possible. They lose their position if they fail at this. We see it in a much larger way when an entire economy does not grow and goes into recession. Jobs are lost, companies fold, governments fall. This is not good for the capitalist order. Unsurprisingly, then, much of post-Keynesian economic manipulation has been aimed at preventing recession (negative growth).

What might well be denied, though, is that Marx, in his focus on capital—that is, the social relations which constitute it—has isolated a fundamental

---

24. Leech (2012), p. 149.
25. Further on the sorry effects of capitalist "development" on the countries of South East Asia, see Sivaraksa (1992), ch. 3. See ch. 4 on the particularly baleful effects of subordinating everything to an increase of GDP.

category which explains the dynamics of contemporary society. Marx' definition of capital as wealth in search of more wealth is intended as a real definition. That is, it is meant to capture its nature, and so explain how we see those relations to function. In the same way, water having the chemical constitution H_2O explains how we see water to behave. One might deny Marx has achieved that.[26]

That he did indeed do so is hardly a self-evident truth. Marx provided a theory of how certain political economies, ones based on capital, function. The theory is certainly an empirical one, and the evidence for it, if there is such, must be whether it provides an explanation of what has happened and still happens. Moreover, the explanation must stand up to the methodological criteria of what counts as a good explanation: it must be relatively simple, unify a large number of different phenomena, be relatively free of *ad hoc* hypotheses, and so on.

Marx' theory fares very well by these criteria. For a start, the varied items enumerated in the last two sections are hard to gainsay, and Marx' theory provides a uniform explanation of why these things happen. More generally, Marx' theory explains events such as why capital is often in confrontation with labour,[27] the need for expanded markets and new capital resources (one important driver of imperialism), the fact that capital becomes multinational when its scope for national expansion wanes, the capitalist imperative to destroy the environment in the cause of growth, and surely many other things. (I will take up some more of these in Chapter 6.) Mandel makes the point this way:[28]

> In fact, it would have been very easy to 'prove' Marx's analysis to have been wrong, if experience had shown, for example, that the more that capitalist industry develops, the smaller and smaller the average factory becomes, the less it depends on new technology, the more its capital is supplied by the workers themselves, the more workers become owners of their factories, the less the part of wages taken by consumer good becomes (and the greater becomes the part of wages used for buying the workers' own means of production) ... then one could indeed say that *Capital* was so much rubbish and had dismally failed to predict what would happen in the real capitalist world a century after its publication. It is sufficient to compare the real history of the period since 1867 ...

26. In philosophy, there is a standard distinction (to be found, for example, in Locke—see Jones (2018)) between real definitions and nominal definitions. Nominal definitions specify the meanings of *words*. Real definitions specify the nature of *things*.

27. In *Capital* Vol. 1, Marx frequently quotes things said by the capitalists of his day in an attempt to justify exploiting their labourers in various ways. I first read *Capital* in the late 1970s, and was struck by the fact that similar things were still being said. Nothing has changed in the last 40 years.

28. Mandel (1976), p. 25.

with what Marx predicted it would be … to understand how remarkable indeed was Marx's theoretical achievement and how strongly it stands up against the experimental test of history.

Of course, socio-economic systems are complex, and attempts to explain what happens in terms of one single thing are risibly simplistic.[29] For a start, capital has not had it all its own way in the last 200 years: there has been resistance: the formation of unions, the creation of some kind of welfare state,[30] Occupy Wall Street. It must be said, however, that these movements were swimming against the historical tide, and gains made by workers in one generation were often undone in subsequent generations.

Perhaps more importantly, what happens in a society is a result of the power structures operating within it (as well, of course, as those which impinge upon it from without). Now, economic power, in the form of the control of capital and the institutional political power which goes along with this, are centrally important in this regard. But these are not the only power structures which operate: there are those of race, gender, and doubtless others. It is clear that there are intimate connections between economic power and these other forms of power. The connection between the antebellum economic system of the United States, slavery, and racism are obvious enough to need no discussion—as are the connections between patriarchy and consigning domestic labour (an integral part of the labour of any society) to women. However, it would be wrong to suppose that one can explain these power structures simply in terms of economic power structure (that is, to reduce them to it). For a start, they cannot be explained by capitalist economic power, since these power structures exist, and have existed historically, in non-capitalist societies. More importantly, racism and sexism can occur between people of the same economic power: black and white workers, men and women employed to do the same thing, and so on. I will return to this matter in more detail in a later chapter.

Marx (and Engels), with their view of historical materialism, held that everything about social attitudes was determined 'in the last instance' by the economic base (relations of economic production, exchange, and consumption) of a society. Whatever determinism in the last instance means (and this is

---

29. Which does not mean that we cannot isolate the "dominant tendency", as it is sometimes put. In the same way, many gravitational forces combine to determine the motion of the Earth. That of the sun is by far the most important, however.

30. This is a complex phenomenon. In Britain it was driven by political parties such as the postwar British Labour Party, an offspring of the British union movement, and devoted—less and less as time went on—to furthering the interests of British workers. And this the welfare state certainly did, delivering great improvements in health care and education. One might well argue, though, that this was allowed by capital only because it mitigated the lot of working people at little capital expense, and so was a cost-effective way of defusing attacks against capitalism.

unclear enough), this is certainly false. (Much more of this also later.) Attitudes concerning race and gender are, at least in part, autonomous. Having said that, the economic power structure of a society is still the most fundamental power structure in one sense: people need to live (have food, clothes, shelter) if they are to do anything else. This is the stuff of economic power.

Whilst on the subject of simplistic explanations, one often hears from the apologists of capitalism that capitalism and its fundamental property of growth is simply a feature of the selfishness and acquisitiveness of human nature. About this, one should note two things. The first concerns human nature. There will be a lot more to be said about this in due course. Here it is necessary to say only the following. People can certainly be selfish; they can also be altruistic. One thing we have learned about human behaviour and its dispositions is that these are highly malleable. Moreover, as I noted above, human selfishness is something that is brought out by capitalism. The relation between capitalism and selfishness is, then, at least a two-way street. Second, and more importantly, the way that capital functions is not a result of individuals' psychological states, but of the "logic" of the system of production. Suppose a capitalist to be altruistic through and through. If they do not make enough profit, they will simply go out of business, not change the system. That's the way the system works; and the system is bigger than any individual.

Before ending this section, it is probably important to deal with the old chestnut that Marx has been refuted, since he predicted the demise of capitalism, which has not happened.

Now, it is true that Marx did expect a revolution to overthrow capitalism. When this would be was unclear. He thought at times, such as the revolutions in Europe of 1848, that it was imminent. He became less optimistic when these periods of political activity came to nothing. Still, I think he would have been surprised to see capitalism thriving, had he come back today. He also expected a communist revolution to occur in the advanced capitalist countries, such as Germany and England,[31] whereas, to the extent that nominally communist revolutions occurred—or to the extent that they were communist for very long—they were in largely peasant countries, such as Russia, China, and Cuba.

Now, why these things did and did not happen one might debate. One might argue that capitalism has survived because of the unanticipated ability of capital to exploit labour in countries of the global South; that the revolution occurred in Russia because it was the 'weakest link in the chain' (as Trotsky put it, in his essay *What Next?*); that the revolutions went awry, much as anarchists like Bakunin predicted, because the Communist Parties involved came to be driven by fostering their own interests, and not those of most people. Books could be (and have been) written on these topics.

---

31. Though, in some of his very last writings, his eyes did turn towards Russia.

But we may simply set these things aside here. It is no part of the account of the dynamics of a capitalist economic system, as explained above, that capitalism will come to an end. It is quite compatible with this analysis that capitalism will go on indefinitely—at least until it hits the wall of finite resources. The economic conditions may (or may not) provide conditions that are ripe for a change of regime; but no change will occur without political action, and this may or may not be forthcoming. Tendencies towards it may be suppressed by violence, ideology, corruption.[32] We may therefore set this objection aside.

3.7 Apologists for Capitalism

Let us now turn from the objections of people who take Marx' theory of how a capitalist political economy functions to be false to those who think it is true, but who wish to justify such a political economy anyway: the apologists for capital.[33]

First amongst these are those who take capitalism to be inevitable. Things just have to be like this. Now, it is true that, from the inside, it is often very difficult to see how things might be otherwise. But we know in this case that they can be otherwise: they have been otherwise. Europe in the year 1000 did not have a capitalist political economy. Still, it might be claimed that now that we have it, it is here for good. The political economy of 3000 will be the same as that of 2000—assuming, that is, that the human race manages to be around for another 1,000 years—which is anything but a good bet at the moment. That claim would be literally incredible. It is like someone saying in the year 1000 that society and economics will be the same in 2000 as it is in 1000. Indeed, the contemporary claim is even more incredible since we now know a lot more about history and the changes this brings than did a medieval European at the end of the first millennium CE. Indeed, even a thinker as economically orthodox as J. S. Mill argued (in 1848) that capitalism would become obsolete:[34]

> The form of association ... which, if mankind continues to improve, must be expected to predominate is not that which can exist between a capitalist as chief, and work-people without a voice in management, but the association of the labourers themselves on terms of equality, collectively

---

32. That the end of capitalism was not inevitable was clear to Trotsky, as he explained in his essay *Socialism or Barbarism*. That disjunction might seem an exaggeration, but given the environmental catastrophes that seem to be looming, perhaps less so now than when he wrote.
33. I note that some attempts to justify capitalism do so—improbably—in terms of the justice of the system. Since the notion of justice plays no role in Buddhist ethics, I ignore these here. In any case, they are thoroughly debunked in Schweickart (2011), ch. 2.
34. Mill (1920), ch. 7, sec 6, p. 773.

owning the capital with which they carry on their operations, and working under managers elected and removable by themselves.

Of course capitalism will not last forever—a simple corollary of the Buddhist doctrine of impermanence (*anitya*). The questions are only 'how will things be different', and 'how can we change them for the better'? I suppose that it might be said that there is no better system. Such a claim would beggar belief. The system we now have has been delivered to us by an uncoordinated series of historical events. And such evolution—biological or economic—rarely finds optimal solutions; its results are usually a kludge. (Think of the results of biological evolution. The creatures produced are generally reasonably well adapted to their environments, but are hardly optimal.) Of course we can do better. Indeed, we need to. Leech puts the matter starkly:[35]

> After all, in reality the issue is not a lack of alternatives to capitalism but rather that there is no alternative to socialism if the human race is to perpetuate itself in a humane and sustainable fashion.

The next kind of apologist admits that a capitalist political economy may have the "downsides" we have noted, but that this is acceptable since, overall, everyone benefits from it. Like most ideological claims which hide the truth, there is a certain plausibility to this claim; but like most ideological claims, its plausibility starts to fade once one scrutinises it.[36]

For a start, the benefit in question is identified with material possessions—wealth, if you like. The objection simply assumes that greater wealth makes for a better—happier, more fulfilling—life. Whether people's lives are more so now than in, say, 1880 is an empirical question. And there is no way we can do the research to find out, simply because we cannot go back and interview people in 1880 to find out. That does not show that the claim is false, of course; but it does not show that the claim is true either. In other words, there is no empirical evidence for this. Moreover, there is evidence which at least suggests that, for the periods for which we do have evidence, people now are not happier than they used to be.[37] And this coheres with further empirical evidence that, beyond a certain amount, more wealth does not make people happier.[38] Indeed, the desire to have ever more wealth generated by capitalist ideology is a prime source of self-defeating *tṛṣṇa*.

35. Leech (2012), p. 112. By 'socialism', he says (quoting Maass (2010)) that he means nothing more than the 'simple idea' that 'the resources of a society be used to meet people's needs'.
36. This line has been pushed most aggressively recently by the "New Optimist" movement of people like Gates and Pinker. The thoroughly misleading nature of the statistics they invoke is exposed in Hickel (2019b).
37. See, e.g., Mental Health Today (2017) and Sustainable Development Solutions Network (2019).
38. See Luscombe (2010) and Dietz and O'Neil (2013), pp. 25 ff.

Next, the blanket claim that people are better off in terms of wealth than they were 140 years ago is, to put it mildly, highly misleading. Clearly, *some* people are. But even if this is true of most people in the global North, it is not true of those in the global South—and it must be remembered that the wealth of the global North has been made possible by exploiting the people, resources, and environment of those countries.[39]

True, in the last 30 years the level of world poverty, as determined by simple numerical measures, has decreased. But the current figures are still shocking. One-tenth of the world lives on less than US$1.90 a day (the official World Bank poverty line); half of the people in the world have a family income of less than US$2.50 a day.[40] And of course, these numbers say nothing about the effects of all the policies enforced on people and their societies by capitalism in order to obtain these somewhat pathetic results—the destruction of communities, environments, healthier work practices, and so on. These bits of arithmetic, in fact, cloak the miserable reality which lies behind them, as explained by Alston, the outgoing UN special rapporteur on extreme poverty and human rights. As he says:[41]

> As I show in my final report as UN special rapporteur on extreme poverty and human rights, almost all of these rosy accounts rely on one measure—the World Bank's $1.90 (£1.50) a day international poverty line—which is widely misunderstood, flawed and yields a deceptively positive picture. It has generated an undue sense of satisfaction and a dangerous complacency with the status quo.
>
> Under that line, the number of people in "extreme poverty" fell from 1.9 billion in 1990 to 736 million in 2015. But the dramatic drop is only possible with a scandalously unambitious benchmark, which aims to ensure a mere miserable subsistence. The best evidence shows it doesn't even cover the cost of food or housing in many countries. And it obscures poverty among women and those often excluded from official surveys, such as migrant workers and refugees. Much of the touted decline is due to rising incomes in a single country, China.

39. Shiva (2005) puts it as follows (quoted in Leech (2012), p. 29): 'The poor [of the global South] are not those who have been "left behind"; they are the ones who have been robbed. The riches accumulated by Europe are based on the riches taken from Asia, Africa and Latin America. Without the destruction of India's rich textile industry, without the takeover of the spice trade, without the genocide of the native American tribes, without African slavery, the Industrial Revolution would not have led to new riches for Europe or the US. It was the violent takeover of Third World resources and markets that created wealth in the North and poverty in the South'.
40. See, e.g., Compassion (2020), Our World in Data (2020), and United Nations (2020).
41. Alston (2020), which contains a link to his draft report to the UN Human Rights Council.

Indeed, it is even a sweeping and misleading generalisation to say that people in the global North are better off. All capitalist countries have people who live below the poverty level. In 2020, about 11%–12% of Americans live below the *official* poverty rate.[42] (And official statistics are always drawn up to put the best possible spin on things.) Moreover, adjusted for the cost of living, the income of a large proportion of US workers has not increased for at least 40 years—if anything, it has declined.[43]

Third, many of the factors that have improved the quality of people's lives have nothing to do with capitalism. Thus, one of the major factors helping to improve the quality of people's lives is the advance in medical science, due to research undertaken in universities, and so not privately funded. True, the improvement also involves the production of drugs and medical technology, much of this by private capital; but this way of producing the technology means that it is then used to make profit, and so made *less* available to people. The general increase of health care has therefore happened *in spite of* capitalism.[44]

But even if none of this were true, three other points are important. The first is that, even if the defence were as stated, it is not at all clear that the result could not have been achieved in some other, and more humane, way. Indeed, it is clear that it can be. Thus, the general level of affluence in Cuba before the revolution of 1959 was pretty miserable, due to the exploitation of workers by local capitalists and international (mainly US) capital. Since the revolution, the level of poverty has plummeted; and notably, the country has an outstanding public health care system. This has been achieved without capitalism—indeed, and again, in spite of the restrictions that have been put on the country by international capital and the actions of its political agents. In fact, it's pretty obvious that cooperation often achieves much better results than competition. A football team that plays as a team will achieve much better results than one in which each player is simply trying to show how good they are. People working together can produce better results than people working in isolation. Part of the ideology of capitalism is that competition always produces better results than cooperation, since people want to do better than their rivals. This is just plain false. Nothing at all could be produced without human cooperation of numerous kinds.

Second, now that the present situation concerning wealth *has* been brought about, that the "historical mission of capitalism" has been achieved, as Marx put it,[45] we could make much better use of the collective wealth than we do. There is now enough wealth in the world that no one need go hungry, we could wipe

42. Poverty USA (2020).
43. Desilver (2018).
44. See, further, Hickel (2019a).
45. *Capital*, Vol. 3, Ch. 27.

out many major diseases, everyone could have decent health care and education, and so on. This is not the case, simply because, this distribution of
wealth having been produced by capitalism, it is lopsided—to put it mildly
—as some simple statistics show:[46]

- Since 2015, the richest 1% has owned more wealth than the rest of the
  planet.
- Eight men now own the same amount of wealth as the poorest half of the
  world.
- Over the next 20 years, 500 people will hand over $2.1 trillion to their
  heirs—a sum larger than the GDP of India, a country of 1.3 billion people.
- The incomes of the poorest 10% of people increased by less than $3 a year
  between 1988 and 2011, while the incomes of the richest 1% increased 182
  times as much.
- An FTSE-100 CEO earns as much in a year as 10,000 people in working in
  garment factories in Bangladesh.
- In the US, [research] shows that over the last 30 years the growth in the
  incomes of the bottom 50% has been zero, whereas incomes of the top 1%
  have grown 300%.

Indeed, another recent report[47] notes the fact that the richest country in the
world (the US) is also the most unequal country in the world with respect to
wealth. In fact, the increase in the world's wealth over the last 30 years has gone
predominantly to the world's richest people, where it can do the least good.[48] It
is not the amount of wealth in the world that is a problem; it is its distribution.
It is about time that wealth was used for the benefit of people, and not people
for the benefit of wealth.

Finally, capitalism cannot go on indefinitely anyway. Capitalism is predi-
cated on economic growth. Yet economic growth is now clearly destroying
the human environment (let alone the environment of other species).
Climate change is causing sea levels to rise, destruction of agricultural lands,
and will soon cause mass migration, heightened international conflict, and so
on. If we do not protect the environment, the environment will destroy us.
Some people may place hope in a technical or market fix of some kind. But
even if something like this could be done, it could be only a stopgap. The
basic point is that growth cannot continue indefinitely in a finite system such
as our natural environment provides. Sooner or later, it will hit the wall. (I
return to this matter in the appendix to this chapter.)

46. Oxfam (2017).
47. Brandmeir et al. (2015). Cited in Gibbs (2017), p. 160.
48. Thus, in the years 1990–2001, for every $100 of global economic growth, only 60c went to
    people living on less than $1 a day. See Dietz and O'Neil (2013), p. 27.

Perhaps this is the place to say something about what has come to be known as 'trickle-down economics'. The view is essentially one to the effect that if one makes the very rich richer—usually by cuts in personal and especially corporate taxation—the poor will get richer too. The view is a staple of contemporary capitalist ideology, and has been appealed to by many capitalist governments in different countries to support their policies—unsurprisingly, since the members of these governments tend to come from the upper side of the class structure and/or are placed there by financial support from business corporations.

The view has been attacked and debunked many times by authoritative economists as factually false, even as a move within the capitalist game. Making the rich much richer does not significantly affect the wealth of the poorer.[49] Joseph Stiglitz, the Nobel Prize–winning economist and erstwhile chief economist of the World Bank, puts matters as follows:[50]

> Some economists disdain even discussing inequality. The job of economists, they say, is to increase the size of the pie. If that is done, all will benefit—as President Kennedy put it, a rising tide lifts all boats. I wish it were true. But it's not.
>
> Many among the wealthy claimed that all would benefit from the riches bestowed on the top—benefits that would trickle down. But this has almost never been so, and certainly not in the period since 1980.

But in any case, as a piece of moral justification it is entirely bankrupt. It is on a par with trying to justify giving the rich more sumptuous food at their banquets, so that there may be more leftovers for those who survive by eating them. It is simply a piece of rationalisation by the rich which functions, consciously or unconsciously, to justify their self-interest.

The capitalist economy which is supposed to trickle down wealth from the super-abundance of the rich to the poor might better be called an economy which pumps up wealth from the labour of the poor to the rich.

Finally in the category of apologists for capitalism, we come to defenders of what one might call "capitalism with a human face". Notable amongst such people presently is Stiglitz himself. In his *People, Power, and Profits*[51] he mounts a well-justified, documented, and damning attack on the contemporary neoliberal American capitalist system and its political entourage.[52]

---

49. See, e.g., Amadeo (2018), Dabla-Norris *et al.* (2015), Keller (2015), Krugman (2017), Lawson (2016), Miles (2014), Perspectives in C (2017), Robinson (2017), Zidar (2018), Hope and Limberg (2020).
50. Stiglitz (2019), pp. 33, 38.
51. Stiglitz (2019).
52. He is particularly scathing about Trump, his administration, and its cronies. As he makes clear, however, they merely bring to fruition tendencies that were already well entrenched in the system.

Stiglitz holds, however, that there is nothing wrong with capitalism as such, and all that is necessary is a more equal distribution of the wealth that it produces. He suggests that this may be achieved by more government regulation in the US: stronger antitrust laws, higher taxation, a national health-care system, an education system not based on wealth, democratisation of the political process, and so on. Indeed, as is clear, Stiglitz is writing to, for, and about the US. (Even though he advised the World Bank, he shows no sign of awareness of the effects of past and present US economic and foreign policy in the global South, for example.)

Stiglitz is under no illusion about how hard it would be to bring about the US regulatory changes he has in mind when the political and ideological power structure is so firmly in the hands of the 1%.[53] He provides, however, no real plan as to how appropriate regulation changes might be brought about, and how one might be able to neutralise the institutional resistance attempts to realise such changes would encounter. Nor does he note that the US has no power over appropriate regulations in other countries—most notably, those of the global South, where capitalism is at its most vicious.

But leave this aside. As he himself points out, the measures he advocates are already in place in many other capitalist countries in the global North. The contemporary problems he notes may not be as acute there as they are in the US; but they are present in those countries none the less. Indeed, this is so because what he is trying to eliminate are not contingencies of the system, but products of the very system itself. Stiglitz assumes that the growth delivered by the profit motive is a good thing. In a world where there is already enough that all may have adequate nutrition, health care, and education, and economic growth is causing environmental havoc, this is hardly obvious. But in any case, it is the very capitalist drive for profit which is the underlying cause of its pernicious effects, as we have already seen.

3.8 Conclusion

In this chapter, I have explained and defended Marx' analysis of the way that a capitalist political economy works. At the core of this is the necessity for capital to grow. The result is that people work for the benefit of capital—that is, wealth—and not the other way around, which would be a much more rational and humane way of configuring human affairs.

The two mainsprings of the analysis of our contemporary socio-economic situation are now in place. I will put them together in Chapter 5. However, before we turn to that we need to look at another part of the story, which is

---

53. Thus, he says (p. 173): 'the greed-is-good ethics of the twenty-first-century American capitalism works against creating the right [regulatory] norms'.

fundamental to tying the two parts together. This concerns what it means to be a person. I turn to this in the next chapter.

3.9   Appendix: Capitalism and the Environment

The relationship between the looming environmental disaster we are facing and capitalism is a crucial one—both for our understanding of capitalism and for the seriousness of the problem. Here I discuss matters in more detail.[54]

3.9.1   The Looming Catastrophe

It is clear that an environmental catastrophe is looming, caused by global warming. Even those who understand the situation well do not know exactly how close it is, or what its precise effects will be. For even if we knew exactly how much global temperatures were going to rise (which we don't), our models of the effects on the Earth, its climates, ecologies, and so on are still imprecise. Moreover, changes may well not be gradual. Quite plausibly, the systems in question are catastrophic, in the technical sense: there can be sudden and irreversible changes: a point of no return.

But that caveat aside, things are obviously not looking good. Even maintenance of the *status quo* will result in erratic weather conditions and droughts, major disruptions to food production, and rising sea levels, resulting in population shifts. (Remember how much of the world's population lives close to sea level.)[55]

But the reality is likely to be worse. The political will for change, if it is to have any real effect, has to be global, and it is presently minimal. Even if the US changed its policy to zero increase immediately (which is not going to happen), many countries that are not yet fully capitalised are understandably loath to stop their capital growth until their standard of living is raised to one approaching the standard of those countries that are. The realisation of this is ecologically impossible. Leech puts the point in the following way:[56]

> [T]he United States, with only 4 per cent of the world's population, consumes 25 per cent of global energy production, and 50 percent of the global production of raw materials, while generating 40 per cent of the world's waste. Clearly, there are not sufficient natural resources, or places on the planet to store the waste generated, to permit 7 billion

54. I take the material here from Priest (2012). There, I go on to argue that we should be preparing for the possibility of a very serious, and perhaps relatively sudden, social collapse caused by environmental change.

55. Remember, also, that it is those in poorer countries, who have done least to generate the problem, who are likely to be hardest hit by it.

56. Leech (2012), p. 87.

people the same materialistic standard of living enjoyed by 300 million
people in the United States.

Moreover, if and when cuts are eventually made, temperatures will still rise for
some time, due to hysteresis in the system.

Even if I were wrong about this, there are reasons to suppose that the capitalist system, which—*pace* Marx—shows no signs of disappearing yet, will
eventually produce an ecological catastrophe anyway. I will return to this in
a moment.

It seems highly likely, then, that we will be facing dramatic socio-ecological
disruption some time this century. The effects of this, though hard to predict,
are likely to include:

* The destruction of major agricultural areas
* Major redistribution of populations away from current coastal areas
* The consequent increased pressure on resources in both urban and agri-
  cultural areas.

The result of this *is* predictable. There will be increasing and intensified
competition for resources: food, clean water, primary resources, and markets—
especially in a context where China and India will be increasingly competing
with North America, Europe—and each other. The consequences of this,
again, are likely to be military conflict, quite possibly outright (even nuclear)
wars. These, in turn, will lead to further environmental degradation and
destruction of resources. This will produce increased competition, leading to
further conflict, and so on—a vicious circle; or, more aptly, a viciously
descending spiral.

Of course, this could all be avoided by radical measures:

* Instituting a world body that can put in place and enforce appropriate
  coordinated international activity.
* The redistribution of the world's resources more evenly across its peoples.
* Capping—or preferably decreasing—the size of the world's population.[57]
* Putting a halt to a form of economic production whose rationale is growth.

But to suppose that these things might happen any time soon is clearly utopian
wishfulness.

It is sometimes suggested that global warming can be solved in due course by
some sort of "technological fix". However, what kind of fix might solve all the
problems is quite opaque. To act on the basis of such hope is like a person

---

57. This should *not* be interpreted as a comment specifically about the global South. As we have
    just noted, the resource use behind the current problem is driven largely by the global North.

doing all the things known to cause cancer in the hope that a cure for cancer will be found. In any case, as we will see, such fixes can never solve the fundamental problem.

3.9.2   The Role of Capitalism in This

What has this to do with capitalism?

Marx thought that capitalism was not sustainable. The ever-increasing pressure for profit (or to be more accurate, surplus value) would make the conditions of workers more and more unpleasant, until they decided that enough was enough, and take over. Clearly this has not happened—at least, not yet. Capitalism has shown a robustness that Marx did not anticipate. Exactly how it has achieved this is a debatable point. Arguably, the globalisation of capital has played a large role in the matter. Not only has the widened market decreased the pressure for a time (the gas has a larger bottle, so the pressure is lower, as it were); but globalisation has moved the worst exploited part of the industrial workforce from the global North to the global South, where expectations are lower, and, in any case, it is easier to control dissent. Conceivably a revolution of the kind that Marx envisaged could still happen, but it seems unlikely that it would happen before the looming environmental catastrophe (though the global near meltdown of the world's banking system towards the end of 2008 certainly gave cause for thought in this regard).

However, Marx was right that capitalism is not sustainable. The reason for the unsustainability is closer to that envisaged a generation before Marx by Thomas Malthus in his *Essay of the Principle of Population*, of 1794.[58] Malthus argued that population growth is geometric—or exponential, as it is also called. (Thus, if every couple has three children, the population goes up by 50% each generation.) In contrast, the increase in resources—and particularly food production—is arithmetic. (That is, it increases only by a constant amount each generation.) Exponential progressions grow much faster than arithmetic progressions; and so in due course, the population must outgrow the means to sustain it, unleashing human suffering. For Malthus, only natural causes (e.g., accidents and old age), misery (wars, pestilence, plague, and above all, famine), vice (which for him included infanticide, murder, contraception, and homosexuality) could check excessive population growth. Malthus favoured sexual restraint (which included late marriage and sexual abstinence) as a check on population growth—though only for the poor and working class. (The rich, I suppose, still had vice.)

Historically speaking, Malthus has proved just as wrong as Marx. Food production has grown at a rate much greater than arithmetic. The reason why, though, should be noted. The increased productivity has been brought about

---

58. For an account of Malthus, see Petersen (1979). For Marx' own thoughts on Malthus, see ch. 5 of Charbit (2009).

by mechanisation and, crucially, the increasingly intensive use of fertilisation. And these form part of the current ecological problem.[59] Many fertilisers emit greenhouse gasses and, heavily used, give rise to salinisation and land degradation; and both the production of fertilisers and mechanisation depend heavily on the petrochemical industry, a primary source of global warming. That Malthus' predictions have not been realised to date is, therefore, somewhat cold comfort in the present context.

Still, even though Malthus was wrong, his view contained an important insight: resource availability is bounded. In particular, then, exponential increase of resource demand must, sooner or later, come into conflict with this bound. To see why this fact is crucial in the present context we have to return to Marx.

As we have seen, capitalism is driven by its need to grow. It requires constant economic growth so that a surplus can be produced, to be reinvested to make more profit, to be reinvested to make more profit, to be reinvested, and so on. The growth requires greater and greater exploitation of the world's natural and human resources. And the world's resources are finite and very limited. True, this was never a factor in Marx' thinking, enmeshed as he was in the period of Victorian industrial optimism. But we are now painfully aware of it. Capital expansion is bound, therefore, sooner or later, to hit the wall, producing the sort of catastrophe we now face.[60] This is why I said earlier that even if I am wrong about the current effects of global warming, capitalism is bound to produce an ecological catastrophe sooner or later. Global warming is the form of the problem in which we now face it; but if it weren't that, it would eventually be something else.

It is also worth noting that capitalism is intrinsically connected with population growth. This is so for two reasons. First, labour power is the prime commodity that produces an increase of capital; second, the more and more commodities which are produced have to be sold, requiring more people. In other words, capitalism is itself a major driver of population explosion.

And it is worth remembering how fast the wall is hit in an exponential progression. Suppose that at midnight we have a jar containing one amoeba. Every second, each amoeba in the jar divides to produce two amoebas—so that at every second the size of the population of amoebas doubles—until, at noon the next day, the jar is full. At what time is the jar half-full? One second before noon.

At any rate, we see why a sustainable economy—one that will not produce, or reproduce, the current grim situation—cannot be capitalism.

---

59. For some discussion, see Layman (2015).
60. It is a notable fact that the few people who are still "global-warming skeptics" come, for the most part, from the political right, and have an investment, emotional and/or financial, in the current economic system.

4

ANĀTMAN AND
GATTUNGSWESEN

4.1 Introduction

In our analysis of the current state of the world, we are dealing with social and ethical matters. Such things concern people. Hence, to understand such things fully, one needs an understanding of what people are. The aim of this chapter is to provide this understanding.

In Chapter 2 (2.4), I noted that according to Buddhist philosophy there are three very important ways in which we are prone to misunderstand the nature of our world and ourselves. These concern *anātman, anitya,* and *pratītyasamut-pāda*. With the first of these, Buddhist philosophy has a very distinctive view of the nature of what a person is. In this chapter I will first explain and defend this view.

After this, we will turn to Marx' account of what it is to be a person, and I will do the same for this. As we will see, this is very similar to the Buddhist view; and where the two accounts differ, the differences do not conflict with each other; rather, they are complementary.

At the end of the chapter I will make a few final comments on the two other Buddhist notions just mentioned, *anitya* and *pratītyasamutpāda*, and their relationship to the Marxist notion of dialectics.

4.2 *Anātman* What

So let us start with the Buddhist notion of *anātman*. This means literally *no-self*, and so is the view that there is no such thing as a self. To discuss this view, the first thing to do is to get straight as to what it means.

DOI: 10.4324/9781003195146-5

The world 'self' is highly ambiguous. One may use the word *self* to refer to a person, as in 'he saw himself in the mirror', 'she thought only of herself'. This is not the sense of self in which Buddhists deny there to be one. There is a very clear sense in which Buddhists take there to be persons.[1] There are also other notions of selfhood such that the possession of a self in these senses is quite compatible with Buddhist *anātman*.[2] However, we do not need to go into all the things that 'self' might mean here.

The self, in the sense in which Buddhist philosophy denies that there is such a thing, is part of a person. This part exists at any time at which the person exists, is constant, and indeed, is what makes the person that very person. In Christian terms, this is essentially what a soul is. The Buddhist view was of course developed in a quite different context. It arose as a reaction against the Hindu view, according to which there was exactly a self—*ātman*—of this kind.

So if a person does not have an essential self, what are they? The standard textual analogy is that of a chariot. Let me update this a little. Take a car. What is this? Essentially it is composed of a bunch of parts. The parts came together at a certain time in a factory. The configuration is maintained for a while. The parts interact with each other and with other things, such as the environment. In the process, parts may wear out and be replaced. And in the end the parts will fall apart, and the car will go out of existence. There is no part that is necessarily maintained throughout the life of the car. Anything can be changed. Even the number plate is changed if the owner of the car moves state. We can coin a concept to apply to it and things like it—*car*. This is certainly useful; but being a car does not presuppose that the car has an essence—whatever, indeed, that might mean.

In all these respects, a person is just like a car. They are composed of parts. Exactly what these parts are is hostage to scientific developments; but given modern science, we may take these to be psycho-biological.[3] The configuration of these comes into existence in the womb, and changes over the years. (The composition of your body changes every morning after breakfast.) And eventually, the parts cease to function together properly; the person dies, and the parts fall apart. These are not random changes, though, but are governed

---

1. Matters are made slightly complex by the fact that Buddhists endorse a distinction between conventional reality (*saṃvṛti satya*)—roughly, the world of our familiar lived experience—and ultimate reality (*paramārtha satya*)—roughly, what there really is behind the familiar phenomenological world. There is disagreement about how to understand the latter notion, but, according to all schools, people are conventionally real, but not ultimately real; and selves are neither conventionally nor ultimately real. In this chapter (and indeed in the whole of this book), we can ignore the ultimate. Ethical and political discourse concerns people and societies and so is located at the conventional level.
2. For example, a "minimal self". See, e.g., Garfield (2015), pp. 99 ff.
3. Early Buddhists had sophisticated taxonomies of the parts, especially the mental parts, but we don't need to go into this here.

by natural laws, such as those of biology and chemistry. One can give a name—*person*—to things of this kind; but crucially, there is no part which must exist throughout the time when the person exists, to make it that very person.[4]

Such is the view; and, it must be said, it is very much in accord with the view of a person delivered by modern science. In particular, a physiologist or anatomist who held, as a professional view, that the soul was a part of a person different from the heart, brain, and so forth would not last long in the profession.

4.3 The Sense of Self

Still, it must be agreed that *anātman* is a somewhat counterintuitive view. We certainly do seem to have a sense of self, of a "*meness*". When one wakes up in the morning after a deep sleep, it is as though a little voice says 'Hello, I'm back again'. Or as Kant put it in more scholarly terms,[5] every mental act can be accompanied by an *I think*, which delivers the unity of my thoughts.

So we have a *sense* of self. But a sense of self is not a self. Quite generally, the sense of *x* is not *x*. I have a sense of time passing, but that itself is not the passage of time. (Time would go on even if I did not exist, and so had no sense of its passage.) In the case at hand, a sense of self is not permanent and does not identify a person as that very person. It can disappear in certain meditation and drug-induced states—or much more obviously, when one is unconscious due to being knocked out or anaesthetised. The person is still that very person without it.

So do we really have a self?[6] We know that the mind—or the brain whose functioning delivers it—plays tricks. At the back of the eyeball there is a place where the optic nerve joins it. There are no rods or cones there, so the joint produces a blind spot in the field of vision. Normally, though, we are quite unaware of this, since the brain "fills in the visual gap". In a similar way, there is a familiar illusion known as the *phi phenomenon* (made use of in the production of movies). Suppose there is a sequence of lights such that from left to right, say, each light flashing momentarily after the one before it. When one looks at this, one actually sees something moving from left to right. The brain "fills in the gaps". Maybe the sense of having a self is just the product of the brain filling in the gaps between mental events, as it were, to create the illusion of something that does not really exist.

That this is so has certainly been argued by a number of contemporary cognitive scientists. Here is Dennett on the matter:[7]

---

4. Further on the view, see Siderits (2007), ch. 3, and Carpenter (2014), ch. 6.
5. *Critique of Pure Reason*, B131–2.
6. What follows draws on Priest (2019).
7. Dennett (1993), pp. 253–4. The book reviews the evidence and mounts the case for the view. See, especially, Part II of the book.

There is no single, definitive "stream of consciousness," because there is no central Headquarters, no Cartesian Theater where "it all comes together" for the perusal of a Central Meaner. Instead of such a single stream (however wide), there are multiple channels in which specialized circuits try, in parallel pandemoniums, to do their various things, creating Multiple Drafts [GP: of a narrative of the self] as they go. Most of these fragmentary drafts of "narrative" play short-lived roles in the modulation of current activity but some get promoted to further functional roles, in swift succession, by the activity of a virtual machine in the brain. The seriality of this machine ... is not a "hard-wired" design feature, but rather the upshot of a coalition of these specialists.

If this view is correct, then, although we have a sense of self, the self of which we have a sense is an illusion, created by various brain processes, just as the apparent motion in the phi phenomenon is an illusion of something that does not exist, created by various brain processes.

Of course, illusions can be useful. If you look in a mirror, what is behind you appears to be in front of you. This is an illusion; but it may be a useful one, since it lets you know what is behind you. And very plausibly, the illusion of self has been hard-wired into us for evolutionary reasons.[8]

Whether for this reason or for some other, the illusion is certainly one which is difficult to shake off. Its appearance is, after all, so insistent. Coming to believe that it is an illusion may help, but the fact remains that things still appear that way. An illusory appearance does not normally disappear when one knows it to be an illusion. As we noted in 2.2.3.3, this is one reason why concentration is important in Buddhism. It is a way of making the illusion disappear.

And for Buddhism, the illusion is certainly a pernicious one. Why so? One might suggest that one can be selfish only if one believes in a self; so getting rid of the belief eliminates the possibility of selfishness; and selfishness is a bad thing. (See 2.3.) But this would be a mistaken argument. A selfish person, action, or motive—as the *OED* reminds us—is one that lacks consideration for other people, and is concerned chiefly with the actor's own personal profit or pleasure. This is to do with a *person*, not an *ātman*.

Rather, the view is pernicious for other reasons. First, if one has a self which is constant and defines one as that very person, then certain kinds of change are impossible. In particular, if there are moral qualities of character attached to the self, then those moral qualities cannot be changed. More broadly, to understand how things in general, and people in particular, can change for the better, one needs to see people as creatures that are what they are in virtue of a whole bunch

---

8. On evolution and the sense of self, see Wright (2017), esp. ch. 6.

of relations, psycho-biological, socio-economic, and so forth. (More on this in a moment.) This being so, changing these relations may change the person.

Moreover, the view that a person has an *ātman*, that there is an essential "me-ness", hides the fact that what a person is, they are because of this network of interconnections. This can certainly make one act unwisely. (It is not a good general policy to act under an illusion. Reality is likely to catch you out.) In particular, it covers up the fact that a person can flourish only given the relations in question. It thus obscures the fact that the flourishing of each person depends on the flourishing of (at least some) others, as I noted in 2.4. And this certainly can lead to selfishness and a lack of compassion for others.[9]

4.4 *Anātman* Why

This all *assumes*, of course, that the self *is* an illusion. Why should one suppose that the sense of self is not tracking something real? In other words, why should one suppose that *anātman* is true?

An articulate—and, I take, correct—case for this was made by Vasubandhu (fl. 4th to 5th century CE).[10] For it to be reasonable to suppose that something exists, there must be some ground for the belief. According to both modern science and Buddhist philosophy, epistemological grounds are of essentially two kinds: perception and inference. (Of course, in practice, most of our beliefs are grounded in neither of these, but on the testimony of others. But for testimony to be authoritative, it must ultimately ground out in one of these kinds.)

So can one perceive the self? Well, clearly not as part of the body: even the brain is in a constant state of change. But, one might think, one can perceive it as part of the mind—by introspection. That view was thoroughly debunked by David Hume (who is often taken to have a view about persons akin to the Buddhist view). In his *Treatise on Human Nature* (I, IV, 6) he says:[11]

> There are some philosophers who imagine that we are every moment intimately conscious of what we call our Self; that we feel its existence and its continuance in existence; and are certain, beyond the evidence of a demonstration, both of its perfect identity and simplicity. The strongest sensation, the most violent passion, say they, instead of distracting us from this view, only fix it the more intensely, and make us consider their influence on *self* either by their pain or pleasure. ...

9. As noted by Carpenter (2014), ch. 2.
10. In his 'Refutation of the Theory of Self' (ch. 9 of his *Abhidharmakośa-Bhāṣya*, Commentary on the Treasury of Abhidharma). See Duerlinger (2003), pp. 71–110. On Vasubandhu, see Gold (2015).
11. Selby-Bigge (1978), pp. 251–2.

For my part, when I enter most intimately into what I call *myself*, I always stumble on some particular perception or other, of heat or cold, light or shade, love or hatred, pain or pleasure. I never can catch *myself* at any time without a perception, and never can observe anything but the perception. … If anyone, upon serious and unprejudiced reflection, thinks he has a different notion of *himself*, I must confess, I can reason no longer with him. All I can allow him is, that he may be in the right as well as I, and that we are essentially different in this particular. He may, perhaps, perceive something simple and continued, which he calls *himself*; though I am certain there is no such principle in me.

But setting aside some metaphysician of this kind, I may venture to affirm of the rest of mankind, that they are nothing but a bundle or collection of different perceptions which succeed each other with an inconceivable rapidity and are in perpetual flux and movement.

There are, in fact, some kinds of Buddhist meditation practice that are exactly exercises in simply experiencing the constant arising and ceasing of mental states.

Hume's point is well taken. But in any case, to suppose that one can see *a self* would seem to be some kind of conceptual impossibility. There is no way that one can *see* that something is constant and enduring, so delivering the identity of the person. At best this is a matter of inference. And it would be a fallacious one, since we know that no mental states are always present. They all vanish when one is unconscious.

If one is to have a ground for the existence of a self, then, perception does not provide it. It would appear that there is better hope for an inferential ground. There are many things in whose existence we have good reason to believe, though we cannot perceive them: electrons, quarks, black holes, dark matter. It is reasonable to believe that such things exist, since this provides an explanation—currently the best explanation we have—for things we *can* perceive. This is a form of inference called *inference to the best explanation*, or sometimes, *abduction*.

Now, for what might the existence of a self provide the best explanation? I suppose that there could be a number of things, but the most obvious is the Kantian one.[12] Some mental states hang together in a very distinctive way. My perceptions, thoughts, emotions all seem to be part of one consciousness— mine—in that my perceptions, thoughts, and so forth are not yours. It is the self that accounts for this unity. All these mental states adhere (as it were) to the same self, which delivers their unity. It accounts for what Kant calls the synthetic unity of apperception.[13] Now, the phenomenon of the unity of

---

12. One might suggest that the existence of a self is the best explanation for the fact that one has a sense of self. But as I have already noted, that fact is plausibly explained by the cognitive architecture of the brain delivered by evolution.

13. For references and discussion, see Rohlf (2015), 4.1.

consciousness is a highly disputable one.[14] But there is clearly a sense in which some mental states do cooperate with each other. For example: today I see a car, and tomorrow I remember it. Could it be the self that is responsible for this kind of unity?

How, exactly, the self is supposed to turn this trick, is, to say the least, opaque. However, there is a standard methodological constraint on inference to the best explanation, usually called *Ockham's Razor*. If there is a perfectly good explanation of some phenomenon which does not appeal to an entity of a certain kind, but which appeals only to things to which we are independently committed, then the explanation which does not invoke the entity in question is the better explanation ('entities should not be multiplied beyond necessity').

So the question is whether the kind of unity of consciousness being appealed to here can be explained in other ways. The unity has both a synchronic aspect and a diachronic aspect. Let us consider each of these in turn.

Synchronic. A motor bike drives past. I see it and hear it. Though one sensation is visual, and the other is auditory, they work together to produce a unitary experience. By contrast: you also see the bike go past, so we both have visual experiences of the bike, but there is no sense in which they are unified in the same way.

This distinction can, however, be explained in simple causal terms. There are causal relations between my auditory and visual sensations which do not hold between your visual sensations and mine. Specifically, the visual and auditory inputs of my brain are processed by different areas of my brain (the visual and auditory cortexes), but these two cortexes communicate with each other in a process of multi-sensory integration to deliver the resulting unity of the mental experience. By contrast, there is no similar causal integration between your visual sensation and mine. (Of course there are also causal interconnections between your perceptions and mine; but they are just of the wrong *kind* to produce the unity in question. Similar points can be made for the examples that follow.)

Diachronic. This can be past oriented or future oriented.

Past oriented. Yesterday I saw a road accident. Today I have a visual memory of it. For me, the visual and memory events are integrated, in a way that any of your visual events are not related to my memory. But again, there is a perfectly natural causal explanation of this integration. When I saw the accident, the results from the visual cortex were encoded in the part of the brain responsible for episodic memory (the limbic system). These can be activated to generate the visual memory. Obviously there is no similar connection between your visual experience and my memory.

14. For discussion, see Brook and Raymont (2017).

Future oriented. Tonight I have a drink. Because of its pleasant effect, I drink too much. Tomorrow I have a hangover, with its painful mental symptoms. This evening's desire and tomorrow's headache go together. However, if you desire to drink, and drink too much, your hangover is not part of my experience. Again, there is a perfectly causal explanation of this. I desire to drink, so I drink. The alcohol enters my body, and the overdose gives me a mild case of alcohol poisoning, which my brain monitors the next day, giving rise to the headache. There is no similar causal chain between your drinking and any headache I might have the next day.

For similar reasons, it makes sense for me not to drink too much tonight if I don't want to have a hangover tomorrow—in a way that it makes no sense for me to try to stop *you* drinking so that *I* don't get a hangover. Thus, the causal relations also make sense of agency without a self.

It would appear, then, that there is a perfectly good causal explanation for the sort of unity at issue here. So the "unity of consciousness" provides no reason to suppose that there is a self.

Hence, without some other essential function for the self (in the relevant sense) to play, there is *no* ground—perceptual or inferential—for believing in it.

4.5   Persons

Let us stay within the realm of Buddhist philosophy, but change the focus of attention from selves to persons themselves.[15] Persons are partite objects— objects with parts. As such, they depend for being what they are on at least their parts. Buddhists standardly take them to depend on something else as well: the way we conceptualise them. I will discuss these things in a moment, but first a brief excursus into Mahāyāna Buddhist philosophy.

Buddhist philosophers in the earlier Abhidharma traditions recognised only these two kinds of dependence at work here. Moreover, they thought that there were partless things which possessed *svabhāva*, a term which means literally something like *self-being* or *self-nature*. It is sometimes translated as *essence*. Perhaps the best translation is *intrinsic nature*. The things with *svabhāva* were called *dharmas*.[16] Dharmas are what they are, in and of themselves; they would be thus even if there were nothing else.

This view came under attack in the Madhyamaka (Middle Way) School of Buddhist philosophy, one of the two schools of Indian Mahāyāna Buddhism, and one which was fundamental to all Mahāyāna Buddhisms (in Tibet, China, and Japan). It arose from the writings of the philosopher Nāgārjuna (fl. ca. 2nd century CE). According to the Madhyamaka School, there is

---

15. For what follows see, further, Priest (2014), ch. 11.
16. A quick warning. The word *dharma* has many meanings in Buddhist philosophy. We are concerned here with just one of its senses.

nothing which has *svabhāva*; everything is empty (*śūnya*) of this. There are no dharmas in this sense. An important part of the case made involved recognising a new kind of ontological dependence: causal. Hence, there came to be recognised three kinds of dependence in play: mereological, conceptual, and causal. (The Abhidharma philosophers recognised that dharmas entered into causal interactions; but they held that such interactions did not determine what they were—their identity.)[17]

Let us now examine the claim that things in general are not what they are in and of themselves, but depend for such on some or all of their parts, causal interactions, and concepts. We will see that people, in particular, are dependent for their identity on all three of these things.

The easiest of the three is mereological dependence. Clearly, a car could not be what it is, namely, a car, if its parts were those of a city or an opera. And a person—say you—could not be a person if you were missing enough of your parts, or even just some very important ones, such as your brain.

So let us turn to causal dependence—the kind of dependence ignored by Abhidharma philosophers. What makes something a rice plant? The fact that it grows out of a grain of rice, delivers further rice grains, and so forth. If it grew out of an onion, and delivered, not grains of rice, but goldfish, it would not be a rice plant. The processes of cause and effect involved here are important. Similarly, what makes something water? This is the kind of thing which puts out fires, quenches thirst, and so on. If something were the kind of thing that burns and poisons people who drink it, it would not be water. Again, the causal processes in play here are important. One might suggest that it is not these phenomenological properties that make something water, but the chemical constitution of the stuff, H_2O. But this is to say that to be water is to be composed of molecules with two atoms of hydrogen and one of oxygen. This is itself a matter of causal interactions.

Exactly the same kind of considerations apply to persons. They are what they are, at least in part, because of the fact that they breathe air, not water, that their parts interact in appropriate ways, that they were produced by a genetic code of a certain kind. These causal processes are important.

Let us now turn to the third, and for present purposes, the most important of these: conceptual dependence. We use concepts to organise the world around us. The network of causation is everywhere. We pick out certain chunks of it conceptually, be they cars, trees, nations; and for a chunk to be an object of a certain kind depends on it satisfying the appropriate criteria for that concept.

Indeed, the role of concepts can run much deeper than that. Thus, as we noted (3.2), for Marx, commodities are what they are only because of being embedded in social practices of a certain kind. Thus, take paper money.

---

17. For fuller accounts, see Siderits (2007), ch. 9, and Williams (2009), ch. 3. On Nāgārjuna himself, see Westerhoff (2014).

Money is the kind of thing which functions as a medium of exchange. To be money it must satisfy the criteria for the concept *money*. In particular, it must operate a certain way in the causal processes of exchange. However, it can do so only because people themselves think of it in a certain way. Something can function in the way that money does only because people believe that others will accept it as a medium of exchange. If and when this fails, the physical stuff is no longer money, just pretty (perhaps) pieces of paper. Thus, something can satisfy the criteria for being money only if people conceptualise it in a certain way. Hence, there is a double conceptual dependence here.

Now, being a person is just like being a car or a tree. A chunk of the causal network is a person if it satisfies the criteria which define the concept *person*. We might well (and people do) argue about what the criteria for being a person are, exactly. But we do not need to go into this here. The point is that someone is a person due to the fact that they satisfy the criteria for the concept *person*—whatever these are. If those criteria do not apply to an alien life form, a foetus, or a piece of software, then these things are not persons.

Moreover, concepts are involved not only in being a person, but in the *kind* of person someone is, that is, their social identity: a professor, a member of parliament, a slave, an asylum seeker, a Jew, a freedom fighter. These things depend on the presence of beliefs about certain social roles which the entity in question plays. Of course, these roles are certainly in part causal. But just as in the case of money, the roles can be sustained only because people have certain beliefs and attitudes. Thus, racism is possible only because people believe that there are races, and that some of these are inferior (morally, intellectually, or whatever) to one's own, and so on. Hence, the second role of conceptualisation is also in operation here, as with money.

I note that the conceptualisation of people does not just apply to *other* people. People conceptualise *themselves* in exactly the same way that they conceptualise others. That is, they have a self-conception of who and what they are. Indeed, this fact seems to be an essential part of how they play their part in the social roles they occupy, such as that of being a parent, or a university teacher.

I hasten to add that none of this implies that if something is conceptualised in a certain way, it is indeed as conceptualised. Other kinds of dependence, especially causal, may also be required. Thus, if I conceptualise myself as the president of the United States, or conceptualise the United States as a neutral arbiter in the Israeli/Palestinian conflict, these conceptualisations are just plain wrong. To be correct, they would require appropriate causal relations (which they do not)—being elected in the first case, and acting impartially in the second.

What we have now seen is that objects in general, and people in particular, have the identity they do because they are located in a web of relations, mereological, causal, and—particularly—conceptual. And as is clear, in the part of the discussion concerning concepts, social categories have appeared. Such categories are not standard fare in Buddhist discussions, but the relevance of such things is obvious once one has seen it. Moreover, it leads us naturally into a discussion of Marx. So let us turn to this.

4.6 Gattungswesen

The first, and most obvious, thing to say about Marx in this context is that he would have agreed entirely with the doctrine of *anātman*. The equivalent of *ātman* in the Western philosophy with which Marx was familiar is the soul. Marx was both an atheist and a materialist, and rejected the existence of any such thing. Of more interest here is Marx' account of a person.

This is articulated at greatest length by writings of the young Marx. Here, he operates with the notion of human *Gattunsgswesen*—species being/nature.[18] And it might appear obvious that this is incompatible with a Buddhist account of persons. True, Buddhist philosophy certainly does not deny that natural kinds have natures: it is the nature of fire to burn, the nature of water to quench thirst, and so forth. But all Buddhists hold that partite things, including people, have no *svabhāva*. If one translates *svabhāva* as *essence*, and translates *wesen* as *essence* too, we do seem to have a conflict here. The conflict is, however, merely apparent—simply a product of infelicitous translation. *Svabhāva* is best translated as *intrinsic nature*. And as we will now see, Marx' *Gattungswesen* is not this kind of thing.

Marx' discussion of species being is mainly in his 1844 *Philosophical and Economic Manuscripts* (sometimes known as the *Paris Manuscripts*, since that is where they were drafted). There are occasional mentions in some other early texts, but the notion is absent from later writings, notably *Capital*. This has led some Marx exegetes to claim that he gave up the notion in a break with his earlier thought.[19] Whether or not this is so (I doubt it), let us see what Marx thinks that species being is. The quick answer is that the species being of a person is whatever it is that can be truly attributed to them, simply in virtue of them being a person. But what are these things?

For a start, like all biological species, humans must survive and reproduce. Hence they need food, shelter, clothing. People are enmeshed in physical and biological laws which require them to do things to live. Moreover, this need depends on many things, their nutritional system, the environment, their genetic inheritance, and so on. This is not, then, intrinsic in the Buddhist sense, as Marx himself points out:[20]

18. For a discussion of species being, see Maguire (1972), ch. 7, Geras (1983), and Wood (2004), ch. 2.
19. For example, Althusser. See Althusser and Balibar (1956).
20. From the *Paris Manuscripts*, McLellan (2000), p. 112. In this and a number of the following quotations, Marx (or his translator) speaks of 'man', and uses male pronouns.

Man is directly a natural being. As a living natural being he is on the one hand endowed with natural vital powers, and is an active natural being. These powers of his are dispositions, capacities, instincts. On the other hand, man as a natural, corporeal, sensuous objective being is a passive, dependent, and limited being, like animals and plants, that is, the objects of his instincts are exterior to him and independent of him, and yet they are objects of his need, essential objects that are indispensable for the exercise and confirmation of his capacities.

An important aspect of Marx' account of human species being is that it is part of this to work. No one, Buddhist or otherwise, is going to deny this. It is a simple corollary of the need to survive that people must grow or gather food, make clothes, and so on. And even if someone is rich and/or powerful enough to get others do these things for them, they are still going to spend at least part of their time working, be it managing and controlling those who labour for them, creating science or art, organising social events, or whatnot. Staying in bed all day sleeping or staring at the ceiling is a pathological human condition.

Marx does think that there is something distinctive about human work, though. It is planned, in a certain sense. A beaver does not plan to make a dam: it just builds it. A human builder, by contrast, plans how to build something in their head or on paper before starting to build. So it is, more generally. No doubt there is work of some kinds which is done by deploying a purely habitual procedure—maybe making breakfast or doing the laundry. But, for the most part, we decide what needs to be done, plan how to do it, and then do it (or attempt to!).

Now, whether there are other species (for example, some of the higher primates) which also do this might be a moot point. However, it is impossible to deny that humans *do* work like this. That this is so is simply a function of the way that the human brain works (and the fact that production is generally social—more of this in a moment), that is, because of the causal processes involved in the laws of physics, biology, and anatomy. And, as we have already seen, causal connections are not intrinsic in the Buddhist sense.

4.7 Social Relations

So far, we have been talking about the biological aspects of species being. However, Marx is clear that there is more to species being than this. Perhaps more importantly, species being requires various social relations—though the precise details of these may vary from society to society. Being a person requires being a member of a society (in the general sense, namely, of a group of people who interact and cooperate with each other). It takes at least two to procreate,

Nothwithstanding the fact that this doubtless says something about his thinking, a more contemporary translation might better use gender-neutral language.

and some kind of social structure is necessary for the rearing of a child. No person can survive in their early years without carers. Adults enter into economic relations connected with the production of the necessities of life. And for good reason: an adult who is not embedded in a bunch of people is very vulnerable (to the elements, to times when sustenance production goes wrong, to other people, and so on) and is unlikely to last for long. For good measure, we might add that it is not just the basic elements of human life that require a society. No one can enjoy the pleasures of the sport of cricket or the game of Go unless there are people to teach them, practice with, and so forth; no one can enjoy the arts unless there are people to create and perform them; and so on. Both work and leisure, therefore, are essentially social activities. It is virtually impossible for people to flourish if they are deprived of their social connections: remember that solitary confinement is used as a form of *punishment*.

Marx notes the social nature of people clearly:[21]

> Exchange, both of human activity within production itself and also of human products with each other, is equivalent to species-activity and species enjoyment whose real, conscious, and true being is social activity and social enjoyment. Since human nature is the true communal nature of man, men create and produce their communal nature by their natural activities; they produce their social being which is no abstract, universal power over against the struggle of individuals, but the nature of each individual, his own activity, his own life, his own enjoyment, his own wealth. Therefore, this true communal nature does not originate in reflection, it takes shape through the need of egoism and individuals, i.e., it is produced directly by the effect of their being. It does not depend on man whether this communal being exists or not.

Or more tersely, as the sixth of his *Theses on Feuerbach* says:[22]

> Feuerbach resolves the religious essence into the human essence. But the human essence is no abstraction inherent in each single individual. In its reality it is the ensemble of social relations.

And whatever is to be said about the role of species being in the thought of the later Marx, the point that people have a social nature most certainly does not disappear. In *Grundrisse*, we have:[23]

---

21. In some notes on James Mill, which he made about the same time as writing the *Paris Manuscripts*. See McLellan (2000), p. 125.
22. Drafted as a critique of Feuerbach in about 1845. See McLellan (2000), p. 172.
23. Nicolaus (1973), p. 265. Or as Sztompka (1991), p. 34, puts it in his discussion of Marx: 'a human being appears as a nodal point, a knot in the wider world of social relationships. This social location—and the consequent fact of social moulding of individuals, as well as

> Society does not consist of individuals but expresses the sum of the inter-relations, the interrelations within which these individuals stand. As if someone were to say: Seen from the perspective of society, there are no slaves and no citizens: both are human beings. Rather, they are that outside society. To be a slave, to be a citizen are social characteristics, relations between human beings.

Note that what are at issue here are social *relations*, and so not intrinsic in the Buddhist sense.

As we have seen, though, Buddhist philosophy is just as clear that people are what they are in virtue of a network of relations. Social relations do not figure notably in the relations in question. However, since people are social animals, they clearly should, and Marx explains how.

Let me finish this section with a comment on the role that conceptualisation plays in Marx' thought. At places in the *Paris Manuscripts* Marx seems to suggest that it is part of people's species being to have some conception of people in general, and themselves in particular, as social creatures.[24] Thus, the first quotation from Marx in this section goes on to say that as long as people do not understand their essentially social nature properly, alienation results:[25]

> but so long as man has not recognized himself as man and has not organized the world in a human way, this communal nature appears in the form of alienation, because its subject, man, is a self-alienated being.

I will return to the matter of alienation in the next chapter. For the present, all we need note is that this is clearly a comment about the unhappy effects of a person mis-conceptualising themself.

Next, in his middle period, Marx stresses the fact that people's concepts are formed, at least in the first place, by their material conditions:[26]

> The production of ideas, of conceptions, of consciousness, is at first directly interwoven with the material activity and the material intercourse of men, the language of real life. Conceiving, thinking, the mental intercourse of men, appear at this stage as the direct efflux of their material behaviour.

the reciprocal impact of individuals on the context of their social life—is a universal of the human condition, whereas the typical combinations of relations networks vary historically, and idiosyncratic bundles of such relations vary individually'.

24. See Wood (2004), pp. 19–21.
25. McLellan (2000), p. 125.
26. McLellan (2000), p. 180.

Neither of these things a Buddhist need deny of course. The first is a fact concerning a form of *duḥkha* which arises because of the way that someone misunderstands their (social) world. The second is an account of the way that concepts are formed; and it is obvious that we often form concepts because they are required for our material practices.

However, beyond these things, one finds little in Marx about the importance of conceptualisation.[27] Thus, though Marx is well aware that certain aspects of someone's identity (being a capitalist, being a worker) are due to their locus in a set of social relations, there is little discussion of the role that conceptualisation and self-conceptualisation play in making those social loci possible, as they certainly must do. For example, how do capitalists or workers conceptualise themselves and others in order to play the social roles they do? Nor is there any discussion of the role that conceptualisation plays in more nuanced social roles (like being a banker or a trades union leader). Perhaps this was because Marx wanted to distance himself from Hegel's idealism. But at any rate, Buddhist philosophy, as we have just seen, does recognise the importance of conceptualisation.

So, let me summarise the whole discussion of personhood as follows. People are empty of *svabhāva*—to put it in Buddhist terms. They are not what they are in and of themselves. They are what they are because of their loci in a bunch of causal and conceptual relations, and these are perforce, at least in part, social. Social relations play little role in Buddhist discussions of personal identity; but in Marxist philosophy, they certainly do. On the other hand, there is no stress in Marxist philosophy on the role that concepts play in the occupation of a locus in a network of social relations. Buddhist philosophy, on the other hand, does emphasise the important role of this.

4.8 *Anitya, Pratītyasamutpāda*, and Dialectics

Let me end with a few comments on the other two Buddhist notions I mentioned in 4.1, and their relation to the Marxist notion of dialectics.

In his philosophy, Marx takes over from Hegel a dialectical view of the world. According to this, reality is not static but is in a constant state of change, in which oppositions arise and are transcended (*aufgehoben*).[28] Marx' exact views on the matter are somewhat unclear, since he never wrote about it in any detail. But one clearly finds an appearance of dialectics in Volume 1

---

27. Thus, for example, there is no entry for 'concept' in Bottomore's *Dictionary of Marxist Thought* (1983).
28. On dialectic in Hegel, see Inwood (1992), pp. 81 ff. On dialectic in Marx and Marxists, see Bottomore (1983), pp. 122 ff.

of *Capital*, perhaps most notably in the first few chapters on the nature of money.[29]

Now, the view that reality is in a constant state of change, in which dynamic laws are ever overthrowing the past and delivering novelty, is clearly a version of *anitya*. Thus, Mandel notes:[30]

> dialectics imply that every phenomenon has an origin and an end, that nothing is either eternal or finished once and for all.

Of course, both Hegel and Marx did take there to be a *telos* to history, in the form of the absolute (Hegel) and the communist state (Marx). Neither of them was silly enough to suppose that, even if this were realised, the cosmos would freeze, and change would come to an end, though.

What to make of the zigzag process involved in dialectics is much less clear. Indeed, how this notion is to be understood is itself very contentious. But I think it fair to say that there is nothing of a similar kind in Buddhist philosophy.[31] Still, however it is best to understand the notion, it is clear that, in some sense, dialectics involves opposites. Thus, for Marx, money is both a *use*-value and an *exchange*-value; and in capitalist production, the means of production are *privately* owned and *publicly* worked.[32] Moreover, to understand the phenomena at issue, it is important to understand how these opposites, or things which instantiate them, interact with one another. Clearly, this sort of interaction is a special case of Buddhist interdependence, *pratītyasamutpāda*. In the rest of the book, we will see many cases of the interdependence of such opposites, such as those of base and superstructure, social and individual, personal and political.

Those who like dialectical contradictions may also appreciate the thought that it is capital (particularly global capitalism) that both connects us with one another and divides us from one another.

4.9 Conclusion

We have now finished looking at the Buddhist and Marxist conceptions of personhood. As we have seen, they have much, and much that is correct, in common. Both, in particular, dismiss the idea of a self or a soul. Buddhism has a view of the pernicious nature of belief in a self; and though we did not

---

29. Whether or not Marx would have agreed with him, Engels spells out his take on the matter in *Anti-Dühring* (Engels (1939)).

30. Mandel (1976), p. 22.

31. Though an interesting exception might be the Chinese Buddhist Jizang (549–623), who has zigzag processes towards the ineffable. See Deguchi et al. (2021), ch. 4.

32. See Bottomore (1983), pp. 93 f.

need to go into it here, Marx, of course, had his own view of the pernicious nature of Christianity and its doctrines, such as that of the soul.[33]

Both Buddhism and Marxism take persons to be, by their nature, embedded in a network of relations. But each emphasises different aspects of those relations. Marxism takes note, in a way that Buddhism does not, of the social relations involved in this matter. Buddhism on the other hand, emphasises the way in which the identity of people is conceptually dependent. These two things are not at all in conflict, though. Indeed, each enriches the picture of the other, drawing attention to things which it really requires, but about which it says little.

What we have here, then, is a way in which Buddhism and Marxism clearly complement each other, each filling out part of the picture concerning which the other is silent. In the next chapter we will look at numerous further points of complementarity.

33. Marx thinks of religion in terms of Christianity, or sometimes Judaism. What his views on Buddhism were—or would have been, had he known anything about it—I've no real idea. I presume that he would have welcomed its atheism, though he might well have regarded (with some justification) the doctrines of *karma* and rebirth as a version of "the opium of the masses", as he puts it in the oft-quoted remark in his *Contribution to the Critique of Hegel's Philosophy of Right*. Whether or not this is so, Buddhism as a religion is not on the cards in this book.

5

THE ELEMENTS AS COMPLEMENTARY

5.1 Introduction

In the last three chapters we have looked at a number of the elements of Buddhist and Marxist philosophy which provide insights into the world in which we presently live and our place in it. In the last chapter, we also saw how, as far as persons and selves go, these two philosophies are complementary. In this chapter we will see many other ways in which the two philosophies are so.

We'll start with the most obvious and general ways in which the two complement each other. Then we'll move to ways in which the two interact more locally. In the final part of the chapter we will see ways in which the two views can be made to converge explicitly.

5.2 Society and Ethics

First, the most obvious large-scale aspects of the picture.

As I observed in 1.2, canonical Buddhist philosophy contains little on matters of social/political philosophy. Indian Buddhism developed in the context of local clans, each with its own ruler—and later, kings such as Ashoka—and a feudal economy. The occasional political comments in the Buddhist texts suggest that nothing beyond this was envisaged. Thus, for example, Nāgārjuna's *Ratnavalī*[1] is a discourse addressed to a local king, which, in the middle of a discussion of Buddhist metaphysics and soteriology, gives him advice to look after the poor, the needy in various ways, the sick, and, generally, be beneficient. Nāgārjuna would surely have given the same

1. Hopkins (2007).

DOI: 10.4324/9781003195146-6

advice to any person to the extent to which it is in their power. The advice is, presumably, more relevant for a king, since he has more resources with which to be beneficent.

Even more obviously, given when they were written, canonical Buddhist texts could say nothing about present-day society and its socio-economic structure. Clearly, Marxist philosophy does both of these things, and hence says much about which such texts are silent—though, it should be noted, many contemporary "Engaged Buddhists" (such as the Dalai Lama, Thich Nhat Hanh, Sulak Sivaraksa) have applied Buddhist ethical lessons to the contemporary socio-political situation, as we will see in the second half of this book.

On the other side of the ledger, Buddhism provides a comprehensive, clear, and defensible ethics. Such is lacking in Marx' writings. This is perhaps more contentious, since there clearly are comments bearing on ethics in Marx, though the exact import of Marx' ethical views is contentious.[2]

Once Marx had developed his historical materialist views, turning Hegel "on his head", he took morals to be part of the superstructure generated, in some sense, by the economic base. Thus, in the *German Ideology*, we find:[3]

> In direct contrast to German philosophy which descends from heaven to earth, here we ascend from earth to heaven. That is to say, we do not set out from what men imagine, conceive, nor from what men as narrated, thought of, imagined, conceived, in order to arrive at men in the flesh. We set out from real active men, and on the basis of their real life-process we demonstrate the development of the ideological reflexes and echoes of this life process. The phantoms formed in the human brain are also, necessarily sublimates of their material life-process, which is empirically verifiable and bound to material premises. Morality, religion, metaphysics, all the rest of ideology and their corresponding forms of consciousness, thus no longer retain their semblance of independence. They have no history, no development; but men, developing their material intercourse, alter, along with this, their real existence of their thinking and the products of their thinking. Life is not determined by consciousness, but consciousness by life.

And in the *Communist Manifesto*, Marx asks rhetorically:[4]

> What else does the history of ideas prove, than that intellectual production changes its character in proportion as material production is

---

2. For a review of some of the literature on Marx and ethics, see 'Marxism, "Ideology", and Moral Objectivism', ch. 3 of Mills (2003).
3. McLellan (2000), pp. 180 f.
4. McLellan (2000), p. 260.

changed? The ruling ideas of each age have ever been the ideas of the ruling class.

It is hard to hear in these comments anything but a relativism about morality. Moral standards change from socio-economic condition to socio-economic condition. As such, there is no objective moral critique of anything. In particular, the capitalist's moral standards are just as good as those of Marx himself. This is sufficient to undercut any moral critique of capitalism.[5]

Perhaps this is reading too much into Marx' comments. It is not that which is true about morality which varies from society to society, but just that which is *believed* to be true. After all, the fact that some people changed their views about the morality of slavery as some enlightenment crept over Europe in the 19th century does not imply that the actual morality of slavery itself changed. Fair enough; but this leaves open the question: what *are* the correct moral principles? And here, Marx has nothing to offer.

A somewhat different view of morality emerges from the early Marx writings, notably in the *Paris Manuscripts* with his discussion of alienation. Marx' account of alienation is itself a contentious matter, and we need not go into many of the details here.[6] But Marx is clear that under capitalism people are alienated; and, whatever exactly that means, he is clear that this is a bad thing. Nor is there any hint of moral relativism in the judgement. Thus, we have, for example:[7]

> [Alienated labour] makes the species-being of man, both nature and the intellectual faculties of his species into a being that is alien to him, into a means for his individual existence. It alienates man from his own body, nature exterior to him, and his intellectual being, his human essence.
>
> An immediate consequence of man's alienation from the product of his work, his vital activity and species being, is the alienation of man from man. When man is opposed to himself, it is another man that is opposed to him. What is valid for the relationship of a man to his work, of the product of his work and himself, is also valid for the relationship of man to other men and of their labour and the objects of their labour.

5. There is a certain "scientistic" view of Marx' work according to which ethics is irrelevant to his critique of capitalism, which is purely scientific: values do not enter into the matter. To what extent this does justice to Marx' view, I leave scholars to argue about (not much, I think). But my own view is that one cannot get a critique out of anything simply from a pure description. See 2.4.
6. For a full discussion, see Wood (2004), ch. 1.
7. McLellan (2000), p. 91.

In other words, under these conditions, workers are alienated from their species-being (*Gattungswesen*). That is, a person's species-being is not fully realised. That is, they are not what they should be. But again, the question is: why *should* they be like that? That is a moral claim, and Marx provides no justification for it. Moreover such claims are apparently false. Aggression of certain kinds, or to certain groups of people, is part of our species-being; it is a trait acquired of necessity in our evolution. But it is no bad thing if we can overcome this aspect of our nature. Similarly, physical and mental ageing are also part of our biological nature. Yet how much better would it be if we did not age after our early adult years? (I am not suggesting that one should live forever; merely that at a certain time one just died without the loss of mental and physical abilities that normally precedes that.)

Struhl suggests that realising one's *Gattungswesen* is *ipso facto* a good thing, since it is a form of human flourishing, and flourishing is certainly a moral good.[8] To flourish is, he says, to realise the potentials of one's human nature. However, and again, letting one's nature flourish is not obviously a good thing. To see this, merely think about Christianity. Human nature is inherently sinful; but human flourishing concerns *overcoming* this. Ethical premises are required to take one from the claim that people are thus and such to the conclusion that they ought to do, or be allowed to do, such and such.

It might be suggested that alienation is bad simply because it is an unpleasant experience. Marx himself seems to suggest this:[9]

> What does the externalization of labour consist in then?
>
> Firstly, that labour is exterior to the worker, that is, it does not belong to his essence. Therefore he does not confirm himself in his work, he denies himself, feels miserable instead of happy, deploys no free physical and mental energy, but mortifies his body and ruins his mind. Thus the worker only feels a stranger. He is at home when he is not working and when he works he is not at home.

But if that is what is wrong with it, alienation is simply a form of *duḥkha*—a very specific social form, no doubt, but just one form.

And as is clear, there are many forms of alienation of this kind other than class-generated alienation, such as those caused by racism and patriarchy. Thus, women often feel alienated in largely male working environments; and black people often feel alienated in largely white working environments.[10] The oppression delivered by these power structures is of a quite distinctive kind, as we will see in a moment—and Marx has little to say about such.

8. Struhl (2016), pp. 89 ff.
9. McLellan (2000), p. 88.
10. Many of the essays in hooks (1994) describe the sense of alienation that she experienced as a black woman in white male teaching establishments.

In other words, if this is Marx' view of ethics, it is a highly partial one. He misses all the other forms of *duḥkha*, and even the other forms of alienation. Buddhism locates all these things in a much larger picture.

Moreover, a corollary of alienation and the other forms of *duḥkha* is, as we have seen, the moral importance of compassion. Marx' account says nothing about this and cognate virtues. There is no entry for *compassion*, for example, in McLellan's (2000) 700-page selection of Marx' core writings or in Bottomore's (1983) dictionary of Marxist thought. Perhaps surprisingly, the same is true of *solidarity*.

Indeed, the Buddhist ethical picture also provides something of which one finds no hint whatsoever in Marx: a concern for other creatures who suffer. For suffering goes a lot further down the evolutionary tree than do humans. How far down it goes is moot, but it is clear that all mammals feel pain. It is also clear that human activity, in the form of contemporary factory farming and related practices occasions a good deal of suffering to the things that we eat. This is quite unnecessary. We do not have to eat them; but even if we do, we do not have to treat them in this way to do so. (Clearly, our farming practices are connected with capitalism. Pain is irrelevant if animals can be raised, distributed, and killed in a way that produces more profit.[11]) The suffering of animals was just not on Marx' agenda.

In other words, Buddhist philosophy has a general and well articulated ethics. Marx does not.

5.3 Other Elements of Complementarity

Let us now turn to some other, and more particular, ways in which Buddhist and Marxist philosophies can be seen as providing interconnected parts of a more general picture. It will be helpful to break these up into a number of separate (but interconnected) areas.

5.3.1 Ignorance and Deception

Let us start with our knowledge of the world—or lack of it.

Buddhist philosophy stresses that we misunderstand the world in which we live (*avidyā*—ignorance). We are deceived—maybe self-deceived—about the nature of this world. We take it that we live in a world of relative independence and permanency, indeed that we ourselves are such a part of it. We are not. As we saw in 2.4, we live in a world of impermanence (*anitya*) and massive interdependence (*pratītyasamutpāda*). And as we saw in Chapter 4, we ourselves are no more substantial (*anātman*). Perhaps these attitudes are simply wishful

---

11. See the essays in Nibert (2017).

thinking; more likely, they are hard-wired into us for evolutionary reasons: evolution engineers us, so to speak, to be disposed to have them.

As we noted in 3.4, according to Marxist philosophy, in a capitalist society we are generally misguided about the nature of the *social* world in which we live. Indeed, we are socially engineered to be so. And the engineering this time is by ideology. In Marxist terms, people are subject to mystification.

I will have a lot more to say about ideology in a later chapter. For the present, the following will suffice. Capitalist ideology teaches people to see everything as a commodity (commodification)—as something to be bought and sold. As Marx puts it in the *Poverty of Philosophy*, capitalism is:[12]

> a time when everything that men had considered as inalienable became an object of exchange, of traffic and could be alienated. This is the time when the very things which till then had been communicated, but never exchanged; given, but never sold; acquired, but never bought—virtue, love, conviction, knowledge, conscience, etc.—when everything, in short, passed into commerce. It is the time of general corruption, of universal venality, or, to speak in terms of political economy, the time when everything, moral or physical, having become a marketable value, is brought to the market to be assessed at its truest value.

Perhaps the most important things which are commodified are people themselves. They are simply something to be bought and sold—or better, who are required to sell themselves—as simple objects of trade. In other words, they are dehumanised. We do not see people as human, but as an unemployment statistic, an illegal immigrant, a disposable resource, and so forth.[13] Correspondingly, we do not behave compassionately, since compassion is applicable to people—or more generally to sentient creatures; and of course, animals are equally commodified in contemporary capitalist farming practices. Buddhism, as noted, is a philosophy of compassion; but the Buddha could have had no idea of the forces that capitalism could bring to bear to undercut this aspect of our humanity.

The first of the octet of the Fourth Noble Truth is Right View: it requires us to see through our ignorance. Marxism, then, provides an important ampliation of Right View, giving it a contemporary social dimension.

5.3.2 Interdependence

Next, let us turn to the matter of interdependence.

---

12. Marx (1963), p. 34. Note that 'alienated' here, just means *sold*.
13. See, further, Marcuse (1964). It is a telling fact that the part of a capitalist organisation that deals directly with the people it employs is often now called the 'Department of Human Resources'. People are simply *resources*, just like raw materials and machinery.

As we have seen, capitalist ideology enjoins us to see ourselves as social atoms; that is, as creatures which have natures, moral rights, interests, and so forth, independently of those of other people. Marxist philosophy, as we have also noted, rejects this as a piece of social ontology. In the *Holy Family*, Marx himself says, somewhat sarcastically:[14]

> Speaking exactly and in the prosaic sense, the members of civil society are not atoms. ... The egoistic individual in civil society may in his non-sensuous imagination and lifeless abstraction inflate himself to the size of an atom, i.e. to an unrelated, self-sufficient, wantless absolutely full, blessed being. Unblessed sensuous reality does not bother about his imagination; each of his senses compels him to believe in the existence of the world and the individuals outside him and even his profane stomach reminds him every day that the world outside him is not empty, but is what really fills. Every activity and property of his being, every one of his vital urges becomes a need, a necessity, which his self-seeking transforms into seeking for other things and human beings outside him.

People are essentially social. The well-being of each person can, then, be assured only if the well-being of the members of the community in which they find themselves is also assured—all of them, since they all contribute to the general weal. The fact of social interdependence clearly provides a reason to be concerned with the well-being of the other members of that community. In other words, Marxism underlines the Buddhist imperative of compassion, providing a quite specific reason for it. Thus, Struhl:[15]

> Dukkha is never simply my individual dukkha in that our suffering always occurs within a social context, which entails that our individual suffering cannot be separated from our social relations and from the suffering of others.

However, the alienation of person from person may prevent one from seeing this.

Turning to Buddhism itself, this says little, as such, about the social interconnectedness of people. However, what it does do is locate social interconnectness in the much bigger picture of quite general interconnecteness: that delivered by the notion of *pratītyasamutpāda*. Social atomism is, then, based not just on a political illusion, but on a metaphysical illusion. And just as for Marx, a misunderstanding of the world, and in particular the illusion of self, covers over these things.

14. McLellan (2000), pp. 162–3.
15. Struhl (2017), p. 105.

This more general interconnectedness also provides another part of the picture of which one finds little evidence in Marx: the destructive nature of capitalism on the environment. He is, of course, aware that people are a part of nature, and that natural resources are crucial to people's existence. But generally speaking, Marx operated in the context of 19th-century industrial optimism. He believed that industrial development is a good thing—at least if it is organised in the right social way. He had no conception, like most people before the middle of the 20th century, that such development can have devastating consequences for our environment, ones which will occasion much suffering, both to those currently alive and to those who will live in the future. We now know better. Our understanding of the interconnecting elements of ecological systems, climatic systems, and so on has shown us that growth—of population, of industrial production, of energy use, and so forth—needs to be curtailed.[16]

5.3.3 Desire

Let us now turn to the subject of desire. As we saw in Chapter 2, Buddhism locates the cause of *duḥkha* in *tṛṣṇa*—of which one important form is desire. But classical Buddhism, at least, says nothing about the social factors which create this. Marxism, as we have noted, says a lot about these. Advertising is a prime source of *tṛṣṇa*. It creates dissatisfaction with what a person already has, and a never-ending series of desires to have other things. It is, to use a well known Buddhist simile, like giving salt water to a thirsty person. Marxism, then, provides an important factor in the genesis of *tṛṣṇa* in a contemporary context.

But Buddhism in turn tells us something about advertising. How is it that the techniques of advertising can get a grip on people? They obviously exploit some sense of insecurity. What? Arguably, it is an insecurity produced by an inchoate sense of the lack of any determinate self. Thus, as Struhl says:[17]

> it is precisely the illusion of our sense of an independent and separate self which provides the desperation that capitalism turns into profit accumulation, competitiveness, and consumerism. Money, in particular becomes a way to avoid *dukkha* and, at the deepest level, a way to evade the recognition that the self is empty.

16. I hasten to add that the need to curtail population growth is not an argument for eugenics, forced sterilisation, or similar things. Such are obviously rebarbative to a Buddhist ethics of compassion. We know that the elimination of poverty, access to techniques of family planning, the education of women, and giving them control over their own reproductive abilities, are all very effective ways of decreasing the birth rate.
17. Struhl (2017), p. 107.

In particular, in a capitalist society, people are socialised to believe that money will create a substantial self. In the *Paris Manuscripts*, Marx says:[18]

> What I have thanks to money, what I pay for, i.e., what money can buy, that is, what I, the possessor of money am myself. My power is as great as the power of my money. The properties of the money are my—(its owner's)—properties and faculties. Thus what I am and what I am capable of is by no means determined by my individuality. I am ugly, but I can afford to buy myself the most beautiful women. Consequently, I am not ugly, for the effect of ugliness, its power of repulsion, is annulled by money. As an individual, I am lame, but money can create twenty-four feet for me; so I am not lame; I am a wicked, dishonest man without conscience or intellect; but money is honoured and so also is its possessor. Money is the highest good, and so its possessor is good. Money relieves me of the trouble of being dishonest; so I am presumed to be honest. I may have no intellect, but money is the true mind of all things and so how should its possessor have no intellect? Moreover, he can buy himself intellectuals and is not the man who has power over intellectuals not more intellectual than they? I who can get with money everything that the human heart longs for, do I not possess all human capacities? Does not money thus change all my incapacities into their opposite?

The questions are rhetorical. Of course it does not. What Marx is describing is a form of fetishism, in which the properties of one thing are transferred to something else. This is part of an ideology which covers up how things actually are. And like all fetishisms, it is an illusion—a form of mystification in Marx' terms. The deceived person thinks that their illusory properties make them a substantial self. But they can no more do so than a person can make the flashing lights that generate a phi effect themselves move. The desire for a determinate self can never be fulfilled. The only way that the *tṛṣṇā* it produces can be expunged is to give up the desire for the unobtainable.

Money and other possessions are, in fact, just one kind of thing people desire in an attempt to cover over the lack of self. Another is power. I will return to this matter in a later chapter.

5.3.4 Concepts

Let us next turn to the importance of concepts. As we saw in the last chapter, Buddhist philosophy—though not Marxist—notes the importance of concepts in our finding our way around the world. Indeed, each of us constructs his or

---

18. McLellan (2000), p. 118. I find it impossible to read this passage without thinking of a certain US president.

her own identity, and those of others, with an array of concepts. But many important concepts are social, and many of these are drawn from the world of economic production. Marxism—though not Buddhism—tells us much about these.

In particular, under capitalism, people are taught to think of themselves in terms of capitalist categories: I'm a truck driver; I'm doing ok. I'm an executive; I'm much better than him. I'm unemployed, so not a valuable person. Much of this is done by the infiltration of notorious business-speak—capitalist categories —into common thinking. People are not deprived of their source of livelihood: they are *let go*. Someone whose money is to be appropriated is an *end user*. Innocent beings killed and maimed in military strikes are *collateral damage*. (True, this last is not an economic term, but things military are closely connected with the maintenance of the dominant power group.) These euphemisms function ideologically to cover up human realities.[19]

In short, people are not taught to think of themselves as simple human beings, interacting with other simple human beings, who need to cooperate with each other so that all may flourish. Indeed, class categorisation, along with the categorisation of race and gender, promote exclusiveness and a corresponding hostility to those in categories of people seen as "others". Loy puts the matter as follows:[20]

> [M]any of our social problems can be traced back to ... a group ego, when we identify with our own race, nationality, religion, etc, and discriminate between ourselves and another group.

The Buddha could have had no idea of the perniciousness of the kind of self-conception engendered by capitalism.

But there is also good news here. As we saw in 5.2, Marx notes that how people think is not a constant. It can be changed, and changed for the better; in particular, by a change in socio-economic practices. He was surely correct about this. One of the things that worked to change the social attitude to women in Europe that occurred in the 20th century was their entry into the

---

19. Many have now become so used to thinking of things in terms of profit generation, that even things that are clearly not of this kind, such as health and education systems are conceptualised in these terms—and so deformed. Thus, in Australian universities, funding a staff appointment is called an "investment"; lecturers are evaluated simply in terms of the "money they make" (students taught, research grants obtained, etc.); if they do not "earn enough" they must "increase their productivity" or be expended by "downsizing"; students are a commodity, who "generate income"; education is a process of "value adding" to a commodity; and so on. Today (10/5/19) I received a press release from the Australian Academy of Humanities, which began, 'Five eminent Australian researchers have been appointed to support *A New Approach*—the independent think tank created to champion effective investment and return in Australia's arts and culture'—as if culture is a profit-making enterprise.

20. Loy (2008), p. 87.

workforce necessitated by the First World War. The presence of so many men at the front required a labour force drawn from a different pool.

Again, concerning self-conception, how people think of themselves is a narrative construction, as we saw in the last chapter. Such constructions can be changed; and they can be changed so that people come to think of themselves as motivated, not by self-interest, but by compassion, and so in a way essentially inimical to capitalism. This may certainly be driven by a change in socio-economic conditions; but it can also arise independently of this, and itself be a driver of socio-economic change.

So, one might ask, should one think of the overthrow of capitalism as a mere means (at least a partial) of eliminating *tṛṣṇa*; or should we think of a reorientation of our attitudes as a means to undermine capitalist ideology? The answer is *both*. The two are, in fact, interdependent. We will come back to this in a later chapter.

5.3.5 Power

Finally, let me turn to the matter of power. Capitalism engenders a particular power structure, with those who own or manage capital exerting great power over those who merely work for it. Power can be used—and usually is—to oppress;[21] and the capitalist power structure certainly is. Marx was, of course, well aware of this. In the *Communist Manifesto*, he says:[22]

> [T]he bourgeoisie has at last, since the establishment of Modern Industry and the world-market conquered for itself, in the modern representative State, exclusive political sway. The executive of the modern State is but a committee for managing the common affairs of the whole bourgeoisie.

At least before the Engaged Buddhist movement, Buddhism, of course, says nothing about this matter.

But there are other, and equally pernicious, power structures which Marxism has largely ignored, notably those of race and gender. To the extent that Marxism has taken these things into account, it has been by trying to reduce gender power and racial power to class power.[23] Thus, in *The Origin of the Family*, Engels bases patriarchal power on the fact that women are the labourers in childbearing and

---

21. *To oppress*: to keep someone in subjection and hardship, especially by the unjust exercise of authority.
22. McLellan (2000), p. 247. The bourgeoisie are those who own and/or manage capital.
23. Here and in what follows, I will use 'class' in its Marxist sense, namely a group of people defined by a certain relationship to the means of production. The capitalist class comprises those people who own/manage capital. The working class comprises those who own/manage only their own labour power. Like most social dichotomies, this is, to a certain extent, vague; that is, it has borderline elements. However, so is the distinction between red and blue. The lack of a clear borderline does not show that there is no distinction.

child-rearing.[24] However, such a reduction does not really stand up to inspection. For traditionally, even if men and women do *exactly* the same job, women have still been paid less. And even where women have had the same economic opportunities—e.g., in the Soviet Union, and China after Mao's revolution—they have not had equal political power. The Central Committee members were/are predominantly men.[25] Thus, even within an economic class, women can suffer some *specific* form of oppression. The methods employed by men to disempower women—such as legislation, an ideology of inferiority, domestic violence, and sexual harassment[26]—have little to do with child bearing/rearing as such—though it is hardly unknown for the supposed interests of children and the family to be invoked to provide a veneer of legitimisation for patriarchy (even within the workers' movement itself[27]). These things are simply the means by which one group maintains its position of power over another.

The matter is clear with racism too. Here, one racial group, be it in a majority or a minority, oppresses another—white and black in the US, Russians and Jews, English and Irish, white and black (or black and white) in South Africa, ethnic Japanese and ethnic Korean in Japan, those in the caste system and those outside it (the Dalit) in India, European and indigenous Australians. Racism is a feature of most societies, past and present, and does not appear to be correlated in any invariant way with economic conditions. Thus, there can be racial oppression within a class, as there is in the current US, with respect to being black within the working class.[28] And, in Australia, indigenous Australians have been the subject of genocide and oppression since the European invasion.[29] This had nothing to do with economic power. Indeed, this could be done with impunity precisely because indigenous Australians never played a significant role in the economy of the white invaders. (Compare black slave labour in the antebellum Unites States. For all its viciousness, this was not genocide. The Australian situation is more like the treatment of native Americans by the European invaders.) Of course, a racial group of subdominant power will often be found over-represented in low-paying and marginalised jobs. But this is precisely because racial attitudes make it difficult for them to get better jobs, or the kind of education necessary for these.

---

24. For a critique of Engels' and other attempts to reduce gender power to class power, see Rubin (2008), Hartmann, (1981), and Arruzza (2013), pp. 82ff.
25. See, e.g., Arruzza (2013), ch. 1.
26. It is perhaps not so obvious that sexual harassment belongs in this category, though perhaps it is becoming clearer, with the #MeToo movement. On the political nature of sexual harassment, see Crosthwaite and Priest (1996).
27. See, e.g., Arruzza (2013), ch. 2.
28. For a discussion of the relative autonomy of racial power structures, especially in the context of the United States, see Mills (2003), esp. chs. 5–9.
29. No one knows exactly how many indigenous Australians there were when the Europeans arrived. However, the number may well have dropped by about 90% in the first 100 years of European colonisation. For some account of the matter, see Jalata (2013).

None of this is to say that there are no connections between the power structures of class, race, and gender. These power structures typically intertwine in various ways. This is patent, for example, in the US, where white racist attitudes and the fact that blacks provided the (slave) labour force for much of the agriculture in the antebellum South reinforced each other.[30] However, class, gender, and race are, in principle, three distinct power structures. And Marxist thinking has done little to recognise the relative autonomy of the latter two—or to aid the elimination of oppression occasioned by these.

Buddhist philosophy is somewhat different. Indian Buddhism rejected the Indian caste system. But the philosophy is also committed to the rejection of status differences on the grounds of race and gender as well—at least in theory.[31] Thus, in the *Vāseṭṭha Sutta*, where the Buddha rejects the caste system, we find:[32]

> While in [various animal] births are differences, each having their own distinctive marks, among humanity such differences of species—no such marks are found. Neither in hair, nor in the head, not in the ears or eyes, neither found in mouth or nose, not in lips or brows. Neither in neck, nor shoulders found, not in belly or the back, neither in buttocks nor the breast, not in groin or sexual parts. Neither in hands nor in the feet, not in fingers or the nails, neither in knees nor in the thighs, not in their "colour", not in sound, here is no distinctive mark as in the many other sorts of birth. In human bodies as they are, such differences cannot be found: the only human differences are those in names alone.

The Four Noble Truths make distinctions of race and gender of no moral significance.[33] There are no differences of colour or gender in *duḥkha*.

Consequently, compassion applies to all, independent of race, gender, sexual orientation, age, or any other category. If something is the cause of suffering, it should be eliminated, whether the cause is capitalism, racial or gender discrimination, religious intolerance, or anything else. The Buddhist view therefore corrects the one-sidedness of the picture that one finds in Marxism.

---

30. On the ways in which the power structures of class, race, and gender interact ("intersectionality"), see, e.g., Crenshaw (2005), Arruzza (2013), pp. 125ff., Fraser (2013), Kinna (2019), pp. 157–64.
31. Sadly, the Buddhist religion—as opposed to its philosophy—has been as patriarchal as all the major world religions. For a discussion of gender and the institution of Buddhism, see Gross (2013). Racism is not absent from Buddhist religion either, as the recent history of Myanmar sadly demonstrates all too clearly. For the experiences of one black woman in an American Buddhist group, see hooks (2006).
32. Suttacentral (2011).
33. Can there be an ethics in which this is not the case? Of course. Merely consider Aristotle on woman and slaves. See e.g., Book 1 of his *Politics*.

5.4 The Elements Converge

Let me now bring our elements of Marxist and Buddhist philosophy into a more explicit convergence.

One way to do this is to return to the three Buddhist *kleśas*. As I noted in 2.4, there are three "poisons" which produce *duḥkha*: attachment (greed), hatred (ill will), and ignorance (delusion). In Buddhist thinking, these concepts are usually applied at the personal level. But they have a social dimension too. One might call the result, following Loy,[34] *social duḥkha*. He describes matters this way:[35]

> Our present economic system institutionalizes greed, our militarism institutionalizes ill will, and our corporate media institutionalizes delusion. To repeat, the problem is not only that these three poisons operate collectively, but that they have taken on a life of their own.

He explains the points one by one. I quote at some length, since it is hard to put the points more forcefully than he does.

- *Greed.* Capitalism institutionalises attachment:[36]

> Who is responsible for the pressure for growth? That's my point: the system has attained a life of its own. We all participate in the process, as workers, employers, consumers, investors, and pensioners, with little if any personal sense of moral responsibility for what happens. Such awareness has been diffused so completely that it is lost in the impersonal anonymity of the corporate economic system. In other words, greed has become institutionalized.

- *Ill will.* Capitalism and its entourage instutionalises aversion:[37]

> Many examples of institutionalized ill will spring to mind: racism, a punitive justice system, the general attitude towards undocumented immigrants—but the "best" example, by far, is the plague of militarism. In the twentieth century at least 105 million people, and perhaps as many as 170 million, were killed in war, most of them non-combatants. Global military expenditures, including the arms trade, amounted to the

---

34. Loy (2008), pp. 151–2.
35. Halkias (2013), p. 492, puts it as follows: 'For Buddhism, human suffering is caused, to a large extent, by unwholesome human actions and state of mind whose origin is greed (*lobha*), hatred (*dosa*), and confusion (*moha*). These three "poisons" do not just affect individuals but contaminate institutions and society at large'.
36. Loy (2008), p. 90.
37. Loy (2008), p. 90.

world's largest expenditure in 2005: well over a trillion dollars, about half of that spent by the US alone. To put this in perspective, the United Nations spends about $10 billion a year. The United States has been a militarized society since World War II, and increasingly so.

- *Delusion.* Capitalist ideology institutionalises delusion:[38]

> With few exceptions, the world's developed (or "economized") societies are now dominated by a power elite composed of the government and large corporations including the major media. People move seamlessly from each of these institutions to the other because there is little difference between their worldviews or their goals—primarily, economic expansion. Politics remains "the shadow cast by big business over society", as John Dewey once put it. The role of the media in this unholy alliance is to "normalize" this situation, so that we accept it and continue to perform our required roles, especially the frenzied production and consumption necessary to keep the economy growing.

Indeed, the more one thinks about it, the more staggering the scale of social *duḥkha* is.[39]

A second way to bring Buddhist and Marxist ideas to a point of convergence is to note that one may formulate a Marxist version of the Four Noble Truths, as follows:[40]

1. Current social life generates suffering in the form of poverty, oppression, and exploitation.
2. Suffering is caused by the need to make a profit, and the greed, competitiveness, hostility, and egoism this generates.
3. The suffering may be removed by eliminating its cause.
4. The route to this is by eliminating the socio-economic conditions which produce it.

The transposition of the Four Truths into a social key is clear enough to require no comment.

Yet a third way to bring Marxist and Buddhist philosophies to convergence is to note how a social dimension bears on the Fourth Noble Truth itself. The *personal* praxis of this needs to be augmented with a *social* praxis, which confronts and aims to change the social institutions that cause suffering. Thus, appropriate praxes should be guided by both Marxist ideas and Buddhist ideas.

---

38. Loy (2008), p. 93.
39. 'Individual suffering and delusion are socially supercharged. Collectively, we commit follies that, if committed individually, would be pathological'. (Jones (2006), p. 111.)
40. The idea is due to Aryiaratne (1982), as quoted in in Waistell (2014), p. 198. I have modified Aryiaratne's version to make the parallels with the Four Noble Truths even closer.

Of course, the social, as described by Marxist philosophy, and the personal, as described by Buddhist philosophy, are deeply interdependent. In Marxist terms, one might say that there is a dialectical interaction between the two. Marx tells us in the *German Ideology* that:[41]

> [a]s individuals express their lives, so they are. What they are, therefore, coincides with their production, both with *what* they produce and *how* they produce. The nature of individuals thus depends on the material conditions determining their production.

But as he insists in the *Eighteenth Brumaire of Louis Bonaparte*:[42]

> Men make their own history, but they do not make it just as they please; they do not make it under circumstances chosen by themselves, but under circumstances directly encountered, given, and transmitted from the past. The tradition of all dead generations weighs like a nightmare on the brain of the living.

Social structures produce individuals; but individuals produce the social structures.

And this being so, they can change them—if they know how. One should remember that capitalism is not some God-given form of social organisation, fallen from the sky. Capitalism is a form of social organisation that has developed over time because of human actions. In that sense, we are the cause of our own problems. But we have it in our power to change that social organisation. So even if we are the cause of the problem, we can also be the solution.

5.5 Conclusion

The general complementarity of the aspects of Marxist and Buddhist philosophies we have been dealing with is, then, clear. Marxist philosophy provides an analysis of the social nature of people, and the (current) society in which they are embedded—about which Buddhism says little. Buddhist philosophy, on the other hand, provides an understanding of persons individually, and their embeddedness in the world more generally, about which Marxism has little systematic to say. Together the two provide a picture—a very disconcerting picture—of the socio-economic world in which we now live.

It remains, in the last chapter of this part of the book, to draw the appropriate conclusion.

---

41. McLellan (2000), p. 177.
42. McLellan (2000), p. 329.

6

FAREWELL TO CAPITALISM

6.1 Introduction

What the preceding chapters have delivered us is an understanding of the socio-economic world in which we currently live—and it is not a lovely one. The world is dominated by a capitalist economic system. But the point of capitalism is not the well-being of people; it is the making of profit. More: people are damaged, both physically and mentally, in the process. This is neither rational nor humane. The conclusion is obvious: we should get rid of it.

I will return to these matters in the second half of this chapter. But first, let me hammer home the point that capitalism *needs* to be replaced, by pointing out how it is behind many of the unlovely aspects of the current world. I can do this fairly briefly, since the cases for many of the points in question have already been made.

6.2 The World With 2020 Vision

Here are a few relatively uncontroversial facts about the contemporary world in which we live, circa 2020.[1] I'll break them up into three kinds—socio-economic, political, and environmental—though these are not entirely distinct categories.

Socio-economic

- Capitalism has now become globalised. It is obviously the socio-economic system of nations in the global North. Equally obviously, it is the system of

---

1. Perhaps the most distinctive thing about the year 2020 is the global outbreak of the Covid-19 pandemic. I'll reserve the remarks I have about this for a later chapter.

DOI: 10.4324/9781003195146-7

the other major economic powers, such as Brazil, Russia, India, and China. One might have some doubts about the last of these, due to the one-party political system; but it is clear that one can have an *effectively* one-party capitalist state. (Merely consider Singapore.) And though many things are still state-controlled in China, private businesses are now booming. More importantly, nationally, China is as locked in to the treadmill of growth as the United States. Moreover, national states are becoming increasingly irrelevant economically anyway, since so much capital is now trans-national, and such capital will operate—with its characteristic effects—wherever in the world it can make most profit. True, there are still a few holdouts, such as Cuba and (maybe) Bhutan; but these are economically insignificant by global standards.

- We are witnessing the economic centre of gravity of the world moving to the East. China has capitalised and developed faster than could have been expected 40 years ago. Its economy is now (2020) second in size only to that of the United States, and will soon overtake it. India is still quite a long way behind China, but it, too, will soon become one of the biggest world economies. It hardly needs to be said that the United States does not welcome the prospect of losing its global economic hegemony.

- There is a staggering inequality of wealth in the world. As report after report shows, most of the world's wealth is locked into a very small percentage of private hands.

- In the global North, people live in a consumer-oriented society, where there is an inordinate amount of waste, and people have a never-ending series of desires generated by advertising and social status.

- In the global South, both the environment and livelihood of many people have been and are being destroyed.

- A substantial part of the world's population, especially (but not solely) in the global South, has inadequate food, water, sanitation, health care, and education. If the world's wealth were more equitably distributed, this would not be the case.

Political

- There are several flashpoints of international (and religious) tension, perhaps most notably in the Middle East. The significance of such points is not local, however, since major international powers, such as the United States, Russia, and China, have interests in these matters.

- Wars and social conflicts (such as those in Syria, East Africa, and Central America) are leading to mass migration. Such migration is causing social and political tension in many countries.

- The manufacture of armaments is a major international industry, and many countries now have nuclear weapons, including countries that have deep and vested interests in international flashpoints.
- We are seeing the growth of nationalist, and often racist, governments and policies (e.g., the United States, Russia, India, Brazil, Hungary, Turkey) or at least a significant rise of the racist right (e.g., Germany, France, Italy).

Environmental

- Human-made global warming is accelerating. By even the mildest estimates, this will cause significant climate change, leading to rising sea levels, destruction of ecosystems, and the despoiling of agricultural areas.
- This will cause further mass migration, scarcity of food and clean water. This will produce, in turn, increased competition for these resources. Such will exacerbate most of the problematic situations already mentioned.

In short, the world is in a very precarious situation (to put it mildly). Of course, national conflicts, migration, poverty, and environmental destruction have always been with us. But we now have these things on a level of magnitude (depth) and global import (width) that we have never witnessed before.

The result of these trends is unpredictable. A worst-case scenario is a nuclear war and the obliteration of the human race (and much of the environment). Perhaps a more likely scenario is a regime—possibly neo-fascist—in which a very small number of people (and corporations) control the world's resources and military. They will live an affluent life in gated communities protected by security forces, whilst the majority of people live in relative poverty in degraded and unpleasant environments. Whatever transpires, however, if things continue to move in current directions, they are going to get much worse for the majority of the world's population.

6.3   The Role of Capital in This

A full explanation of all of the facts I have mentioned is clearly complex, and undoubtedly many factors, both global and local, are required for a complete understanding. But one thing stands out as a central factor behind all the things noted: capitalism and its need for incessant growth. Again, let me break matters up into the same three categories as before, but this time in a different order.

6.3.1 Socio-economic

One way for a quantity of capital to grow is to pay workers as little as possible. By contrast, those who own or manage capital—its agents—are going to acquire more of it. Hence we see the increasing disparities of social wealth. Another way for a quantity of capital to grow is for it to take over smaller quantities of capital. Hence, we see capital becoming concentrated in larger and larger amounts in fewer and fewer hands. Yet a third way for capital to grow is by economies of scale. Size matters. The United States exploited this fact in the 20th century. India and China are much larger, and are exploiting (and will exploit) this fact in the 21st century.

Next, to grow, capital requires continuing increases of raw materials and markets. Hence, it is in the nature of capital to expand beyond individual nations, and so become global. That this was happening was already clear to Marx in 1848. As he and Engels put it in the *Communist Manifesto*:[2]

> The bourgeoisie has through its exploitation of the world-market given a cosmopolitan character to production and consumption in every country. … All old-established national industries have been destroyed or are daily being destroyed. They are dislodged by new industries, whose introduction becomes a life-and-death question for all civilized nations, by industries that no longer work up indigenous raw materials, but raw material drawn from the remotest zones; industries whose products are consumed, not only at home, but in every quarter of the globe. In place of old wants, satisfied by the production of the country, we find new wants, requiring for their satisfaction the products of distant lands and climes. In place of the old national seclusion and self-sufficiency, we have intercourse in every direction, universal interdependence of nations.

Marx is obviously discussing countries of the global North; but his comments now apply to countries of the global South even more acutely.

Moreover, capital is not used for people; people are used for capital. Hence, the increasing amount of wealth is not used for health, education, and so forth—or it is used for this only to the extent that it produces the labour force required. Hence, the dire living conditions of much of the world are of no consequence.

Finally, for the products of a quantity of capital to realise a profit, they must be sold, so people must be made to buy them (rather than, say, the similar products of a rival quantity of capital). Hence we see mass advertising and the generation of a consumer society, with all its waste and dysfunctional psychological states.

6.3.2 Environmental

Capital growth cannot continue indefinitely in a finite system, such as the Earth provides. Exploitable land, primary resources, and population are all finite.

2. McLellan (2000), pp. 248 f.

Capitalism is bound, therefore, to hit the wall sooner or later; and it looks as though we are fast approaching it. In the process, natural resources, such as forests and fish stocks, are being depleted; the waste products of production and consumption—such as the byproducts of fertiliser use—and greenhouse gasses, are wreaking havoc with ecosystems; energy use is multiplying fast, the effect of which is increased global heat production; and so on. Moreover, capitalist systems are not going to stop this. It is against their very nature. The only thing that could stop it is (global) political intervention to stop capital expansion.

Note that capitalist competition is particularly vicious in its environmental effects. The drive for profit means that goods should be produced as cheaply as possible. This means that as much expense as possible should be offloaded onto someone or something else. (Economists call such things 'externalities'.) And this something else is often the environment. The costs to the world of the destruction of the environments, pollution, global warming, and so forth, which the capitalist produces, is something the capitalist does not have to pay for.[3]

Note also that one of the major causes of the economic damage to the environment is population growth. (We would not be in the current situation if the world's population were three or four billion.) But capitalism is a major driver of population growth. Since labour power is not only a commodity in and of itself, but central to the production of surplus value (profit), growth in capital requires growth in the number of those who labour. Moreover, the growth of capital requires more and more to be sold. Again, more and more people are required to buy these things.

6.3.3 Political

This brings us to the political effects of capitalism. In some countries it is the rich who control the government. In contemporary societies, their wealth comes from owning and managing capital. They are not going to bring the system to a halt. In other countries, the members of government are not necessarily rich. However, in contemporary "liberal democratic" systems, one cannot get elected without huge amounts of capital support, or by being a member of a party which depends on capital support; and fortunes, both individual and collective, can be made or broken by what the media say. The media are controlled largely by enormous business corporations, such as News Corporation and Facebook. In other words, the politicians are beholden to capital and its agents. These agents are going to do everything possible to ensure that the political system works for the benefit of capital. Finally, those in power, because of the avaricious mind-set encouraged by consumerism, are going to want to

---

3. The phenomenon where each pursing their own interests produces something that is against the interests of all is sometimes called the *tragedy of the commons*.

stay in power, and exploit their positions to make as much money as they can. As with governments whose members are the rich, they will support a capitalist economy.

This brings us to international relations. First, wars, international conflicts, and invasions obviously predate capitalism. However, since the rise of capitalism, capitalist economic concerns have clearly played an enormous role in generating these things. The contemporary political ruling class of a country, as just noted, act as agents for the quantities of capital they control, or that maintain them in their positions. Hence, we have seen imperialist wars and expansion for the control of resources and markets (especially, in the last 40 years, oil); the support of dictatorships and repressive regimes by so-called liberal democracies, in their national (aka capital) interests; and so on. There is something of an irony here, though. More and more, power is being taken away from national governments, because the biggest quantities of capital are now international; and global capital can manipulate national governments by moving its resources from country to country (or at least threatening to do so).

One bullet point remains to be addressed: the international rise of nationalism and racism. In explaining this, the specific conditions in each country must play an important role. However, it would be too much to suppose that the fact that this is happening in so many places is coincidence. There must be something more systematic going on. I suspect that it is this. In the global North, for a couple of decades after the Second World War, there was a period of economic growth and prosperity of an historically unusual kind. Since the 1980s economic conditions have reverted to something historically much more normal, with recessions, pressure on wages, attacks on collective labour, and so on. In particular, it has become clear to large sections of the working class, particularly after the 2008 economic crash, that the capitalist economy is not working for them. Stiglitz (himself a defender of capitalism) puts the situation in the US like this:[4]

> The elites had promised that lowering taxes on the rich, globalization, and financial market liberalization would lead to faster and more stable growth from which everyone would benefit. The disparity between what was promised and what happened was glaring. So when Trump labelled it "rigged", it resonated.

The ideology of capitalism, which assures people that they all benefit from capitalism, is therefore wearing thin. Hence, the political agents of capital must be kept in power by something other than this. Nationalism (and especially war) has always been a highly effective way of raising support for a government. Racism often goes hand in hand with nationalism. Moreover, though many

4. Stiglitz (2019), p. 21.

people know that the system is not working for them, they do not understand why; nor is it in the interest of capitalism for them to know. Hence is peddled a spurious explanation of why the system is not working. Blaming migrants (against all the economic evidence) who are 'coming here and taking our jobs' is such a strategy. More racism.

We see, then, that it is capitalism which is behind this litany of world problems and the present dystopian tendencies.

6.4 Humanity and Rationality

In light of the above considerations, it is clear that capitalism is neither rational nor humane. As the Bible says: by their fruits, ye shall know them.[5] Let me underline a couple of elements of this.

First, we have the absurdity that there is easily enough wealth in the world to eliminate poverty, starvation, and provide a decent level of health care for all. Yet much of this wealth is not only wasted; it is centralised in the hands of a global few. They have so much wealth that most of it can do them no detectable good at all for them; whilst so many have so little that it could do them an enormous amount of good.

Another index of the irrationality and inhumanity of capitalism is that it wastes human labour, not only in producing things that have little value, but also in keeping many people unemployed, simply because, though their labour could produce things of value, this is not mobilised since it cannot make anyone a profit. Stiglitz again:[6]

> there is work that needs to be done and people wanting to do that work, and yet our economic and financial system is failing both our society and these individuals.

Or Schweickart, more colourfully:[7]

> Here is a … paradox. A visitor from another planet would be perplexed to discover that in a purportedly free and rational society there are millions of people who want to work more, living with millions of people who want to work less. The visitor would be even more perplexed to learn that new technologies allow us to produce ever more goods with ever less labour, and yet the intensity of work—for those who have work—has increased.

5. Matthew 7:16.
6. Stiglitz (2019), p. 196.
7. Schweickart (2011), p. 107. Chs. 4 and 5 list the rational shortcomings of the current system on a number of fronts, including: inequality; unemployment; overwork; poverty; economic instability; environmental degradation; democracy.

Moreover, the unemployed—who are usually unemployed through no fault of their own—tend not only to be poor, but suffer the psychological traumas of being put on society's scrap heap.

Finally, even those people in employment, whether they are rich or poor, are conditioned by an economic system that privileges the simple acquisition of wealth; the capitalist advertising system produces desires that cannot be fulfilled; and people lose sight of the fact that the real things that give life value are not money.

In short, capitalism is both irrational and inhumane since it uses people for the benefit of wealth—that is, people are sacrificed at the altar of Mammon. Clearly, in a sensible economic system it should be the other way around: wealth should be used for the benefit of people. That is, it should be used to promote human well-being.

6.5 And So?

So where does this take us?

To get rid of the sorry effects of capitalism, we have to get rid of the cause: capitalism itself. It is sometimes suggested that capitalism would be perfectly fine if there were an appropriate welfare state (perhaps on the Scandinavian model). Now, it is true that a welfare state does alleviate the hardships of those in a capitalist society who are not rich—at least to a certain extent. However, this has limitations, functioning mainly as a safety net for poverty. And in any case, as should be clear from the preceding discussion, this suggestion addresses only one of the problems caused by capitalism. Tinkering with capitalism will not change the fundamental structure or the way it functions, and therefore the effects of this. Consequently we should work to destroy the illusions and power structures which support it—and so to dismantle the capitalist socio-economic structure itself.

We need to work towards a better socio-economic system. A system of humanity, compassion, tolerance, and cooperation; where wealth is used to provide the basic needs of health, education, and so forth for all; where social decisions are not made by a minority of vested interests; and where production is sustainable and does not cause havoc with the environment. In short, a society where *duḥkha*, though it may not be eliminated, is at least minimised—and certainly not brought upon us by our own actions. In short, we should think first of human well-being, and then see how we can achieve this (or more of this), starting from where we are now.

Of course, the most important question is: how? That is the topic of the second part of this book. And I should say straight away that neither Buddhism nor Marxism offers a magic bullet to achieve the end. Neither do I have one to offer. But here are a few thoughts to orient us towards the discussion in the second part of the book.

History has taught us some important lessons, and so alerted us to many traps along the path. Arguably, one of the most important lessons that history has taught us is a simple one: power tends to corrupt. It feeds the ego; people who have it want to retain it and—usually—get more of it. Those who have power, then, even if they sought it for the most altruistic of reasons, soon come to exercise it to feed the beast. Change, and the power structures which this requires, must therefore be bottom-up.

Relatedly, contemporary social life requires the solution to many coordination problems, especially in the realm of economic production, distribution, and consumption. What is produced? In what way is this to be distributed? How are these decisions to be made? It is necessary to figure out how these problems may be solved in a bottom-up fashion.

Another thing that is important, as both Buddhism and Marxism stress, is that people fundamentally misunderstand the world in which they live. So education is of central importance—not the sort of "education" that simply pushes some capitalist ideology, or the ideology of some other power structure; but education that allows us to see the world aright, including an understanding of interconnectedness, the need for compassion, and the negative effects of *tṛṣṇa*—that is, an education which overcomes the three *kleśas* of Buddhism: greed, hatred, and ignorance.

A further part of the story must surely be the construction of appropriate social structures. Human behavioural dispositions are very malleable. Thus, there was a time when people regarded torture, public executions, and slavery as perfectly acceptable. No longer so (at least for enlightened people). And the institution of Nazi concentration camps engendered dispositions to act apallingly in those who ran the camps. On a more contemporary note, penal incarceration is well known actually to promote anti-social behaviour; on the other side, working with groups who help those with particular needs promotes a more benevolent attitude. We need to develop social structures (and the practices which go with them) which promote the human tendencies to compassion and cooperation, and inhibit the tendencies to aggression and dysfunctional antagonism—which, instead of promoting a "dog eat dog" mentality, promote the realisation of interdependence and a consequent solidarity. At this point, one should remember the Buddhist theory of personhood. Persons are dynamic sequences of parts held together by causal chains. Change the causes and you change the person. Though—I hasten to add, if this is not already entirely obvious, given Buddhist ethics—this most certainly does not imply that the end justifies the means.

Even given these preliminary thoughts, one thing is clear. What is required for change are practices which are absent from traditional monastic Buddhist orders and from Marxist groups—indeed, from both. Buddhism has always laid stress on personal practice; Marxism has always laid stress on social (economic) practice. But the personal and the social interact dialectically. Change will then require the interlacing of action in both domains, in ways that both complement and reinforce each other, to dismantle the old and build the new.

6.6   Conclusion

In this part of the book, I have discussed and defended certain aspects of Buddhist and Marxist philosophy. As we have seen, together they provide us with an understanding of central aspects of the contemporary world, each providing parts of the picture on which the other is silent.

But understanding should not be an end in itself. As Marx said in the 11th of his theses on Feuerbach:[8] philosophers have only interpreted the world in various ways; the point, however, is to change it. The Buddha, I am sure, would have agreed. And that takes us to the second half of the book.

8. McLellan (2000), p. 173.

PART II

Right Action

If the revolution does not start from below, if it does not enlarge the "base" of society until it becomes society itself, it is a mere *coup d'état*.

Murray Bookchin[1]

1. Bookchin (2004), p. 173.

DOI: 10.4324/9781003195146-8

7
PROLEGOMENON TO PART II

7.1 Introduction

In the first part of the book I melded ideas from Buddhist and Marxist philosophy to analyse the current unhappy socio-economic state of the world. In this part of the book I will turn to the much harder question of what to do about it. The lessons we have learned from Marxist and Buddhist philosophies will still inform our discussions, but a third element will inform matters also: aspects of anarchist thinking. And as might be expected, this will involve explicitly rejecting some parts of standard Marxist philosophy (ones that I have not endorsed).

Replacing capitalism with something more rational, humane, and sustainable is clearly not going to be an easy task. Doing so will attack the wealthy and powerful minority. And one thing we have learned from history is that those with power do not give it up lightly. Indeed, it must be said, as have a number of people, that presently the end of the human race is easier to envisage than the end of capitalism.

However, if we are to avoid going down the dystopian path I indicated in 6.2, we must attempt to make the necessary changes. As I noted in 3.7, someone who holds that capitalism will not come to an end is living in a fantasy. The question is not whether capitalism is replaced, but only when, how, and what can replace it for the better.

Even how to approach the problem is a difficult question, however. In the rest of this chapter I will outline the approach I will follow in this part of the book.

DOI: 10.4324/9781003195146-9

7.2 How Not to Proceed

How, then, to proceed? Here is one way. First of all, design the perfect socio-economic system. Then, figure out how to get there. This is useless, for at least two reasons.

First, socio-economic systems are complex, and we have very limited understanding of how the pieces of an hypothetical system might fit together. We have no idea how a perfect system—even if we could figure out what one would be like—would, or could, work. It is like designing a machine with no knowledge of the laws of physics. People are complex; societies are complex; economies are complex. And we have only the barest grasp of the ways in which these things might work and their parts interact.

For what it is worth, I note that Marx himself, whether for this reason or for some other, said virtually nothing beyond a few platitudes about what a post-capitalist society would be like. It was left to the Bolsheviks after the Russian revolution to try to figure out what to do, and things did not go well, for reasons which we will come to in due course.

Second, even if we did know where we should get to, we have no good grasp of how to get there—or even if it is possible to get there—for exactly the same reasons. Where one is places constraints on where one can get to.[1]

For these reasons, we cannot but start from where we are, and move in what seems to be the best direction, learning from our successes and failures as we go along. The way forward will require a constant reevaluation and critique, in the light of what we learn. As Chomsky puts it (in answer to a question):[2]

> Well, I suppose I *don't* feel that in order to work hard for a social change you need to be able to spell out a plan for a future society in any kind of detail. What I feel should drive a person to work for change are certain *principles* you'd like to see achieved. Now, you may not know in detail— and I don't think that any of us *do* know in detail—how these principles can best be realized at this point in complex systems like human societies. But I don't really see why that should make a difference: what you try to do is advance the principles.

We will, then, have to work out a lot of things as we go along. Metcalf puts it this way:[3]

---

1. There is an old joke about a tourist who asked a local farmer how to get to such and such a place. The farmer pondered for a moment, and then said 'Well, I wouldn't start from here'.
2. Chomsky (2013a), pp. 31 f. As he goes on to note, the view can be thought of as some kind of reformism, which comes with its own dangers. I will take these up in due course.
3. Metcalf (2015), p. 36.

The dream of changing everything at once is only a dream—or more often in the real world, a nightmare. There can be no single revolution that sweeps away all the oppressive institutions and replaces them with better ones. The work of creating a good society is never done.

Of course, the fact that we cannot design a utopia and plan how to get there does not, as Chomsky notes, mean that we have to fly blind. Indeed, we have to have *something* to guide us, fallible and revisable as this is, or we have no guide to action at all.

What is that? What are the principles, to use Chomsky's expression? The obvious answer, given the first part of the book, is that action should be driven by compassion. But that doesn't take us very far. To go further, let us start from the fact that capitalism has to be replaced.

7.3   The Shape of a Post-Capitalist Society

To replace capitalism, the group of people who own or manage capital (call these capitalists) at the expense of those who are merely employed by it (call these workers) must be eliminated. (I should emphasise that when I am talking of the elimination of a group, I am not talking about destroying the individuals. I am taking about a restructuring of society such that there is no group of this kind.) One could not eliminate the other group (the workers) if anything at all is to be produced.

I have sometimes heard it suggested that, in due course, all production could be done by technology (especially with the development of artificial intelligence and machines that teach themselves), making a workforce entirely unnecessary. The thought is utopian. We are clearly nowhere near this at the moment, if ever we will be. More to the point, without a paid workforce, there would be no one to buy what is produced, and so no way of realising the profit required for the growth of capital. In other words, for such a system to work, capitalism would already be gone.

Perhaps not, it might be suggested. Capitalists might simply *give* some of their profit to people (maybe via taxation). But why would they do that? Capitalists could simply purchase from each other directly. People as workers would have become redundant; and people as buyers would have become redundant too. In other words, capitalists could just dispense with everyone else and let them rot. Clearly, that is obviously not compassion.

If the class of capitalists is to be eliminated, the control of production must not rest in the hands of a group of private individuals. And if the means of production are not to be privately controlled (and in a capitalist country, this means owned), control must lie either in the hands of those who work them, or of some public body—most obviously the state.

The first is a bottom-up power structure. The second is a top-down power structure. There are reasons for much preferring the former—or at least, for preferring a structure with as much bottom-up control as possible. The main reason for this concerns the nature of top-down power. This is important, and I will turn to a substantial discussion of the matter in the next chapter. For the present, the following will do. Eliminating the private ownership/control of capital is a necessary condition for the elimination of capitalism; but it is by no means a sufficient one. State control of the means of production is quite compatible with a capitalist system. The economy of the old Soviet Union was thus, as is that of contemporary China. We must, then, think carefully about the details of a society that is organised in a bottom-up fashion.[4]

7.4   The Structure of Part II

To organise the discussion of these matters and others they bring in their train, the second half of the book has the following structure. In the next chapter, Chapter 8, we will look at questions of power and the state, and see why bottom-up organisation is to be preferred to top-down organisation.

In Chapter 9, we will turn to look at what a society organised in a bottom-up way might be like, and problems associated with this form of organisation. In Chapter 10, we move to the obvious next question: how one might move society in this direction?

Two matters related to this are so important that they deserve separate chapters. The first is ideology and its control of people's thinking—their consciousness. Chapter 11 examines this. The second is changing ourselves. Societies produce people, but people produce societies. Chapter 12 discusses changes we may make in ourselves to move society in the right direction. Buddhist themes will be present in much of the discussion of this part of the book, but they are at their most obvious in this chapter.

Finally, what this book is about is capitaism and its replacement. However, we have, or will have, touched on many other important matters in the course of the book. In the final chapter, Chapter 13, I comment on some of these, and simply point out a few implications of our discussions.

7.5   The Time Frame for Replacing Capitalism

Let me end with some final thoughts which provide a backdrop to our discussion. These concern the time frame pertinent to change.

Clearly, replacing capitalism is not going to happen overnight. It will be a slow process, with its successes, setbacks, false starts. One should think, here,

4. For a trenchant critique of the state and the arguments often used in support of it, see Sylvan (2007).

of the Western transition between a feudal economy and a capitalist economy. The exact origins of capitalism are contentious; but arguably it starts with the rise of mercantile capitalism in about the 14th and 15th centuries, and it is not in full swing till urbanisation and industrialisation in the 19th century. The process, then, took 400 years—indeed, longer, since capitalism is still developing its global form now. Perhaps the transition to a post-capitalist economy will take just as long. In his essay of 1895, 'Fédéralisme, Socialisme, et Anti-Théologisme', Bakunin puts it thus:[5]

> How to organize society in such a way that every man and woman who comes into the world may find approximately equal provision for the development of his or her various faculties and for their exercise through labour; how to organize a society which, by making it impossible for one man to exploit the work of another, allows each to share in the enjoyment of social wealth—which in fact is produced only by labour—only to the extent that he has contributed his own to its production.
>
> The complete resolution of this problem will probably be the task of centuries.

Indeed, the transition from feudalism to capitalism should remind us that a nascent socio-economic system can be developing at the same time as the old system flourishes. Indeed, as Marx points out, a new society cannot appear *ex nihilo*: it must ferment within the old:[6]

> new higher relations of production never appear before the material conditions of their existence have matured in the womb of the old.

In other words, without the appropriate causes, you cannot have the appropriate effect. Marx warns us, moreover, not to expect a new system to emerge fully formed, like Athena from the head of Zeus: it will show its provenance. When a post-capitalist society forms, it will be:[7]

> in every respect, economically, morally, intellectually, stamped with the birth marks of the old society from whose womb it emerges.

Indeed, it could be argued that the transition to a post-capitalist socio-economic formation has already been under way since at least the late 19th century, with the rise of workers' movements, unions, popular revolutions—though perhaps the result of what we have seen here is no more than the analogue of merchant capitalism.

5. Lehning (1973), p. 108.
6. *Preface to a Critique of Political Economy*, McLellan (2000), p. 426.
7. *Critique of the Gotha Program*, McLellan (2000), p. 614.

All this underlines the importance of patience and persistence. One is not going to change the world overnight. There will be times of hope and times of frustration. One has to accept the good times and the bad. Thus, Ray:[8]

> At a certain point in our political work, the going can become very difficult. We find that the anticipated results are not materializing as expected, that the people we are working with are frustrating, and we find ourselves losing our original inspiration. In that situation—which is the rule rather than the exception—the willingness to continue on, regardless of our own feelings of fulfillment and frustration, is critical. Without that, nothing of benefit is ever going to be possible.

As we noted in 2.3.3, patience and persistence are important Buddhist virtues.

Having said all this, the contemporary situation is very different from that which turned a feudal economy into a capitalist one. As I discussed in Chapter 3, a looming ecological catastrophe threatens to bring the whole pack of cards down around our ears fast. Time may be a luxury we can ill afford. Thus, Lowey:[9]

> There will be no radical transformation unless the forces committed to a radical socialist and ecological programme become hegemonic, in the Gramscian sense of the word. In one sense, time is on our side, as we work for change, because the global situation of the environment is becoming worse and worse, and the threats are becoming closer and closer. But on the other hand, time is running out, because in some years—no one can say how much—the damage may be irreversible. There is no reason for optimism: the entrenched ruling elites of the system are incredibly powerful, and the forces of radical opposition are still small. But they are the only hope that capitalism's 'destructive progress' will be halted.

All, sadly, true.[10] We may be working for change under steadily worsening environmental circumstances and the social conditions these engender.

7.6 Conclusion

Moving to a more rational and humane society, and moving within the time we have available to do so, will clearly, then, be a difficult task for many reasons. But here is a thought to motivate:[11]

8. Ray (2006), p. 70.
9. Lowey (2006), p. 307.
10. But for a note of optimism, see 'Letter to the March 15, 2019 Climate Strikers', pp. 171–5 of Solnit (2019).
11. Slott (2011), p. 350.

Put aside for the moment the question of whether [an ideal post-capitalist] society, or even some relatively close approximation can actually be established some time in the future. Try for a moment to imagine the life of an individual in such a society. Certainly, many of the problems which make our current life so difficult would no longer play a significant role. Insecurity would be diminished as people are guaranteed the basic necessities of life. Competition and striving for advantage over others would also be less prominent in a world in which everyone experiences nurture and support for their human potential. The horrors of war, famine, and environmental devastation would disappear, allowing us to lead lives marked by peace and security. Technology would be used to free human beings from uncreative, physical difficult labour while reducing the total amount of time needed to work. We would have more time to spend with our families and friends, as well as to develop our talents and interests in a variety of areas.

It hardly needs to be said this is a goal for which it is well worth striving—something to be kept in mind when we meet the many obstacles, in both theory and practice, surely to be encountered.

8
POWER AND THE STATE

8.1 Introduction

The matters we are concerned with in this book are intimately connected with questions concerning power, and especially that of the state. In this chapter we will look at such matters. First, we will look at power in general, and the psychology of top-down power in particular. Next, we will turn to state power in a capitalist society, and then to matters of power in a post-capitalist society.

In the previous chapter, I indicated that for a post-capitalist society one should prefer a bottom-up power structure to a top-down one—or at least, a society with as much bottom-up power as possible. The reason for this will have become clear by the end of this chapter.

8.2 Power and Oppression

For a start, then, what is power? Power is the ability to do things; and power over other people is the ability to get them to do things. That is, power, in this sense, is the ability of a person or group of people to have control, authority, or influence over the behaviour of others (*Merriam-Webster Dictionary*). Notably, since organisation requires coordination, organisation requires power.

Power can be of various kinds. For a start, it can be personal or institutional —where by an institution I mean some kind of entrenched social configuration. Institutional power can itself be of several kinds: political, economic, gender, racial. Our concern in this chapter will be with institutional power.[1]

---

1. Perhaps the contemporary writer who has thought most about institutional power is Michel Foucault. One thing he stresses is the effect of power relations on subjectivity. (See his essays

DOI: 10.4324/9781003195146-10

A crucial distinction that will concern us is that between top-down and bottom-up power structures. In a bottom-up power structure, those who are subject to power have an active say in what happens. They can agree with the decision made, or at least agree to accept it. Failing this, they will just have to take whatever consequences follow. But in all cases they have at least had the opportunity to be part of the discussion which determined the decisions and policies.

In a top-down power structure, however, matters are different. Decisions are taken and policies are made and implemented by a certain group in society. Those subject to the power are consulted in no significant sense, but the consequences of the decisions, policies, and practices are imposed on them, whether they like it or not.[2]

I note that any complex social system will be composed of a number of different and interconnected power structures; some of these may be top-down, and some may be bottom-up. It is this which makes it meaningful to talk of moving to a *more* bottom-up structure (i.e., one with fewer top-down elements).

As is clear to even a somewhat cursory inspection, top-down power is used, if not always, then nearly always,[3] to the benefit of the powerful, and so to oppress the disempowered group.[4] Thus, patriarchal power is used for the benefit of men. Racial power is used for the benefit of a dominant race, and so on. Political power is no exception to the rule.

What I have to say in this chapter concerns mainly the power of the state. This is top-down power of a political kind—and an economic kind, which is not far behind. I will make a few comments on other kinds of power in a later chapter.

8.3   The Psychology of Power

Let us now turn to the psychology of top-down power, with especial reference to political power. Why do those in positions of such power tend to use it in an

in Faubion (1994), especially pp. 326–48, 'The Subject and Power'.) We will look at the effect of ideology (one important channel of power) on subjectivity in a later chapter.

2. As Sharp notes, however, in the last instance, top-down power can be held only because of the cooperation of at least a certain group of those over whom power is wielded: 'every ruler needs the skill, knowledge, advice, labour, and administrative ability of a significant portion of his subjects. The more extensive and detailed the ruler's control is, the more such assistance he will require'. (Sharp (1973), Vol. 1, pp. 12–3.) Top-down power structures therefore have a built-in vulnerability.

3. The case of parental power is an interesting case. This is certainly top-down. Thus, Chomsky reminds us that a parent may grab a child in order to stop them running into traffic (Chomsky (2013a), p. 110). And with overbearing parents, parental power can certainly be used in an oppressive fashion. However, it need not be used in this way; with good parents, it generally is not. Why such power is an exception to the more general rule is a fair question. It is perhaps something to do with the unique nature of a parent/child relationship.

4. *Collins English Dictionary*: to oppress people means to prevent them from having the same opportunities, freedom, and benefits as others.

oppressive fashion? Doubtless there are as many answers as there are people involved. However, many general things can be said.

For a start, psychological research suggests that people who attain positions of power of this kind start to see the world from only their perspective, and they lose the ability to see it from the perspectives of others. There are even physiological reasons for this: power tends to inhibit "mirror neurons", which fire in such a way as to reproduce the subjective experiences of others. Thus we have what Keltner has called the 'paradox of power'. Those who attain power lose the ability to experience the empathy which may have put them in positions of power in the first place. Tellingly, the phenomenon can be mitigated if a person in power takes time to reflect on incidents of suffering and powerlessness in their own life.[5]

Of course, this phenomenon will be magnified when people mix with others of like mind. All our views and behaviours are reinforced if we mix largely with others who see the world in the same way that we do. Thus, associating with those who have little sympathy with, or compassion for, others will do this. It is hardly surprising, then, if business executives and politicians, who mix mainly with each other, lose any sense of solidarity with those over whom they wield power. So, Stiglitz says:[6]

> It is not an accident that bankers exhibit the extent of moral turpitude that they do. It has been shown by experiments how bankers—especially when they are reminded that they are bankers—act in a more dishonest and selfish way. They are shaped by their profession.[7] So too for economists; while those who choose to study economics may be more selfish than others, the longer they study economics, the more selfish they become.[8]

The next observation concerns the fact that many people are driven to acquire power; and, more importantly, those in positions of power want to hang on to them. It is a striking fact, for example, that of all the leaders of the UK, the US, and Australia, since the Second World War, only two have voluntarily resigned from office, as opposed to being removed from power by losing an election (or the immenent inevitability of this), being dismissed by their own party, death, reaching the limit of their term, or threatened by imminent impeachment. One was the Australian Prime Minister Robert Menzies at the age of 71. The other was the British Prime Minster Harold

5. On all these things, see Useem (2017), Miller and Xu (2015), Fisk and Dépret (1996), Keltner (2016), Owen and Davidson (2019).
6. Stiglitz (2019), p. 30. Footnotes his. One might recall here, the point about Right Livelihood in the Eightfold Noble Path.
7. See Cohn et al. (2014).
8. See Bauman and Rose (2011).

Wilson in 1976—and so unusual was it that it took everyone outside of his immediate circle by surprise.

When we move from individuals to groups, the phenomenon is even more striking. It is very hard to think of any powerful group, be it a political party, company board, or military group, which has voluntarily given up power. The loss of power typically seems to be brought about by external circumstances which force matters.[9]

Thus, what we often see in both individuals and groups is that, whatever motives brought them to the positions of power they occupy, retaining power and keeping others out of it becomes an end in itself.

Why is this? Power has the effect of enhancing and strengthening the sense of self, or, if you like, the ego. It is, hence, addictive. Having it magnifies one's sense of self. Losing it is a blow to the ego. Indeed, there is physiological evidence that power releases dopamine in the brain, the same chemical that disposes one to a drug addiction.[10] Some have suggested, moreover, that power, like drug addiction, makes one want more power by its very nature:[11]

[T]he desire for power is in principle insatiable, because its essence is to overcome resistance, yet once resistance is overcome, the evidence of resistance vanishes.

Buddhist psychology provides an acute analysis of what is going on here. There is no such thing as a determinate self; yet we try to construct one. We all tell ourselves stories about who and what we are (see Chapter 4). Power allows someone to define themself—or suppose themself defined—by their title and their position.

As we saw in 5.3.3, Struhl argues that it is the insecurity produced by an inchoate grasp of the fact of having no determinate self which is behind the desire for money as an end in itself. Loy puts the point this way:[12]

Our repressed sense of unreality [of the self] returns to consciousness as the feeling that there is something lacking in my life. What is it that is lacking? How I understand that depends on the kind of person I am and the kind of society I live in. The sense that *something* is wrong with me is too vague, too amorphous. It needs to be given a more specific form if I'm to be able to do something about it, and that form usually depends on how I've been raised. In modern developed (or

9. An interesting exception to this rule is the nation of Bhutan, where a monarch constructed a functioning democracy for his country, making himself a constitutional—and (theoretically) removable—monarch. See Long (2019), ch. 4.
10. See Al-Rhodin (2014).
11. Winter (2018), p. 327, quoting Riezler (1942).
12. Loy (2008), pp. 19 f.

"economized") societies such as the United States, I am likely to understand my lack as not having enough money—regardless of how much money I already have. Money is important to us not only because we can buy anything with it, but because money has become a kind of collective *reality symbol*. The more money you get, the more real you become. That's what we tend to think, anyway. (When a wealthy person arrives somewhere, his or her presence is acknowledged more than the arrival of a "nobody".) Because money does not really end *dukkha*—it can't fill up the bottomless hole at one's core—this way of thinking often becomes a trap. You're a multi-millionaire but still feel that something is wrong with your life? Obviously, you don't have enough money yet.

And as he points out in the next paragraph, fame (of the usual kind and of the very transient kind delivered by social media) and—especially—power can fill the same function as money:

> We crave power because it is a visible expression of one's reality. Dictators like Hitler and Stalin dominate their societies. As their biographies reveal, however, they never seem to have enough control to feel really secure. Those who want power the most end up the most paranoid.

Indeed, a running theme of Loy's book is that the desire for money, fame, power, and so on is generated by an awareness of a lack of a determinate self. The more one has of these things, the more one is *something*.

In fact, similar insights, to the effect that there is no determinate self, and that the realisation of this causes trauma, are to be found outside of the Buddhist tradition. Thus, famously, Sartre argued that the fact that a person has no determinate being (essence) is wont to generate a sense of anguish which, by an act of bad faith, makes them attempt, forlornly, to be a being-in-itself (*être en soi*), rather than a being-for-itself (*être pour soi*).[13] They find comfort in supposing that they have a determinate nature.

The Buddhist analysis may, indeed, be pushed one stage further—not in terms of *anātman*, but in terms of *anitya*. Everything is impermanent. Moreover, it is clear that we all have a sense of this, much as we might try to suppress it. It is simply an obvious generalisation of all that we see around us. And much of this change we have no control over at all. Naturally, this causes insecurity—*duḥkha*.[14] (The connection between this and the desire for a determinate self is obvious. If we have such a self, there is part of us, indeed the essential part

---

13. The matter is spelled out at length in Sartre's *Being and Nothingness* (Barnes (1956)), but perhaps most dramatically in his plays and novels, such as *Nausea* (*La Nausée*).
14. Indeed, Carpenter (2014), ch. 1, argues that this is the most fundamental cause of the *duḥkha* we experience.

of us, which is immune to the vicissitudes of change.) Now, it is clearly natural to suppose that things like wealth and power are a means of controlling these vicissitudes, and thus protecting ourselves from them. Desires for these things are, therefore, eminently explicable by our inchoate grasp of impermanence.

Such desires are, however, pernicious. Not only are permanency and determinate self unachievable—*anātman* and *anitya* are features of reality; the desires (*tṛṣṇa*) for these things generate the very *duḥkha* they are meant to overcome. It is wise, therefore, to work to break such desires—and in particular, in the present context, the desire for power. (More of this in a later chapter.)

The upshot of all these matters is that there are deep psychological reasons why, for those (at least unenlightened) persons in positions of power, the first imperative will become maintaining, or, if possible, increasing their power. Using the power for the benefit of others, if this was ever a motive, will fall by the wayside. As the 19th-century British politician Lord Acton noted: power corrupts, and absolute power corrupts absolutely.[15]

8.4   The Capitalist State

Let us now turn to political power and its exercise in a capitalist society. This is certainly of a top-down kind. We may call the organ of this power *the state*.

But what, exactly, is the state?[16] The first thing that is likely to occur to someone who ponders the matter is that it is the government (parliament, the presidency, etc.); and certainly this is a central element of it. But in a capitalist state, the loci of state power are many: the government, the judiciary, the police (and more generally, the penal system[17]), the military, capital (both local, for example, in the workplace; and international, for example, in the form of the International Monetary Fund and the World Bank), the press, the education system.[18]

Let us set education aside for the moment; I will return to it in a later chapter. That the judiciary is part of the state and its enforcement of power is clear enough. There is a view to the effect that the law is neutral: all are equal under the law. This, however, is not true. The wealthy have a power in the system that the poor do not have. They have the ability to pay for expensive lawyers who know how to operate the system; not to mention the fact that they tend to have influential contacts within the system.

---

15. 'Power tends to corrupt and absolute power corrupts absolutely. Great men are almost always bad men, even when they exercise influence and not authority; still more when you superadd the tendency of the certainty of corruption by authority'. Letter to Bishop Mandell Creighton, 5 April 1887. Published in Figgis and Laurence (1907).

16. One does well to remember in what follows that the state is not a uniform monolith (as Wright (2018), ch. 5, reminds us). There can be tensions between different sections of capital, between long and short term goals, etc.

17. As emphasised by Foucault (1977).

18. And, one might add, in those countries where a religious group has political power, the church (whether it be Christian, Islamic, or some other).

That the police have a role in the state and its enforcement of power is equally obvious. Neither are *they* neutral. The police target blue-collar crime, not white-collar crime, such as the shady dealings of the financiers who caused the 2008 economic crash, or the illegal acts of invasion and torture committed by the politicians and those whom they controlled in the 2003 invasion of Iraq and its aftermath. (Notoriously, also, in many countries, such as the United States and Australia, the police are not racially neutral. Black and indigenous people have higher rates of arrest, incarceration, and so forth than white people.)

The military, equally, is an organ of state power. This is usually used in international matters. Rarely is it actually used for defence. Much more commonly, it is used in acts of aggression, to further the ends of the government that controls it (and the capital that controls this)—though of course, for ideological reasons, this will be called *defence*. Just occasionally, military power will be used nationally. It will be used in this way when enforcement requires greater force than the police can muster—for example, in the case of mass civil disobedience, or strikebreaking.

The press tends to be a locus of state power as well. In many countries the organs of the press are state institutions, or if this is not the case, they are heavily controlled by government. Many countries, however, boast a *free press*. This means that they are not subject to explicit state control; but it does not mean that they do not reinforce the general political *status quo*. The press may be free to support this or that political party, but the parties are usually in agreement in endorsing a capitalist economy. Neither is this an accident. Though there may be no explicit state control, most presses are themselves capitalist organisations, subject to the imperative of making a profit through advertising, circulation, and so on. Moreover, other forms of capital have the ability to manipulate the press with the way they use their money (say, by the placing of advertisements). What appears in the press is, then, largely the capitalist state line.[19] It might have been hoped that the internet would break this kind of power structure, and at one time it seemed possible that this might happen. But no longer so. There is now so much information available that the question of its control is crucial. The control is largely in the hands of private companies, such as Google and Facebook, and the algorithms they decide to deploy. Indeed, we all think that we use the internet; but in reality, capitalism has now engineered the internet to use us.[20]

---

19. For a detailed and telling analysis of this, see Herman and Chomsky (1988). I will return to the details of this in ch. 11.

20. How so, is explained in detail in Zuboff (2019). And thus Stiglitz (2019), p. 133: 'Unfortunately, those who would use the new technologies for manipulation understand the limitations of our regulatory framework [GP: supposed to keep it under control], and work hard to exploit its gaps. It is war, and at this juncture, those who would undermine democracy seem to be winning'.

This brings us to capital itself. Whether or not one calls capital part of the state, it should be clear from what I have said that it is the power of capital which is, in the last analysis, the dominant and driving force behind the (other) organs of state power. Thus, take just a couple of small examples. The capitalist Koch brothers have wielded enormous political power in the United States, through their funding of capitalist propaganda, think tanks, political parties, and individuals.[21] Or again, in 2008 the American insurance company AIG suffered a speculation-induced collapse. The US government bailout of the company with $180 billion delivered:[22]

> more corporate welfare in one fell swoop than had been provided to all of America's poor through our welfare programs aimed at children over a period of more than a decade.

As Marx and Engels put it in the *Communist Manifesto*:[23]

> The executive of the modern State is but a committee for managing the common affairs of the whole bourgeoisie.

This does not mean that every action of a political party, president, or prime minister is clearly in the immediate interest of capital. A government may make concessions against the short-term interest of sections of capital for long-term benefits, be they defusing dissent and undercutting hostile class action, or remaining in power so that they can make more important decisions in the interest of capital. And there is always, of course, the lure of power itself. But in the end, all roads lead back to capital.

It is often claimed that in a so-called liberal democracy of the kind one finds in most of the countries in the global North, people do have an active say in the decisions of a government which affect them. There is a grain of truth in this; if there were not, it would be harder for the view to retain any credibility. Once every three, four, or five years, those who are enfranchised (which is usually only some of those whom the political decisions affect) are given the power to choose a governing party, president, or prime minister. But to suppose that this is a significant say in political decisions and policies is largely an illusion. All they are doing is, as Marx says:[24]

> deciding once in three or six years which member of the ruling class [is] to misrepresent the people in Parliament.

21. As noted by Schweickart (2011), pp. 154–5.
22. Stiglitz (2019), p. 107.
23. McLellan (2000), p. 247.
24. From 'The Civil War in France'. McLellan (2000), p. 588.

On those rare occasions when people have a voice, they are faced with a choice between a handful of parties (often two), which largely agree on most things, including the desirability of a capitalist economy and its growth. Nor is this an accident. Who gets to stand for election, or at least, who gets to stand for election with any significant chance of winning, is determined by money put up by capitalist institutions, or political parties beholden to such money. Moreover, the process is under the sway of a media controlled by those same capital interests.[25]

Moreover, for the rest of the time, between elections (which is most of it), those subject to the political power have no say whatsoever in what it does. Those elected can do exactly what they like: they are bound in no way by election "promises". Again, those who have real influence on what happens are the capitalist lobbyists whose deep pockets politicians cannot afford to ignore— even if they wanted to, which, generally speaking, they have no inclination to do. Thus, CEOs and other executives of corporations wield an enormous amount of power in a capitalist economy; and it is entirely obvious that they are in no way democratically responsible to those whom their actions affect.

Indeed, many of those in political and economic power are clear (usually in private) that they are the ones who should be making decisions, and that the illusion of democracy is a good one for maintaining the *status quo*. Thus, consider, for example, James Madison, one of the main architects of the American Constitution. Using Madison's own words, Chomsky summarises matters as follows:[26]

> In the debates on the Constitution, Madison pointed out that if elections in England 'were open to all classes of people, the property of landed proprietors would be insecure. An agrarian law would soon take place,' giving land to the landless. The Constitutional system must be designed to prevent such injustice and 'secure the permanent interests of the country,' which are property rights. ...
>
> Madison foresaw that the threat of democracy was likely to become more severe over time because of the increase in 'the proportion of those who will labor under all the hardships of life, and secretly sigh for a more equal distribution of its blessings.' They might gain influence, Madison feared. He was concerned by the 'symptoms of a leveling spirit' that had already appeared, and warned 'of the future danger' if the right

25. 'In the United States there is very little space in which to espouse anti-capitalist views. The US Congress is overwhelmingly dominated by pro-capitalist Republicans and Democrats; all supreme court justices are appointed by the two dominant parties; alternative parties are barred from participating in election debates and have difficulty accessing funding (even public funding); and the corporate-owned mainstream media refuse to present perspectives that challenge the hegemonic discourse of capital' (Leech (2012), p. 136).
26. Chomsky (1999), pp. 47–8.

to vote would place 'power over property in hands without a share in it.' Those 'without property, or the hope of acquiring it, cannot be expected to sympathize sufficiently with its rights,' Madison explained. His solution was to keep political power in the hands of those who 'come from and represent the wealth of the nation,' the 'more capable set of men,' with the general public fragmented and disorganized.

And as Bernays, the father of modern advertising and political propaganda, says:[27]

> The conscious and intelligent manipulation of the organized habits and opinions of the masses is an important element in democratic society. Those who manipulate this unseen mechanism of society constitute an invisible government which is the true ruling power of our country. ...
> [W]e are dominated by the relatively small number of persons ... who understand the mental processes and social patterns of the masses. It is they who pull the wires which control the public mind, who harness old social forces and contrive new ways to bind and guide the world.

Thus, *liberal democracy* is an entire misnomer. What we have is clearly a plutocracy. Indeed, *dictatorship by capital* would be a much more apt description.

At any rate, as should be clear, to move to a post-capitalist society, the link between wealth and political power must be broken. Positions of political power should not be in the gift, direct or indirect, of wealth. Wealth must be removed from whatever election and decision-making processes there are. The flip side of this is that persons should not be able to use positions of political power to make themselves rich.

8.5   The State in a Post-Capitalist Society

Let us now turn to matters concerning the state and state power in a post-capitalist society. This was the central theoretical (as opposed to personal) issue that separated Marx and Bakunin in their struggle over the First International. According to Bakunin, abolishing the state was a necessary condition of a move to a post-capitalist society. According to Marx, it was not. Indeed, at least in a transition period, it was necessary to have a state, though a "proletarian" one, a "dictatorship of the proletariat (working class)". Thus, in his 'Critique of the Gotha Program', Marx writes:[28]

27. Bernays (2005), p. 37.
28. McLellan (2000), p. 611. Indeed: 'Every political set-up following a revolution calls for dictatorship, and an energetic one at that'. From an article in the *Neue Reinische Zeitung*. (McLellan (2000), p. 197.)

Between capitalist and communist society there lies the period of revolutionary transformation of the one into the other. Corresponding to
this is also a political transition period in which the state can be
nothing but the revolutionary dictatorship of the proletariat.

Exactly what he meant by this was never very clearly explained, and in the
context, the word *dictatorship* might have meant no more than *government*.
There is no particular reason to suppose that Marx had in mind what was
later to be made of the notion by Lenin and the Bolsheviks.[29]

It is clear, however, that Marx endorsed a centralised state of some form after
the demise of capitalism: something that had the power to enforce new social
relations. True, Marx and Engels claimed that it would eventually 'wither
away'. In *Anti-Dühring*, Engels puts matters as follows:[30]

The interference of the state power in social relations becomes superflu-
ous in one sphere after another, and then ceases of itself. The government
of persons is replaced by the administration of things and the direction of
the processes of production. The state is not "abolished", it withers away.

However, Marx and Engels gave no reason for, or mechanism for, the disappearance of the state. It was simply a hope—and, as we have seen, a somewhat
forlorn one.

The points were forcefully made by Bakunin:[31]

Even from the standpoint of the urban proletariat who are supposed to
reap the reward of the seizure of political power, surely it is obvious
that this power is but a sham? It is bound to be impossible for a few thousand, let alone tens or hundreds or thousands of men to wield power that
effectively. It will have to be exercised by proxy, which means entrusting
it to a group of men elected to represent and govern them, which in turn
will unfailingly return them to all the deceit and subservience of representative bourgeoise rule. After a brief flash of liberty or orgiastic revolution, the citizens of the new State will wake up slaves, puppets and
victims of a new group of ambitious men.

This is the real contradiction. If the State is really going to be a
people's government, then why should it abolish itself, and if its abolition
is essential for the real emancipation of the people, then how dare they
[Marxists] call it the people's government? By the polemic we have
used against them, we have made them realize that liberty or anarchy,

29. See Draper (1987), ch. 1.
30. Engels (1939), p. 307.
31. From letter to the Editorial Board of *La Liberté*, 1872 (Lehning (1973), pp. 254 f.) and Baku-
    nin's *Statism and Anarchy* (1873) (Lehning (1973), pp. 269 f.).

that is the free organization of the working masses from the bottom up, is the final aim of social development, and that any State, including their people's State, is a yoke, as it gives birth to despotism on the one side and slavery on the other.

On this contradiction we must for the time being end our argument. They affirm that only dictatorship, *theirs* of course, can create a popular will. We reply that no dictatorship can have any other aim but to perpetuate itself, and that it is capable of instilling and fostering only slavery in the masses that endure it. Liberty can only be created by liberty, that is, by mass rebellion and the free organization of the working masses from the bottom upwards.

Though written decades before the Russian Revolution and the Soviet Union it produced, it is hard to read these words without hearing them as a prescient vision of what was to come.

The causes of the derailment of the Russian Revolution are many: the need to fight a civil war and to repel counter-revolutionary invasions from Britain, France, and the United States; the need to rebuild the economy, and so maintain people's livelihood after this collapsed as a result of the First World War and the revolution; the need to turn a largely peasant economy into an industrial country very fast, so that the country could compete with more advanced capitalist countries; being threatened by a remilitarised Germany; and, if you like, add in the autocratic and paranoid personality of Stalin.[32] Be that as it may, Bakunin got it right, and was vindicated by history. Once the Bolsheviks were able to take power away from the relatively democratic soviets and workers councils, and place it in their own top-down power structure, the rest was all downhill.[33]

Drawing on his analysis of the psychology of power, Loy diagnoses the matter as follows:[34]

Even if our revolution is successful, we will merely replace one group of egos with our own. If I do not struggle with the greed inside myself, it is quite likely that, if I gain power, I too will be inclined to take advantage of the situation to serve my own interests. If I do not acknowledge the ill will in my own heart as my own problem, I am likely to project my anger onto those who obstruct my purpose. If unaware that my own sense of

32. On the complex personality of Stalin, see Montefiore (2005).
33. On the destruction of democracy by the Bolsheviks, see Berkman (2003), chs. 14–19, Goldman (1923), and Schapiro (1965). Interestingly, as early as 1918, some members of the left wing of the Bolshevik Party, including Bukharin—executed by Stalin, after a show trial in 1938—argued that Lenin's policy of top-down centralisation 'amounted to nothing more nor less than state capitalism; and that unless the masses exercised economic dictatorship, their political dictatorship would inevitably disappear' (Schapiro (1965), p. 138).
34. Loy (2008), p. 142.

duality [GP: of self and other] is a dangerous delusion, I will understand the problem of social change as the need for me to dominate the socio-political order. Add a conviction of my good intentions, along with my superior understanding of the situation, and one has a recipe for social and personal disaster. History is littered with examples.

The lesson, then, is a quite general one. Top-down power structures do not dismantle themselves. For whatever reason they arise, they start to run things for their own benefit. Such is the fate of all bureaucracies, be they of the major kind of the Soviet communist *nomenclatura* or the minor kind of bureaucracies that have taken over Australian universities.

In short, a post-capitalist society, if it is to work, must be organised in a bottom-up fashion, as endorsed by many anarchists. I note that nearly all those who do or did endorse such a kind of structure, argue for it on the basis of the value of liberty and its role in human flourishing.[35] As is clear, we are approaching matters from a very different direction. It is Buddhist ethics which is driving the picture, not libertarianism (though the oppression caused by a lack of freedom can certainly be a cause of *duḥkha*).

8.6 Conclusion

So much for power, its nature, the way it functions in a capitalist society, and the way it ought not to function in a post-capitalist society. In particular, it should now be clear why I take it to be desirable that the power structure in a post-capitalist society be a bottom-up one as largely as possible. A top-down power structure will not be a compassionate one, functioning for the well-being of all.

Having established this, we may now turn to the issue of what a society organised in bottom-up fashion might be like. This is the topic of the next chapter.

---

35. On the varieties of anarchism, and the moral justifications offered for them, see Ward (2004) and Fiala (2017).

9

SOCIETY—FROM THE BOTTOM UP

9.1 Introduction

In Chapter 7 I noted that if control of production is not to be in private hands, then we face a choice as to whether control resides in the state or in those themselves who produce; in other words, a choice between whether the power to organise is top-down or bottom-up. In the last chapter, we saw that the nature of top-down power is such that it is to be avoided—or at least, if it is impossible to eliminate it entirely, then avoided in as far as possible.

Is it possible to have a society with entirely bottom-up organisation? I don't know—and neither does anybody else. Maybe some top-down elements will always be necessary. And one cannot deny that top-down power can (and sometimes does) do good things. However, these provide no reason *not* to get rid of top-down power, in as far as possible.

In a top-down organisational structure, decisions are taken by a person or a group, who then tell those below them what to do (though maybe it will be left for them to decide some of the details of how this is to be achieved—which of course conveniently provides someone to blame if things don't work out). These, in turn, tell those below them in the same terms, who tell those below *them*, and so on, until the people at the bottom of the chain have to do it. McEwan describes such a structure thus:[1]

> First we have the model current among management theories in industry, with its counterpart in conventional thinking about government in

1. McEwan (1963). The passage is quoted by Ward (1996), p. 51.

DOI: 10.4324/9781003195146-11

society as a whole. This is the model of rigid pyramidical hierarchy, with lines of 'communication and command' running from the top to the bottom of the pyramid. There is fixed delineation of responsibility, each element has a specific role, and the procedures to be followed at any level are determined within fairly narrow limits, and may only be changed by decisions of elements higher in the hierarchy. The role of the top group in the hierarchy is sometimes supposed to be comparable to the 'brain' of the system.

In a bottom-up structure, by contrast, decisions are taken by those who they immediately affect. If more coordinated decisions are needed, they are made by "higher-level" groups comprising those who are delegated from below. The structure is, thus, much less rigid and more flexible. Thus, McEwan continues:

> The other model is from the cybernetics of evolving self-organising systems. Here we have a system of large variety, sufficient to cope with a complex, evolving environment. Its characteristics are changing structure, modifying itself from continual feedback from the environment, exhibiting redundancy of potential command, and invoking complex interlocking control structures. Learning and decision making are distributed throughout the system, denser, perhaps, in some areas than in others.

We are very familiar with top-down organisational/power structures. Clearly, they are implemented in military organisations. They are equally implemented in familiar capitalist business models, where the CEO assumes the role occupied by the general in a military organisation. And such top-down power/organisational structures are thoroughly thought through in military manuals, corporate business plans, MBAs, and so forth. Bottom-up power/organisation structures are much less familiar, however, and the principles involved in how they work—their structure, features, and problems—are much less (or less commonly) thought through systematically. It is the function of this chapter to do so. As will be obvious to anyone who knows some of the relevant literature, we are in the vicinity of societies as conceived of by many anarchist theorists.

In what follows, I shall certainly outline a kind of society I take to be preferable to the society in which we live. But let me emphasise again what I said in Chapter 7. I am not providing a blueprint for a future society, much less a utopia or an "end of history". Rather, what follows is simply a very rough, provisional, and fallible map of a sort of society with bottom-up organisation, and the problems that such organisation faces. Its aim is, as it were, to provide a lodestar by which to navigate.

We will start with a description of the structure itself. We will then turn to some of its features. Lastly, we will have a look at some of its problems.

9.2   Bottom-Up Socio-economic Structures

9.2.1   Self-Organising Cooperatives (SOCs)

So what sort of structure does such a society have? Let us start with the simplest cells of such an organisation, and work our way to more complex matters. Each of these cells is what we might call a *self-organising cooperative*, SOC for short. (I prefer pronouncing this as *essosee*, rather than as *sock*.) An SOC is a group of people held together by a common interest, and who organise their affairs in that common interest. Decisions are made collectively, by consensus. (So one might call the power structure at this level horizontal, rather than bottom-up.) Natural sites for an SOC are where people work or where they live—which may or may not, of course, overlap. There is obviously a maximum size that an SOC can have if it is to function in this way. How large this is may depend on many matters, but truly collective decision-making becomes very difficult if numbers run into the hundreds.

Though the principle behind an SOC is collective decision-making, this does not mean that an SOC cannot have a committee of management or other sub-groups for particular purposes (sub-committees, if you like), but such a committee will be chosen by the group and responsible to it. There is no blueprint for how an SOC is organised, however. Since it is *self-organising*, details are for the members of the collective to decide.

The notion of an SOC is, in fact, not at all an esoteric one. Many sports clubs, recreational clubs, and social clubs are run in exactly this way.

9.2.2   Cooperation Between SOCs

Naturally, some interests are such that SOCs will want to cooperate with each other. They will then form a higher-order committee of management to organise cooperation for their mutual interests. The higher-order committee of management will, however, ultimately be responsible to the lower-order structures. Again, this type of organisation is a familiar one. A bunch of sports clubs (say cricket clubs, or chess clubs), can cooperate together to form a league. Natural higher-order SOCs might be the workshops or sections of a factory, and the neighbourhoods of a town.

Such higher-order cooperatives may themselves wish to band together to pursue higher-level coordination. The iteration will work in essentially the same way. In this way, district sporting leagues may band together to form a state (or national) sporting league. Or the groups in a bunch of factories or towns may cooperate to act in their collective interest. We may hence have a network of SOCs of wider and wider generality. I will call such a configuration a *structure of SOCs*, or SSOC (*essessosee*).

One might also call this kind of structure a (con)federation, as does Book-chin. These are, he writes:[2]

> based on a network of policy-making popular assemblies with recallable deputies to local and regional confederal councils—councils whose sole functions ... [is] to adjudicate differences and undertake strictly administrative tasks.

A simple example of the structure of an SSOC might look something like this. (Mathematicians call this sort of structure a finite partial order.)

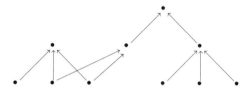

Note that, being finite, the structure will always have top elements; but there may be no unique top element (though there may be). The important feature of such a hierarchy is, however, that the power relation is bottom-up. Decisions are devolved to the lowest possible level, and where decisions are made which affect lower-order SOCs, those who make them are responsible to those SOCs.

Examples of the sorts of thing on which the parts of a large social structure of this kind might wish to cooperate are the raising of a communal pool of money (taxation), and its use for matters of common interest, such as, perhaps, health services, education, public transport, help in periods of unemployment, a fund for emergencies, setting up and/or monitoring banking services, self-defence, and so forth. It should be remembered that any of these things that can be set up and imposed by a top-down government, if they are worth having, could be achieved by bottom-up coordination—on which, in practice, they normally depend—except that they will be administered less rigidly, and more democratically.

9.2.3   General Policy

There are, in fact, many *general* issues on which parts of an SSOC are likely to wish to cooperate. These might concern, for example, policies involving

2. Bookchin (2015), p. 40. He calls this sort of structure *confederalism*, as opposed to federalism, which he takes to refer to a way of organising a structure of top-down states. On this kind of federation, see also Chomsky (2013a), pp. 136 ff.

environmental issues, equality of a material, racial, or gender kind, moving between SOCs (migration), resolving disagreements or disputes between groups (for example over water rights or conditions of trade), stopping some SOCs exploiting others (perhaps because they have more natural resources), and so on. The policies and practices concerning things like this would also have to be agreed upon by committees at the appropriate level of administration. Most cooperative enterprises have such policies and procedures, agreed informally or formally. Thus, for example, sports clubs have rules for how the club is to be run, and federations of sports clubs have policies and procedures that apply to all clubs. Call these constitutions, if you want to make it sound formal.[3]

Of course, these rules and policies could not be imposed in a top-down fashion. Like all things in an SSOC, they would have to be formed with the agreement of the groups lower down the structure. Bookchin describes how this might work as follows:[4]

> Decisions made at the base are moved to the top and then back again in modified form to the base until, by a majority vote at the base, they become policies whose implementation is undertaken by special or standing committees.

Neither could policies be fixed. They would have to be flexible, being changed when circumstances—or understanding of them—changed.

It is likely to be suggested that such procedures on a large scale are impracticable. Certainly, changes could not be made as fast as in a top-down system. They would therefore not be efficient—if one identifies efficiency with speed; but that is a short-sighted identification. In most cases, speed is not important; making the best decision is. And collective thought, discussion, and consideration generally produce a much better result than heavy-handed, top-down action. As Mansbridge notes, given her observation of one organisation that worked in this way, by spending time on a decision the organisation:[5]

> produced a much better informed decision and had made it acceptable to a significant minority who might otherwise have disowned it.

Of course, there would be times when fast action is required—for example, to handle a natural disaster. Such do not allow the luxury of time for lengthy reflection. There is no reason, however, why, in general, the kind of action required could not be covered by general regulations. And even when it is

3. For a discussion of various anarchist-oriented "constitutions", see Kinna (2019), pp. 177–203.
4. Bookchin (2015), p. 183. Interestingly, something like this back-and-forth procedure was used to determine the current Cuban constitution.
5. Mansbridge (1983), p. 174.

not, action taken can still be subject to subsequent communal scrutiny, with whatever consequences this might have.

Naturally, how effective general practices are at achieving generally agreed-upon goals may well not be obvious, especially with a large and complex SSOC, perhaps stretching over several continents. This would need to be monitored against appropriate standards. Such a thing is already in place in a capitalist economy. Thus, GNP (Gross National Product) is used by national governments, the IMF, and the World Bank, to monitor and promote growth.

In the present context, it hardly needs to be said how inappropriate such a measure is.[6] Alternative measures are, however, certainly known. Thus, Bhutan uses a measure of Gross National Happiness (GNH). ('Happiness' is probably rather misleading here. 'Well-being' is closer to the mark.) This includes not only living standards, but things such as health, education and life satisfaction.[7] GNH is clearly a better measure than GNP, though one may certainly be able to improve on it.[8] No doubt, any such measure would also have to evolve as circumstances and our understanding of them evolve.

The key to note in all of this is that the committee of management at some level of an SSOC is *not* a policy-making entity. Policy is determined by democratic decisions, ultimately coming from the individual SOCs. The role of the committee is purely to coordinate actions. Of course, there need to be checks and balances to prevent the overstepping of these limits. I will return to this later in the chapter.

9.2.4 Production and Consumption

In a society of the kind we are discussing, there is a further, very specific coordination issue that needs to be addressed: how to organise production, distribution, and consumption.

Such matters are organised most easily in a small SOC which is self-sufficient in resources (goods and services). The group can decide what needs to be produced/provided, and how this is to be achieved. The result can then be made

6. Thus, Brown (2017), pp. 107 f., notes that when Hurricane Katrina hit New Orleans in 2004, devastating the city and causing its inhabitants trauma and hardship, this actually caused the US GDP to grow, due to relief efforts and insurance payouts!

7. Bhutan is a small independent Himalayan, largely agricultural country, squeezed between its two large neighbours, India and China. In the last hundred years it has moved from a theocracy to an absolute monarchy to a constitutional monarchy. The state religion is Buddhism, and its current constitution is explicitly based on what it sees to be implications of Buddhist values, including equality, the right to work, free health care and education, promoting the elimination of discrimination on grounds such as gender. The society is in a rapid state of transition, and it remains to be seen what will develop. However, it must be said that the constitution looks much more like a constitution for the 21st century than the US Constitution, which appears very much like a constitution for the 18th century. For an account and discussion of Bhutan, see Long (2019).

8. See Brown (2017), ch. 6.

available on a "help yourself" basis, people taking only what they need. The fact that things are always there to be taken means that people never have to take more than their needs. Of course, if demand exceeds supply, the goods and services in question may need to be rationed, with appropriate oversight. Both the nature of the rationing and the monitoring of the distribution may be determined collectively by the decision-making process of the SOC.

However, short of a global catastrophe (which could, unfortunately, all too well happen), no sort of socio-economic system we have in the future is going to take us back to a pre-industrial, pre-urban, society—that is, simply a bunch of SOCs. Given this, no SOC would be self-sufficient—in food, accommodation, clothing, health care, education, "luxury goods", and so on—and so cooperation between them would be necessary.[9] Hence, a very distinctive coordination problem arises.

To a certain extent, such coordination problems could be eased by localisation. The closer the locus of production to the locus of consumption, the easier coordination is. Nor is there any reason why, for example, the food each of us eats should have to travel, on average, some thousands of kilometers to reach us.[10]

However, it seems likely that much production (e.g., of manufactured goods) could not be significantly localised. In a self-sufficient SOC, it will be clear where resources (labour and otherwise) need to be mobilised to create enough of what is needed, and to ensure that resources are not wasted on over-production. That solution to the coordination problem cannot work on anything but a very local level. How might it be solved in a complex structure?

In a capitalist economy, the problem is solved by "the market". If there is not enough of a good, the price will go up, encouraging more groups to make it; conversely, if there is an over-supply, the price will go down and fewer people will be inclined to make it.[11] It seems to me that such market determinations could well work in an SSOC.

To see this, note that there is nothing essentially capitalist about markets.[12] Markets are simply places (literal or metaphorical) where people go to exchange things they have—usually that they have produced—for those of others in the same situation. As such, markets exist in most societies, and certainly in many

---

9. Though there may still be *relatively* isolated communities, such as the Amish in Northern America.

10. See Jones (2010). The desirability of localisation and suggestions as to how it might work can be found in Schumacher (1973).

11. I note that Marx is quite well aware of the role of markets in determining price, which is not the same as value (as determined by the labour theory of value). The latter is dealt with in Volume 1 of *Capital*; the former is dealt with in Volume 3 of *Capital*.

12. As emphasised by Schweickart (2011), p. 25. For his discussion of how markets might regulate supply and demand in a post-capitalist society, see pp. 51 ff.

societies that predate capitalism.[13] Of course, they play a distinctive role in capitalism. They are the loci where commodities are exchanged for money as part of
the process of capital growth (as explained in 3.2)—not to mention the fact that
capitalist stock markets are simply a casino of the rich. However, their functioning in the regulation of supply and demand is not *essentially* connected with
capitalism.

Suppose I make shoes. If I can exchange a pair of shoes that I have made for
one chicken with one chicken owner, and two chickens with another, then
ceteris paribus I will prefer the latter exchange. Once the facts about what is
going on in shoe and chicken exchange become common knowledge, a standard rate of exchange (an equilibrium point between supply and demand) will
develop, determining the price of shoes—in chickens, but if money is used as a
general means of exchange, in money. If at some point I find that I have too
many shoes to sell at this price, I will make fewer shoes. It does me no good
to make shoes and have them just sitting there. It is a waste of my labour.
So there will be fewer shoes on the market. If the demand for shoes is constant,
this means that people will give more chickens (or money) for them. So the
price will go up, and I will be encouraged to make more shoes—likewise
other shoe producers, until something like an equilibrium point emerges
again. There is nothing specifically capitalist about this. In terms of information
theory, what prices are doing is simply providing information about supply and
demand. Those exchanging their products are simply responding to this
information.

As is well recognised, however, using markets to solve coordination problems
of supply and demand has problems. As is clear from the simple-minded description of the last paragraph, market responses take time—and the more widespread
the market, the more time it takes. Market responses can, then, take years. Hence
it is that we see regular over-production and under-production in capitalist
systems. These deliver the well-known phenomenon of the trade cycle.[14] We
certainly ought to be able to do better than that, especially with the resources
of modern information technology.

One way of doing so in an SSOC is suggested by Albert and Hahnel.[15]
Requests are submitted up the chain of an SSOC, where, at the appropriate
level, resource needs are determined, and the information about what should
be produced and how it should be distributed is then passed back down the
chain. Albert and Hahnel in fact give a fairly detailed account of how this
could work with certain examples; but these are only examples. In practice,
details of how any such system might be implemented would be strongly

---

13. On markets, see Herzog (2017). Herzog is quite clear that markets are much more general than
    a capitalist economy, though much of her discussion focusses on markets as embedded in cap-
    italist institutions.
14. Also known as the business cycle. See Niggle (1999).
15. Albert and Hahnel (1991).

affected by many contingent and variable factors. As ever in such a system, details would have to be worked out by those involved in the contexts in which they are working.

As is clear, what Albert and Hahnel describe is, in a sense, a planned economy; and, it is likely to be said, we know that planned economies do not work. No. We know that some of them did not work. Notoriously, a planned economy crashed spectacularly in the Soviet Union. (It seems to be working quite well in contemporary China—for the moment.) However, there were many reasons why this did not work. One was that it was inefficient. The relevant information could not be collected and processed in real time. As Albert and Hahnel explained (already in 1991!), we now have the information technology resources to do better. Another problem was that the top-down (and totalitarian) power structure of the Soviet Union produced corruption, and the alienation and consequent non-cooperation of producers. A bottom-up organisational structure would avoid these issues.

9.3   Examples of Bottom-Up Organisation

Examples of societies instantiating many of the organisational features I have just described are, in fact well known, though not commonly acknowledged.

I have already mentioned sports clubs and federations. One of Kropotkin's favourite examples is the British Life Boat system, organised and run on such lines.[16] But there are, or have been, much larger social structures of the kind in question. Let me mention a few of these.

The first is that of the traditional Israeli kibbutzim. These approximate to relatively self-contained SOCs—though kibbutzim have now lost a number of of these features due to an increasing integration with the wider state.[17]

The next example is a crisis-management organisation studied by Mansbridge in an unnamed US city in the 1970s, which she refers to as Helpline Inc. She describes how this functioned as follows:[18]

> The entire organization still functioned primarily as a direct democracy. Each service group sent a representative to the long range policy making body (CRC) and to the second committee on personnel and daily policy (DPW), both of which met once a week. Yet these representatives were delegated little power. They made decision by consensus, and, in theory, had to report back all questions on which they suspected there might not be complete community wide unanimity to their service group for final

16. Priestland (2015), ch. 11.
17. On the organisation of kibbutzim, see Spiro (1963), esp. ch. 4. See also Pateman (2005), pp. 134 f., and Chomsky (2013a), pp. 23 ff.
18. Mansbridge (1983), p. 144. I presume from her discussion that the organisation no longer exists.

determination. Moreover, any interested member could participate in either CRC or DPW deliberations. At any stage, a community member could demand a full community meeting (called a Community Day) either for a day or a weekend, to discuss and decide on any issue collectively. All major policy decisions were to be made by the entire staff assembled at Community Day.

A much more large-scale example of the pertinent structure is the anarchist system which appeared in Spain during the first part of the Spanish Civil War.[19] As Chomsky (2005, p. 134) notes, this was remarkably successful. However, it was hardly typical, since it was a wartime society and one, moreover, that did not last for very long, since it was crushed by the Communist and Republican forces.

A fourth example is the current society of Cuba. McKelvey describes the Cuban system (somewhat over-generalising, and perhaps romanticising) as follows:[20]

> As an alternative to representative democracy, socialist nations have developed popular democracy, which is established on a foundation of a multitude of small popular assemblies. The people meet in numerous local small groups in order to discuss problems and issues and make recommendations, and this structure of face-to-face dialogue weakens the capacity for ideological manipulations by a wealthy class. The popular assemblies also meet to select delegates to serve in a higher level of popular power. The elected delegates in turn select delegates to serve in still higher level, until ultimately the highest political authority of the nation is established. In socialist nations, citizens who serve in the highest levels tend to have the same demographic characteristics as the people: They are professionals, workers, peasants, students, women, and members of ethnic groups. Political parties tend not to participate in the selection of those who hold political authority. Political parties play more of a role in educating, disseminating ideas, and participating in public discourse. Citizens who hold political authority are selected by the people without mediation by political parties, and are selected on the basis of personal characteristics they possess.

Clearly, this is a bottom-up democratic decision-making structure, though one with a top element. The Cuban Communist Party plays no constitutional role in this; in particular, people elected do not have to be party members.

19. See Dolgoff (1974).
20. McKelvey (2018), p. 237. See further, ch. 5 of McKelvey's book. See also Leech (2012), pp. 131 ff.

However, the party is officially written into the constitution, according to which it:[21]

> organizes and orients the communal forces towards the construction of socialism and its progress toward a communist society. It works to preserve and to fortify the patriotic unity of the Cuban people and to develop ethic, moral, and civic values.

The party, then, wields a good deal of *de facto* top-down power.

The final example is the Spanish worker cooperative, Mondragon, founded by José María Arizmendiarrieta in 1956, and still going.[22] Schweickhart describes how this operates thus:[23]

> This worker-owned, worker-managed "cooperative corporation" is in essentially a federation of cooperatives, each of which is wholly owned by its workforce. The workers of each cooperative meet at an annual general assembly to elect a board of directors, which then appoints the cooperative's management and selects delegates to the MCC [Mondragon Corporación Cooperativa] Congress. The delegates, some 350 in all, then meet to pass judgment on the strategic plan for MCC presented by a congress board, whose twenty-two members include the division heads of MCC (the member cooperatives are grouped in divisions) plus representatives of the special institutions (the bank, the research organizations, and so forth).

Metcalf describes Mondragon as follows:[24]

> We can imagine what a network of worker cooperatives might look like at scale in modern times, because such a network already exists in Spain, with the Mondragon cooperatives. Founded in 1956 in the Basque region of Spain, Mondragon has grown into a network of more than one hundred worker-owned industrial and retail cooperatives, with more than thirty thousand worker-owners and another forty thousand nonowner employees. Mondragon sets aside money for workers' pensions and for reinvesting in business. Profits and workers' savings are kept in a workers Bank (Caja Laboral Popular), which has the mission of making investments to start new cooperatives.

21. Comparative Constitution Project (2019), Article 5.
22. On Mondragon, see Whyte and Whyte (1988).
23. Schweickart (2011), p. 69.
24. Metcalf (2015), p. 54.

Of course, each of the institutions I have mentioned is a creature of its time and place. And I am certainly not suggesting that any of them provides an ideal model—something to be emulated in detail. But they show that social structures which have a different political economy from a capitalist one are indeed possible, and they provide insights and ideas for further reflection.

9.4 Scholarly Interlude

Perhaps this is an appropriate place to make a few comments on the relationship between the sort of bottom-up society I have just described, and the thought of some well-known anarchists.

The advocacy of something like the SSOCs I have described can be found in the "collective anarchism" of Kropotkin, as described, for example in his *The Conquest of Bread*.[25] However, writing around the turn of the 20th century, Kropotkin did not have to face the coordination problems delivered by the complexities of the industrial economy of the 21st century.

In his *Anarcho-syndicalism*, Rocker—very much inspired by the anarchist movement at the beginning of the Spanish Civil War—also advocates something like this.[26] However, it must be said that Rocker focusses very much on the workplace, and seems to ignore other and interdependent aspects of social life, such as the neighbourhood. He also has a somewhat idealistic view of trades unions. (I will take up the matter of trades unions in the next chapter.)

Perhaps the kind of bottom-up organisation I have outlined is closest to what Murray Bookchin calls *libertarian municipalism*, or sometimes, *communalism*, which he defines as:[27]

> a system of government in which virtually autonomous local communities are loosely bound in a federation.

He hesitates to call this anarchism because of the fact that some anarchists have refused to be part of any centralised decision-making process altogether. But as he says, correctly:[28]

> the truly pertinent issue that confronts anarchism is not whether power will exist but whether it rests in the hands of an elite or in the hands of the people.

25. See, e.g., Priestland (2015), esp. chs. 3, 10.
26. Rocker (1989), esp. ch. 5.
27. Bookchin (2015), p. 16. See also pp. 64–8, entitled 'Confederalism and Interdependence' where, as the title indicates, he emphasises the interdependence of communities in a confederation.
28. Bookchin (2015), p. 143.

Bookchin takes the lowest-level organisation-groups to be local municipalities, but this does not address the question of how workplaces are to be organised—especially since these may well cross municipalities—or of how the parts of a large municipalities are to function with respect to the whole.

Finally in this context, one cannot omit mention of the many pertinent comments sympathetic to the general ideals made by Noam Chomsky, though these may not be as systematic as those of the above three thinkers.[29]

9.5   Solidarity and Interdependence

So much for the structure of societies organised along bottom-up lines. Let us now turn to some general features of such societies, especially in comparison with capitalist societies.

To start with: a very obvious feature of the sort of structure we have been dealing with is that it requires people to act in a cooperative, as opposed to a confrontational, way. That is, to put it in political terms, solidarity[30] is needed to deliver, as Marx and Engels put it in the *Communist Manifesto*, 'an association in which the free development of each is the condition of the free development of all'.[31]

Solidarity is most easily obtained within a small group of people, and thus in an SOC. In such a group, people can all know each other, meet collectively to discuss, and hence realise that no individual can flourish without the flourishing of the group, and so the other people in it. In other words, the interdependence of each of its members is manifest. One comes to understand the need to cooperate with others so that all may flourish together.

Of course, groups may have "free-riders". Free-riders are individuals who are part of the group, and who benefit from the actions of the collective, but do not contribute to the collective well-being. In a capitalist economy, tax-dodgers are free-riders. SOCs would have to have ways of dealing with free-riders. These might involve persuasion, penalty, or even expulsion. What is best may very well depend on the circumstances of the SOC and the parties involved. What this might be could be left to the SOC in question.

The maintenance of solidarity is much harder when groups become larger, and so relationships become largely impersonal, as they are liable to be in an SSOC. (Indeed, I think it is fair to say that a central problem of building a bottom-up society is how to preserve collegiality and empathy up the levels of the organisational structure.) Free-riding (of individuals or of SOCs) therefore becomes more likely. Hence, steps would be necessary to make people

---

29. See, for example, in Chomsky (1976), (2013a), (2013b).
30. *OED*: Unity or agreement of feeling or action, especially among individuals with a common interest; mutual support within a group. Indeed, the insistence on solidarity is a feature of many left-wing anarchist thinkers. See Nightingale (2015).
31. McLellan (2000), p. 262.

understand the *general* interdependence of people—a central (and correct) part of Buddhist metaphysics, as we noted in 2.4. Education would therefore be of crucial importance in any well-functioning SSOC. I will return to the matter of education in a later chapter.

As I also noted, even with a much larger degree of localisation than we have now, given contemporary methods of production and communication, economic interdependence is likely to be global. And even if this were not so, it remains the case that the Buddhist imperative of compassion requires solidarity to be global. Lebowitz puts matters thus:[32]

> Building a solidarian society means going beyond our own particular interests—*or more accurately, understanding that our particular interest is that we live in a society in which everyone [can attain] full human development.* It means that our premise is the concept of human community. ... [O]nly when our activity is consciously an act for others can we go beyond the infection of self-interest, exchange relations, and inequality.

And Schweickart:[33]

> an adequate theory of the transition from global capitalism to democratic, sustainable socialism will stress the need for an international social movement, not in the sense of a unified centrally directed party, but in the sense of a common consciousness that recognizes a kind of unity in diversity and allows for cross-national cooperation and inspiration. The counter-project is nothing less than the project of our species.

The failure of solidarity is, of course, a blatant feature of capitalism. Quantities of capital, and those beholden to them, compete with each other by the very nature of capital. A quantity of capital has no regard for those who work for another quantity. A central aim is, in fact, to *under-cut* their interests. Indeed, those who operate a quantity of capital have no regard even for the interests of their own workers. These are simply sacked if they fail to produce the required profit. And as the example of the tax-dodger reminds us, free-riding is very much a feature of contemporary capitalist society. Never mind the tradesperson who takes a cash payment to avoid declaring it on their tax return. This is small fry, dwarfed by the tax-dodging activities of major corporations using shell companies and tax havens.

Such a failure of solidarity is, then, a feature of capitalism itself. It is what capital does by its nature (i.e., how capitalists relations function); and it is

32. Lebowitz (2010), p. 144. I have taken the liberty of substituting *can attain* for Lebowitz' *has the right to*. Rights have no part in Buddhist ethics. The notion of a moral right is one from deontological ethics, closely tied up (historically and conceptually) with capitalism.
33. Schweickart (2011), p. 16.

what individuals do because they are under the influence of the ideology of capitalism, which legitimises selfishness. One might well, therefore, hope that much of such behaviour would largely disappear as capitalism disappears. Thus, for example, in his discussion of Mondragon, Schweickert notes:[34]

> A principle of solidarity also operates amongst member coops. When an enterprise has to cut back production, an attempt is made to transfer workers to other cooperatives within the system rather than simply laying them off and solidarity funds are made available to companies to help them through bad times.

Finally, could a system of the kind described revert back to a capitalist one? Yes of course it could; everything is impermanent. As we have seen, however, a sense of solidarity is inimical to capitalism, and so would counteract this. How, then, to maintain a sense of solidarity if one has been achieved? The answer to this concerns both education and the kind of people such a system would make us. I will return to these matters in a later chapter.

9.6   Natural Cooperation

It might be suggested that to expect cooperation and solidarity of this kind is unrealistic. However, it should be remembered that cooperation and solidarity are, and always have been, features of human society. As Mansbridge notes:[35]

> unitary democracy [her term for consensual decision making in a community] is the oldest and longest lived form of human organization … equal status or respect, consensus, common interest, and face-to-face contact … recur in unitary democracy throughout history.

The spontaneous cooperative nature of human society is well documented and argued for by Kropotkin in his 1902 book *Mutual Aid*.[36] Indeed, as Kropotkin argues, there is a strong biological basis for this. Struhl summarises as follows:[37]

> [Kropotkin] offers the following thought experiment. What is more likely to enable a species to survive—mutual aid or ruthless competition amongst its members? A moment's reflection should make it clear that the former has greater survival advantage than the latter, as animals who can support each other, work together, and protect each other are more likely to reproduce than those who are constantly at each other's throats.

34. Schweickart (2011), p. 68.
35. Mansbridge (1983), pp. 8, 10.
36. Bookchin (2008).
37. Struhl (2016), p. 96.

This leads Ward to comment:[38]

> How would you feel if you discovered that the society in which you would really like to live was already here, apart from a few little, local difficulties, like exploitation, war, dictatorship and starvation? ... [A]n anarchist society, a society organising itself without authority, is always in existence, like a seed beneath the snow, buried under the weight of the state and its bureaucracy, capitalism and its waste, privilege and its injustices, nationalism and its suicidal differences and their superstitious separatism.
>
> [O]nce you look at human society from an anarchist point of view you discover that the alternatives are already there, in the interstices of the dominant power structure. If you want to build a free society, the parts are all at hand.

Of course, a top-down power structure will claim, for its own ideological reasons, that society can function only because of the imposition of its power. Such is false. As Marx puts it in the *Holy Family*:[39]

> it is natural necessity, essential human properties, however alienated they may seem to be, and interest that hold the members of civil society together. ... Only political superstition today imagines that social life must be held together by the state whereas in reality the state is held together by civil life.

In other words, human cooperation is a natural phenomenon. Building a whole society on it is not asking for the moon. It is simply allowing the moon to shine.

9.7 "Human Nature"

It will frequently be said at this point (often by the apologists of capitalism) that a society organised along bottom-up lines could never function—at least for long—because people are inherently selfish because of human nature, and this will destroy any such society.

Such armchair psychology is worthless. Human behaviour is the product of both biology and sociology—not that these are entirely distinct, since the two are interdependent. Our grasp of biology and its potentials is basic enough; but our knowledge of the potentials of socialisation to affect behaviour is minimal. This is an empirical question, and has to be determined by appropriate

---

38. Ward (1996), pp. 18, 20. The detailed case for his claim is made in ch. 2 of his book.
39. McLellan (2000), p. 163.

empirical investigations. Such have hardly been carried out. Nor could they be. The number of kinds of society there could be may not be infinite, but it is surely very large. By comparison, the number of kinds of society there are or have been, is very small. To make a universal generalisation from a small and non-random sample of this kind is terrible methodology.

What we *do* know is that human behaviour is incredibly malleable. There was nothing very unusual about those who worked in the Nazi concentration camps. They were mostly ordinary people like you and me. Yet they did the most atrocious things to people because of the circumstances in which they found themselves. We find what they did shocking, but most of us would probably have behaved in the same way had we been put in the same circumstances.[40] On the other side of the agenda, it is well known that during the Blitz of London in the early 1940s, for all the hardship this imposed on the citizens, there emerged a cameraderie, compassion, and cooperative spirit of a kind rarely seen in the more usual circumstance of life in Britain before the war.

Social circumstances, then, very much affect how people behave, as one would expect, given a Buddhist account of persons in the network of *pratītya-samutpāda*. Change the causes, and you change the effects. Indeed, one thing that needs much further investigation is how causation works in this regard. What kind of social arrangements is it that produce compassionate and cooperative people, as opposed to competitive and selfish people? Lebowitz puts matters as follows:[41]

> The essential problem for building the solidarian society, however, is how to incorporate *into communities themselves* the concept of solidarity, so that people produce directly for the need of others. How, in short, is it possible to make requirements predicated upon the principle of "from each according to his abilities; to each according to her need for development" appear to all members of the community as "self-evident and natural laws".

One needs to render the fundamental human solidarity and cooperation as obvious as it is real.

For all this, the kind of people we are is integral to the problems at issue here, and we cannot expect that just changing social arrangements will do everything required. But let us set this point aside for the present; I will come back to it in a later chapter.

40. On the banality of evil, see Arendt (1963).
41. Lebowitz (2010), p. 145. The first quotation is an allusion to a passage from Marx' *Critique of the Gotha Program* (McLellan (2000), p. 615). The second is from *Capital*, Vol. 1, and is, in fact, a description of how capitalism appears to people in a capitalist society (Fowkes (1976), p. 899).

9.8   Problems Facing SSOCs

Finally, let us turn to problems a structure organised in a bottom-up way may face. In the above discussions, I have noted some of these. Let me now take up others. The point is not so much to try to solve the problems as to render them visible, so that they may be addressed when and where appropriate. The issues fall into a number of rather disparate categories. One is so important that I will devote the whole of the next section to it. I will break up the ones to be dealt with in this section into five groups.

1. First, there is a group of old chestnuts often directed against anarchist-type structures. Thus: what does one do about the division of labour? In particular, who is going to do the jobs that no one wants to do? If there are such jobs, the answer may depend entirely on what these are and how they fit into the overall structure. (Are they within an SOC? Do they involve the social function of an SOC within an SSOC?) And one might address these matters in many ways: with a roster for doing such jobs; with some kind of compensation (such as greater pay or shorter working hours), and maybe others.

Another issue: what does one do with anti-social people? Again, the answer may depend on the kind of anti-social behaviour and its effects. (Is it being persistently offensive, theft, murder?) And there are many possible measures that might be taken: counselling, conflict resolution, restorative justice, ostracism, ejection from the group, fines, incarceration. In fact, these procedures are not so different from the options available to currently structured societies. The main difference is that they would be determined in a collective fashion, and not imposed top-down. And, one might hope, they would be decided upon and implemented in a more thoughtful and humane way than is done under current penal systems.[42]

In short, for both of these issues, there is a wide variety of measure that may be taken. Which ones are appropriate will depend on many matters, and would be up to the relevant groups to decide.

2. Next, there are issues that may arise in collective discussions. First, there are people who would rather not take part, but prefer to be doing something else. If so, so be it. Nothing has to force people to take part, and as long as they are informed about what is happening, they always have the option of doing so.

More of a problem are those who want to take part, but feel inhibited, for whatever reason, about speaking in a group. On the other side, there may be those familiar individuals who like to speak too much and dominate meetings.[43] To a certain extent, this matter can be taken care of by appropriate and sensitive chairing. The chair needs to maintain a collegial atmosphere

---

42. In this context, it is interesting to consider Nāgārjuna's comments on the just but wise and compassionate treatment of those needing correction, in vv. 328–338 of the *Ratnāvalī* (Hopkins (2007)).

43. On these issues, see Mansbridge (1983).

(open, non-confrontational), encouraging all to speak their mind, politely shutting people up sometimes, perhaps asking people to reflect on their own behaviour, and determining an appropriate mechanism for reaching a decision that respects the views of all parties. Of course, how these things are best achieved will depend on circumstances, the people involved, and so on. Matters have to be left to the group involved to arrange the best psychodynamics of its meetings. However, it is important that chairs always remember that they work for the group, and not vice versa.

Another issue in this category is that, with respect to some issues, some individuals are likely to know much more about them than others; and as the old saying goes, knowledge is power. Of course, there is nothing problematic about knowledge as such. Knowledge of a situation is highly desirable when making a decision about it. The problem will arise if the knowledgeable individual uses the fact that the others know that they know more, to impose their view on the group unreasonably. It is important, then, that those with the power of knowledge share it with the group in such a way that others can understand it and respond appropriately. Reciprocally, the others must hold the knowledgeable person to account to do this.

3. Another issue that needs to be faced concerning group decision-making is the following. Within a group it is quite possible for a majority to "gang up" on an individual or a minority group, giving rise to what is sometimes called the tyranny of the majority. Of course, such things can happen—and notoriously do—in a top-down power structure. However, it is less likely to happen in a bottom-up structure if there is an appropriate sense of solidarity—that is, a general concern for all—and the sense of tolerance this promotes. There certainly need be no sense of this kind in a capitalist society: indeed, the whole ethos of a capitalist society is to destroy such solidarity, as I noted. There is therefore more hope of realising an appropriate sense of solidarity in the kind of post-capitalist society envisaged here.

Group pressure may of course be exercised openly, but it can act at a much more subconscious level. People simply want to be "part of the group", and this may lead to conformism.[44] Now, certain kinds of conformism are not necessarily bad. They can engender "team spirit", that is, working together to get things done. They can even engender a sense of solidarity. What is pernicious is an uncritical conformism. Again, we see this in spades in capitalist societies. People—be they those in positions of power, such as politicians and economists, or simply run-of-the-mill citizens—have an uncritical conformism to the ethos of capitalism, generated by advertising and the organs of ideology. Arguably, it would be much less likely to arise in a de-centred society where uniformity is not enforced by a top-down mechanism—as long as those in any group in the network are educated enough to understand the variety

---

44. As noted by Chomsky (2013a), pp. 23ff.

and cultural differences of different groups in the network. I will come back to the matter of education in a later chapter.

4. The next problem to consider is the following. Could not a society organised in this bottom-up fashion simply reproduce capitalism? The worry is something like this. Take a bunch of workplaces organised as SOCs. What is to stop them all competing with each other and so producing a capitalist environment of unchecked growth? Obviously this is some kind of possibility, and there would have to be some awareness of this so that it can be dealt with. At the very least, there would have to be some kind of procedure in place at an appropriate level to prevent untoward growth, simply for environmental reasons—perhaps where supply and demand are coordinated in the Albert and Hahnel model, if that is in place.

But I think that the likelihood of capitalism re-emerging is much less than one might have thought. First, let's be clear what the situation is. Each SOC will generate a product. Call this their wealth. What happens to this wealth is entirely under the control of the members of the SOC. Some of it they will want to use to provide things for the collective good, such as the funding of health and education, an emergency fund, and so forth. Some of it will have to be used to buy the materials they need for their production. The rest is for the members of the SOC themselves. Why would they want to eat into this even more, simply to grow?

Recall the dynamics of a capitalist society which cause growth. One is the fact that bigger capitals eat smaller capitals. But why on earth should an SOC use some of its wealth just to buy up another? As far as I am aware, there was never a case in a feudal economy of one village trying to purchase another. Moreover, why should the workers in one SOC even *want* to sell themselves to another? Clearly, they would lose their autonomy.

Another dynamic of capitalist growth is a producer aiming to sell more and more of their product. But if they are selling all the product they have, why would they want to make and sell more? For a start, it means more work, simply for the sake of it. It might be suggested that the members of the SOC would do this simply because they have a natural desire to possess more wealth. Now, the desire to have more wealth, if not generated by capitalism, is certainly strongly exacerbated by it, and so would not be so strong without it. But in any case, if this argument has a point, it is close to self-defeating. If people are keen to acquire wealth simply for the sake of it, they are hardly likely to give their own wealth away when they do not have to. Recall that a decision of this kind is not in the hands of a capitalist, who can use what amounts to the wealth of others to make more for themself. It is in the hands of those people whose wealth it is.

And finally, there are very good reasons why a collective would not want to produce more. Significant increase of production requires more labour, and so more labourers. The SOC would therefore have to grow in size. The growth of the labour force means less share of the wealth per capita, as well as making the SOC more impersonal and watering down the control that the current members have over their affairs. Such is not in their interests.[45]

5. A final issue is this: suppose that an SOC—call this S—in a cooperating bunch of SOCs makes a decision that the other SOCs think to be a bad one. Suppose, to make matters concrete, that S implements procedures that would clearly seem to be harming some of its members. At the appropriate level of organisation, the others should try to persuade S to desist. (Perhaps, for example, the actions of S are in violation of general principles that S has already agreed to.) Suppose they fail? Given the tight economic interconnections between parts of an SSOC, it is quite likely that the others could impose effective sanctions on S which would bring about change. If all else fails, they may simply have to expel S from the cooperative (at least until it changes its mind)—the ultimate sanction.

It is perhaps here that a clash with Buddhist ethics might be sensed most acutely. If the actions of S really are making some of its members suffer, perhaps the other SOCs, being greater in number, could simply *force* S to change its procedures by taking control of it top-down. After all, as I emphasised in 2.6, absolutely hard and fast rules for ethical action are not to be expected. There always has to be room for *phronesis*. Maybe a case could be made for such action in things like genocide and child abuse (for example, female genital mutilation). However, given the negative ramifications that any such action is likely to have, and dangers of the systematic misuse of top-down power, the case had better be a good one.

9.9 Collapse Into a Top-Down Structure

Let us now turn to the important issue I flagged at the start of the previous section. Power in an SSOC is designed to be bottom-up. But those who are part of organising committees are clearly in a position of power, in some sense; and power corrupts. Could not the system morph into a top-down power structure?

An (S)SOC is a democratic structure—much more democratic than any parliamentary "democracy" could ever be. And Plato famously argued in Book VIII of the *Republic* that a democracy has a tendency to collapse into a tyranny—government by a tyrant. The core of Plato's argument is that in a democracy everyone has liberty to pursue their own interests, which they do. The result is a completely disorganised society—anarchy in the common usage of the word. When things fall apart in this way, a "strong man" will arise who gathers support on the promise that he will run things for the benefits

---

45. On these matters, see, further, Schweickart (2011), pp. 88–9.

of all. Once in power, though, he becomes a tyrant, and simply runs things in the interest of his own power.

It cannot be denied that Plato's vision (or perhaps nightmare) has a certain ring of current verisimilitude. Contemporary "democracies" are manifesting a notable tendency to elect "strong men" (even if the election process is corrupt): Trump (US), Putin (Russia), Bolsonaro (Brasil), Erdogan (Turkey), Modi (India), Orban (Hungary).

However, Plato's analysis does not apply to an (S)SOC. For such a structure is not anarchic (in the popular sense). It is highly organised and structured, albeit the case that the organisation is driven from the bottom up. And the solidarity of the structure prevents people going off and acting simply in their own interests. So this is not a problem.

What is a problem is this. Those who are appointed to serve on a higher level committee are there as delegates, not representatives. That is, they are delegated to maintain the view of those who delegated them. They are not there as a representative of the group—something that stands in its place. That is, they may not take decisions that are not in accord with those of the body that delegated them—at least, not without taking them back to the group for ratification. But it is clear that those involved are, none the less, in positions of power. It is therefore possible that individuals on a committee, or groups thereof, driven by the psychology of power, come to assume an executive role, making decisions and organising policies that are not generally agreed upon; and indeed start to organise things for their own benefit. Perhaps this might happen covertly at first, and then overtly, as the person/group feels more secure. In such a way could the bottom-up power structure be subverted.

Possibly, this could happen even within an SOC, but I think it is less likely to happen there. When a group is small, and regular meetings of the group can monitor the actions of its committees. It is much more likely to happen at higher-level committees, which are more remote from the base, so that oversight is more tenuous and the actions of the committee are much less personal. As Mansbridge notes:[46]

> Once representatives are cut off from daily face-to-face interactions with their constituents and enter into face-to-face interactions with other legislators, they inevitably develop different interests from their constituents.

A major point of a democracy—and a good one—is that it acts as a control on those in positions of power, to ensure that they do not misuse it. The question, then, is how to ensure that a democracy stays a democracy. Clearly, there should be checks and balances built into the system to ensure this. A number

---

46. Mansbridge (1983), p. 240.

of these have been suggested. They all have their merits, but all have limitations as well.

One of these is to ensure that such delegates are subject to "immediate recall" if they overstep those limits. The obvious drawbacks of this are two. Continual recall and replacement is likely to completely clog up administration. Second, because decisions are being made remote from the collective group, there is a risk that the actual actions of the representatives will not be effectively transmitted to the group, or may even be covered up.

Another obvious policy is to have a person's period of tenure on a committee limited, so that they cannot serve more than a certain time. The obvious problems with this are, again, two. First, understanding all the affairs that a committee deals with, and how the committee operates, takes time—especially for high-level committees dealing with complex matters. It may not be a good idea to remove someone who has mastered all this, and who is acting effectively. Moreover, even though limited terms constrain the power of an individual, they do not constrain the power of groups, who can simply permute their members in these positions.

Another strategy is sortition: appointing people to positions, on a periodical basis, by lot (in the way that the membership of jury is determined), as suggested by Burnheim.[47] The problem with this is, again, clear. People do not all have the same abilities. Some are taller than others; some are naturally more athletic, or more musical; some are better administrators; some are better, or more effective, communicators. Naturally a group will wish to have its affairs administered as effectively as possible, and its views communicated to higher-level committees as effectively as possible. It will naturally prefer, then, to have the people in those positions who can best do the job, not those chosen at random.

There may, of course, be many other possibilities to address the problem; we have hardly exhausted the fount of human wisdom here. In the last analysis, perhaps the most robust approach to the issue is to attack the psychology of power directly. People can be changed in such a way that they are no longer attracted by power—though this is a very long-term solution. I will return to the matter of changing ourselves in a later chapter.

So much for a discussion of a number of pertinent problems for an SSOC. As I said at the start of the last section, the point of the discussion here has not been to solve them. Given the de-centred nature of an SSOC, and the fact that its elements are self-organising, one would not expect there to be uniform solutions to these matters. They have to be addressed *in situ* by the relevant groups. The most important thing is that people are aware of such matters, and so primed to face up to them. It should be remembered that problems will arise in *any* form of social structure. However, in general, problem-solutions

---

47. Burnheim (2006).

produced in a bottom-up fashion are liable to be better, not only because they preserve solidarity and so are more functional, but because they are more flexible (locally adjustable) and unmediated (not deformed by extraneous considerations, such as the lures of power).[48] I will return to the virtues of group decision-making in the next chapter.

9.10 Conclusion

In this chapter we have looked at the structure of a society organised in a bottom-up fashion, some of its features, and some of its problems. It is to be expected, of course, that there will be a wide variety of ways in which individual parts of such systems function. The details are to be determined by deliberation of the relevant groups; and there is no reason to suppose that the outcomes will be uniform—though of course, groups may learn from each other. But, crucially, the deliberations should be based on an educated understanding and a sense of solidarity.

The next obvious question is how one might go about moving towards a society of this kind from where we are now. We will turn to this matter in the next chapter.

---

48. As argued in more detail in Ward (1996), ch. 4.

10

A TRANSITION TOWARDS THIS

10.1 Introduction

In the last chapter I discussed what a society organised in a bottom-up fashion, with solidarity and hence greater compassion, might be like. In this chapter we move to the question of how one might move towards such a society—always bearing in mind that we have to learn about all things as we go along. Call this a revolution if you want, though I think that the word is best avoided, since it comes with such heavy historical baggage.

It would be absurd, of course, to suppose that such a transition could happen overnight. Even if there were an episode of violent change, this would be just one phase of matters. And in any case, such an episode is unlikely to deliver what is required, for reasons that we will come to in due course. (Basically, one cannot produce a bottom-up power structure by imposing a top-down power structure, of a kind a violent revolution requires, and hoping that it will then dismantle itself.) Change, then, has to be gradual. Gradual change comes with problems of its own, though, to which we will also come. And of course, any change—sudden or gradual—is likely to face a fightback by the rich and powerful. So there may be retrograde periods as well.

In discussing actions for change, it will be helpful to distinguish between those that are reformist and those that are radical—though in the end the difference may be more one of degree than kind. Reformist actions are ones that aim to modify the system, though leave it essentially in place. Radical actions are those which which aim to change the system fundamentally (from the Latin, *radix*, meaning root). In what follows, I will start by discussing the first of these. We will then turn to the second. When we do so, I will

DOI: 10.4324/9781003195146-12

distinguish, in turn, between dismantling the old, and constructing the new. There are, then, three moving parts of the picture. The three naturally interact, however. In particular, aspects of each can function to complement and reinforce aspects of the others. And I am not suggesting that one should attack matters in the order I discuss them. Just because of their interconnection, one may move on all fronts at once, though some are clearly more important—or urgent—than others.[1]

10.2 Reforming Action

First, then, let us consider reformist actions.

10.2.1 Improving What We Have

In the *Communist Manifesto*, Marx and Engels advocate a communist revolution. But, as they are aware, one may certainly use government action of a familiar kind to move towards this. They say:[2]

> the first step in the revolution by the working class is to raise the proletariat to the position of ruling class to win the battle of democracy.

The steps taken to do this, they note, will 'of course be different in different countries'. However, they suggest the following for the 'most advanced countries':[3]

1. Abolition of property in land and application of all rents of land to public purposes.
2. A heavy progressive or graduated income tax.
3. Abolition of all rights of inheritance.
4. Confiscation of the property of all emigrants and rebels.
5. Centralisation of credit in the hands of the state, by means of a national bank with State capital and an exclusive monopoly.
6. Centralisation of the means of communication and transport in the hands of the State.
7. Extension of factories and instruments of production owned by the State; the bringing into cultivation of waste-lands, and the improvement of the soil generally in accordance with a common plan.

---

1. There are standard Marxist debates concerning reform *vs* revolution. (See, e.g., Bottomore (1983), pp. 409 ff.) I regard this choice as something of a false dilemma. One should work within the system where this helps; but the aim is eventually to replace it. Some of the things that follow are similar to strategies that Wright (2017), ch. 4, describes as 'eroding capitalism'.
2. McLellan (2000), p. 261.
3. McLellan (2000), pp. 261–2.

8. Equal liability of all to work. Establishment of industrial armies, especially for agriculture.

9. Combination of agriculture with manufacturing industries; gradual abolition of all the distinction between town and country by a more equable distribution of the populace over the country.

10. Free education for all children in public schools. Abolition of children's factory labour in its present form. Combination of education with industrial production, &c, &c.

Item 4 is relevant only to the political situation in Europe in the 19th century. Strikingly, several of the other items have been achieved: 2, 8 (depending what is meant by an industrial army), 9, 10. And several others have been achieved at least in part—at least at some times: 5 (there are state banks in most countries), 6 (there is public transport and communication in many countries), 7 (most countries have general agricultural policies). That leaves only 1 and 3, on which no progress has been made.

This reminds us of a number of things. The first is that appropriate actions of this kind will vary from place to place. Another is that appropriate measures will change from time to time. I am sure that if Marx and Engels were writing the *Manifesto* now, the list would be significantly different. The third, and the most relevant for present purposes, is that positive change can be made by using the prevailing system for well-determined ends. In this way, for example, female suffrage and the establishment of the National Health System were achieved in the UK. Where positive things can be achieved in this way, then they should indeed be achieved.

Of course, virtually any social change, reformist or radical, requires the action of more than one person, though undoubtedly in the present system there are individuals who wield a lot of power, and so have the ability to change things for the better—if they are so inclined, or can be persuaded, to do so. It remains the case that for change of the kind we are talking about collective action is absolutely essential.[4]

In the present context, what things might be achieved by such changes?—at least for countries in the global North: doubtless, as noted, in many other countries (such as China, Saudi Arabia, Nigeria) they will be somewhat different. Many progressive thinkers have, of course, made important suggestions in this regard, which I can but echo.[5]

4. Further on the power of collective action, see 'A Hero is a Disaster', pp. 143–54 of Solnit (2019).

5. In particular, Naomi Klein's *This Changes Everything: Capitalism vs the Climate* (2014), see esp. p. 460; Claire Brown's *Buddhist Economics: An Enlightened Approach to the Dismal Science* (2017), see esp. ch. 7; Hans Baer's *Democratic Eco-socialism as Real Utopia: Transitioning to an Alternative World System* (2018), see esp. p. 205; Michael Lebowitz' *The Socialist Alternative* (2010), see esp. pp. 164–5; David Schweickart's *After Capitalism* (2011), see esp. pp. 143 ff; Erik Olin

First, and perhaps most urgently at the present time, are environmental policies, such as:

- Underwriting the research and development of cleaner technologies. For example, taxing the production and use of fossil fuels, and using the tax to subsidise development of renewal energy—and sharing the results with countries in the global South.
- Winding back coal and oil production, and setting strict emission limits on cars, power plants, and other heavy polluters—all of this with concern for those who will have to move to different jobs as a result.
- Expanding public transportation and diminishing the reliance on private motor vehicles and air travel.
- The implementation of sustainable food production and forestry, and encouraging people to move away from a meat-consuming diet, which is energy inefficient and environmentally destructive. (Recall how many governments have been able to decrease the number of smokers.)
- Encouraging measures to stop population growth (education, family planning).

Next are policies to reduce the obscene levels of wealth of a few, and the poverty and hardship of many:

- Creating a guaranteed minimal income to ensure that everyone can meet basic standards of a decent life.
- Instituting a wealth tax on individuals and corporations, and closing tax havens.
- Capping exorbitant executive salaries, and implementing a ceiling on how much wealth any particular person may amass.

Then there are policies aimed at improving the conditions of workers and communities:

- Introducing health and safety regulations that ensure that workers can veto practices harmful to health.
- Ensuring community control over industrial practices of workplaces in their localities in order to prevent environmental destruction and conditions harmful to health.
- Shortening the working day and providing people with opportunities for education and self-development.

Wright's *How to Be Anti-Capitalist in the 21st Century* (2018), esp. ch. 4; and the *Guardian* columnist George Monbiot in a number of articles, e.g., (2019a), (2019b), (2020).

Then there are policies aimed at helping countries that have been exploited—and continue to be exploited—by the global North:

- Increasing humanitarian aid.
- Implementing fair trade practices.
- Rescinding large parts of the international bank debt of such countries.
- Not supporting corrupt governments.
- Not supporting the exploitative conditions imposed by bodies such as the IMF and the World Bank.

Though results of this kind may be achievable through orthodox political channels, it should be remembered that very often such changes occur only because of extra-parliamentary action—as the example of the British suffragettes reminds us. In such action, lobbying, harnessing, and building public pressure, targeting the weakest points of resistance, and a judicious mixture of cooperation and confrontation, can all be effective.

The methods of animal-rights activist Henry Spira (1927–1998), are illuminating in these matters.[6] Spira's success highlights a number of strategic insights. Some of these are as follows: choose a fight you have a good chance of winning; success can be used to breed further success, and to change public opinion, orthodox political agendas, and so on, in such a way that what was unachievable before becomes achievable; learn from successes and failures—your own, and those of others; don't expect immediate success; be prepared for a "war of attrition". With an eye on the bigger picture, Bookchin puts matters this way:[7]

> we might see the practice as a process. Indeed a transitional program in which each new demand provides the springboard for escalating demands that lead towards more radical and eventually revolutionary demands.

10.2.2   Political Domestication

Notwithstanding, the fact that improvements may be effected by reformist action, there are well-known problems with working within the system. Groups who do so have a tendency to become "domesticated", or to put it more bluntly, to sell out.

We certainly see many examples of this tendency. Thus, the British Labour party started off as a grassroots party of the 19th-century British workers'

---

6. See Singer (1998), esp. ch. 6.
7. Bookchin (2015), p. 29.

movement. And undeniably it achieved significant things, most notably with the post–Second World War government of Clement Attlee, which completely reformed the health service and education, and nationalised power and public transport. But in due course the party became that of Tony Blair, and is now simply a wing of the establishment, no more radical than unions—indeed less so.

Thus, as Rocker put it, commenting on the socialist parties of his day (the 1930s):[8]

> Participation in the politics of the bourgeois state has not brought the labour movement a hair's-breadth nearer to Socialism, but, thanks to this method, Socialism has almost been completely crushed and condemned to insignificance. The ancient proverb: "Who eats with the Pope, dies of him," has held true in this content [GP: context?] also; who eats of the state is ruined by it. Participation in parliamentary politics has affected Socialist labour movements like insidious poison. It destroyed the belief in the necessity of constructive Socialist activity and, worst of all, the impulse to self-help, by inoculating people with the ruinous delusion that salvation always comes from above.

It would be wrong to put such changes down simply to personal corruption, however—though doubtless such happens. The point is that to achieve most things requires the taking of orthodox political power, and hence obtaining and retaining power becomes an end in itself. (Recall the discussion of power in 8.3.) Rocker continues:[9]

> It would be a mistake to find in this strange about-face an intentional betrayal by the leaders, as has so often been done. The truth is that we have to do here with a gradual assimilation to the modes of thought of capitalist society, which is a condition of the practical activity of the labour parties of to-day, and which necessarily affects the intellectual attitude of their political leaders. Those very parties which once set out to conquer political power under the flag of Socialism saw themselves compelled by the iron logic of conditions to sacrifice their Socialist convictions bit by bit to the national policies of the state. They became, without the majority of their adherents ever becoming aware of it, political lightning-rods for the security of the capitalist social order. The political power which they had wanted to conquer had gradually conquered their Socialism until there was scarcely anything left of it.

8. Rocker (1989), p. 83.
9. Rocker (1989), p. 84.

Perhaps one can do some things to reduce such domestications. There is at least a lesson to be learned from the Buddhist virtue of non-attachment. In particular, being invested in something may mean that one does not give it up and change strategy when it is not (or is no longer) working.[10]

At root, we are back with the problem of succumbing to the lures of power. And this time the problem is exacerbated by the fact that those involved are operating in a power structure which is already top-down. In the end, I suspect, the only thing that might succeed in making matters better is attacking the psychology of power, and so the kinds of relationships that this engenders. I will return to this matter in a later chapter.

In any case, one should not expect fundamental changes to be brought about by reform—at least until many people have become different from what they are now. Moreover, such changes are likely to be limited by the fact that they work essentially within national boundaries, whereas the aim, in the end, is to transcend them.

10.3   Radical Action

Marx and Engels were, of course, well aware of this. More radical change is required. So let us turn to this. Two of the issues here are so important that I will deal with them in separate chapters: ideology and education, and changing ourselves. In the rest of this chapter I will deal with other matters which fall under this rubric.

Here again, we need to draw a distinction: that between dismantling the old system and engendering the new. These two strategies are not incompatible, however. Indeed, they are complementary, and can be pursued in parallel, perhaps in a kind of "pincer movement". Let us start with the first strategy, and move to the second in due course.

10.3.1   Dismantling the Old

Actions to implement the first strategy concern dismantling top-down power structures and organisation, most notably those of the state and its parts. Let us return to the facets of the state I noted in 8.4, and think about things that might work to achieve this.

One obvious step here is devolving decisions as far down the chain of command as possible, from national governments to state/province/regional governments, to town governments, and even to more local communities.

10. 'Even though good people pour their passion and hope into the work of creating an alternative institution, even though it takes so much time and energy, even though it's fragile and precious, we have to be resigned to impermanence. If dedication to the institution comes to overshadow dedication to the goal the institution is supposed to achieve, we have been co-opted' (Metcalf (2015), p. 121).

Of course, such decisions might well require coordination between the groups to which decisions are devolved, but this could be obtained by instituting appropriate committees to manage the cooperation.

Another major step is making the election to all such bodies truly democratic. (We have already noted the importance of democracy as a control on power.) This can be done by implementing voting systems such as proportional representation, single transferable votes, and so forth; by removing obstacles to democratic voting, such as the gerrymandering of constituencies; and so on.[11]

A third step is by removing undue power from those who would use it for their own interests, such as religious groups, business groups, and so on. Indeed one might define democracy roughly as a system in which the relevant electorate is reasonably well informed, and unobstructed by a privileged special interest group.[12]

A major part of this is decoupling political power from capital, and religious groups in those places where it is entrenched in politics. In particular, there should be stiff limits to the amount of money any one person or group can "donate" to individuals standing for election, and to any parties to which they may belong.[13] Moreover, those in power should also not be able to exploit their position for financial gain, for example by using it to obtain lucrative business positions either during or after their terms.

The situation concerning religion is a bit more complex. First, there are countries that are theocracies, such as Iran. The obvious thought here is that progress would be made by moving to a democracy. But of course religion plays a role in countries that are (nominally) democracies. Part of the answer to the question of what could be done here is the same as that in the case of capital. Religious groups have an influence by funding political parties, lobby groups, and so forth. This can be controlled in the same way in which economic influence is addressed: take the money out of politics. There is more to matters than this, though. Since religious leaders can clearly influence the political views of their adherents. (Merely consider the evangelical Christian right and anti-abortion in the United States.) Here, I think it is important to note that even *within* most religions there are significant differences on social matters. Thus, in Christianity, Islam, Judaism, Hinduism, there are both conservative and reactionary voices, and progressive voices. The important thing is that all should be heard. The aim should not be to stifle disagreement, but to make sure that all views are aired, so that people are better placed to make an informed decision. J. S. Mill made important points concerning this matter, which I will pick up in the next chapter.

11. On the democracy of mass action, see Monbiot (2020).
12. Following Schweickart (2011), p. 153.
13. Schweickart (2011), p. 186, suggests a ban on *any* funding to those running for election, except for a small "voter credit" provided by the government, given to each voter, which may be donated (anonymously) to any candidate the voter decides.

Of course, real democracy requires people to be well informed, so access to information should be prioritised. This means exposing all aspects of government that are hidden by those in power as a matter of self-interest—notably those where an official secrets act is usually invoked—unless making the information available really *would* have socially damaging consequences. Information, of this and all other relevant kinds, needs to be accessible to the public, and this requires impartial and authoritative journalism of the kind delivered by relatively independent bodies such as the BBC, which should therefore be strengthened and developed. Moreover, so-called news programs should be taken entirely out of the capitalist media altogether—especially those who clearly peddle capitalist ideology, such as Fox News. (I will return to this matter in the next chapter.) Finally, in this category, lifelong education should be freely available to all.

Let us turn now to the police and military. Policing should be brought under genuine community control. The military should be reduced and restructured in such a way that it can function for purely defensive action only, and so cannot be used for acts of aggression.

Finally, steps can be taken to reduce the power of large capital institutions. Banks can be tightly legislatively controlled; or better, nationalised; or still better, replaced by community (co-operative) banks. The crasser aspects of financial profiteering can be legislatively controlled, such as gambling on the money markets, usurious rates of credit card interest, and so on. Government money can be used to encourage and develop community and worker-run businesses and to promote workplace democracy and control of established businesses.

Doubtless, reflection would suggest many other measures to emasculate the organs of top-down power. Perhaps some of the things in question could be obtained by parliamentary action, but because of their radical nature, probably not. Radical activity is liable to require grassroots action, including taking to the street, general strikes, civil disobedience and non-cooperation, organised boycotts.

10.3.1.1 Dealing With the Forces of Reaction

Clearly, action which challenges top-down power of the kind currently operative poses a direct challenge to those in power. One can therefore expect to see a reaction from these. That is, we are likely to witness a backlash from capital and its political entourage. Of course, even the sorts of reforms mooted in 10.2.1 are likely to meet stiff opposition. For example, as Stiglitz points out:[14]

---

14. Stiglitz (2019), p. 116.

the banks will fight tooth and nail against both regulations that curb their bad practices and those that encourage good behavior.

How much more so, then, those things which challenge the very essence of power? Call this a counter-revolution, if you want to sound dramatic. Whatever one calls it, one must be prepared to take this on.

The reaction will be executed by governments, by law, by the media, and, in all likelihood, by the police and sometimes, perhaps, the military. If moves against the capitalist state seem to be gaining the upper hand, one might even expect an extreme top-down power reaction to emerge—perhaps some kind of fascism. Thus it was, for example, that the German capitalist class backed Hitler in the 1920s and 1930s, as a defence against the burgeoning threat of the Communist Party. Plato was not right about a democracy necessarily turning into a tyranny (as we noted in 9.9); but a major threat to capital and its power structure may certainly give rise to tyranny.

So the question arises as to how one might counter the use of naked violence. Non-violent action can be effective, as both Gandhi and Martin Luther King demonstrated.[15] But that depends on the fact that the other side is not prepared to use violence ruthlessly over a long term. Such is not impossible in certain situations. Police, in particular, may not have the discipline to inflict such violence. Though the police are certainly violent sometimes, most of their work is not physically violent, and they are not used to a continual infliction of indiscriminate violence. Moreover, the individuals in the police are ordinary community members. They go home at night and live next door to those against whom they would have to commit such violence. Especially if they have started to feel solidarity with those they confront, they may well refuse to act in the required way.

The military is a quite different story. Generally, the military live in gated communities away from the general public; their training is all about using violence; and military training conditions them to do what they are told by those who command them without demur. It is, of course, known for units of the military to "defect", and join those against whom they are ordered to use violence; but rarely, if ever, does the whole of military force do so—though it did happen in Russia before the 1917 revolution, where the troops were completely demoralised by the First World War and how it had been handled. Confrontation with the military, at least while it is organised as present, is, then, to be avoided. Matters would be quite different if progressive

---

15. Sharp (1973), Vol. II, provides an encyclopedic (but incomplete!) list—with historical examples—of 198 methods of non-violent action including protest and persuasion (demonstration and propaganda), social non-cooperation (disrupting various social arrangements and conventions), economic non-cooperation (various kinds of boycotts and strikes), non-violent intervention (various kinds of disruptive action). For the positive effects of non-violent action on solidarity, even after the action, see Vol. II, pp. 744 ff.

political action could change the nature of the military; notably, if it were reduced in size and reconfigured simply as a *defence* force; in particular, if it were constituted as a militia system, as in Switzerland, where it is much more a part of the community.

One might suggest that military force should be met with organised counter-force. Such is the standard of violent revolutions; and it is doomed to failure. For a start, a largely amateur force has absolutely no hope against the modern military, with its overwhelming superiority of weapons—on land and in the air—and logistic support. Moreover, in a confrontation with police and military, violent resistance of a bottom-up kind is, by nature of this kind of organisation, going to be at a great disadvantage. It was for essentially this reason that the Communist and Republican regiments were able to crush the anarchist militia in the Spanish Civil War. Effective fighting requires tight top-down control. Even to give it a chance, counter-violence would have to be organised along highly disciplined lines, and this requires a top-down power structure, as the need of the Bolshevik Red Army reminds us. And as already noted, top-down power structures do not voluntarily disband themselves. Forming a top-down power structure in the cause of producing a bottom-up power structure is a forlorn prospect.

10.3.1.2 Violence

Since the topic of violence has arisen, let me say a few more words about this.

I have said that non-violence can be effective, and that all-out confrontation with the military is not a sensible strategy. But I have not said that violence is entirely to be eschewed. The transition to a non–capitalist society will be one with many episodes, small and large; and it is not impossible that violence could be appropriate sometimes. Perhaps, after all, the assassination of Hitler in 1930 could have stopped Germany from descending into Nazism.[16]

It might well be wondered how this sits with Buddhist ethics. Buddhist ethics is, after all, about getting rid of suffering (*duḥkha*). And undeniably, violence causes suffering. Buddhism is therefore a philosophy of peace. Indeed, it has a number of precepts (codes of conduct), the first of which expresses the principle of *ahiṃsā*, non-violence.[17] (Not that so-called Buddhist states have always done justice to this ideal—think only of current Myanmar.)

---

16. And even according to Gandhi, violence may sometimes be necessary: 'some active form of Satyagraha [GP: lit., holding firm to the truth], not necessarily civil disobedience, must be available in order to end an impossible situation. ... There must be either effective non-violent action or violence and anarchy within a measurable distance of time'. Quoted by Sharp (1973), Vol. III, p. 622.

17. See Harvey (2000), p. 69.

But there are times when the only realistic way to prevent greater suffering is to occasion lesser suffering.[18] Moreover, for this reason, Buddhism, unlike Jainism, is not a form of pacifism. Thus, the *Upāyakausalya* (Skilful Means) *Sūtra* tells a story of the Buddha in one of his lives prior to the one in which he achieved enlightenment.[19] Though the Buddha was not yet enlightened, he was still very good at doing the right thing. In the tale, the Buddha-to-be is the captain of a ship, and he discovers that one of the people on board is planning to murder the other passengers and steal their belongings. The only way to prevent this is to murder him, which the Buddha does, taking on himself any negative consequences this may have.

Moreover, there is nothing in Buddhism which is against the use of violence in self-defence against violence. If the only way to protect oneself from suffering is to inflict pain on one who would inflict it, that is a perfectly ethical choice.[20]

Of course, when violence is used, it must be appropriately justified. It must prevent greater suffering, it must be the only way to do so, and it must be the minimum required to be effective. In practice it is hard to know that these criteria are met, though we may well have good reason to suppose so sometimes. At any rate, if violence is used, it should be used without hatred or anger (themselves forms of *duḥkha*), but out of compassion, even—strange as this may sound—for the subjects of the violence.[21]

Moreover, it should not be forgotten that oppression is often enforced by physical force and violence. In such cases, one might well see the use of violence as a form of self-defence. As Freire puts it:[22]

> With the establishment of the relationship of oppression, violence has *already* begun. Never in history has violence been initiated by the oppressed. How could they be the initiators, if they themselves are the result of violence? How could they be the sponsors of something whose objective inauguration called forth their existence as oppressed? There would be no oppressed had there been no violence to establish their subjugation.

18. This is, of course, the standard reason given for the Americans dropping nuclear bombs on Hiroshima and Nagasaki in 1945. Frankly, I doubt that this was the real reason. There were ways that the Americans could have demonstrated the power of nuclear weapons to the Japanese without targeting innocent civilians. The truth is that they had spent years developing such weapons, but they didn't really know what they would do to a human population. They wanted to find out, and dropping the bombs on Hiroshima and Nagasaki was a way to do so. Indeed, a number of cities, including these two, were spared the conventional carpet bombing which flattened most major Japanese cities in the Second World War, for just this purpose.
19. See Tatz (1994), pp. 73–4.
20. Further on Buddhism and violence, see Jenkins (2010) and (2013).
21. For a very thoughtful Buddhist essay on violence, see Hanh (2006).
22. Freire (1970), p. 29.

Violence is initiated by those who oppress, who exploit, who fail to recognize others as persons—not by those who are oppressed, exploited and unrecognized.

Let me be clear. None of this is an argument for using violence. Violence inflicts suffering, and so is bad. It is also often ineffective; very often, it makes matters worse, triggering further rounds of counter-violence. The point is just that sometimes it may be the least worst option; and if it is, there is no moral argument against it from a Buddhist perspective. We are back to the issue of *phronesis*.

10.3.2 Engendering the New

This brings us to the second category of radical action: engendering the new; that is, creating the bottom-up organisations to eventually supersede the top-down ones. Thus, if the steps suggested in 10.3.1 were at all effective they would certainly weaken the top-down power, and so erode it from within. They would not, on their own, however, do much to generate the kind of bottom-up society envisaged in the previous chapter. This requires something of a different kind. Thus, Bookchin:[23]

> There can be no separation of the revolutionary process from the revolutionary goal. *A society based on self-administration must be achieved by self-administration.* … Assembly and community must arise from the revolutionary process itself; indeed, the revolutionary process must *be* the formation of assembly and community, and with it, the destruction of [GP: top-down] power.

As noted in 7.5, a transition to a post-capitalist society should be expected to be an extended process. A post-capitalist society must develop "within the womb of capitalism", as Marx put it. Grassroots organisations must be built and sustained. That is, nascent SOCs must be formed, decisions being taken collegially. (More of this in a moment.) These might start, perhaps, as *ad hoc* groups for particular organisational purposes, and gradually expand into things of wider vision.[24]

In fact, we are already familiar with bottom-up organisations of this kind: grassroots political parties, cooperative stores, and even banks, neighbourhood groups, workers' associations, free schools, community health clinics,

---

23. Bookchin (2004), p. 104.
24. 'Rather than try to reform the "government" as a whole in a systematic way, we create new experiences of democratic decision-making from the ground up' (Metcalf (2015), p. 45).

women's centres, community newspapers, and so on.[25] Thus, Metcalf notes that:[26]

> [m]any of the existing alternative institutions in the United States trace their roots to two waves of activity—the first in the 1920s and 1930s, which centered on consumer cooperatives, including food co-ops, rural electricity co-ops, and credit unions, and the second in the 1960s and 1970s, which included free schools, alternative media, community health clinics, and communes. A more recent wave of activity includes developing local currencies, community land-trusts, and carsharing cooperatives.

In fact, as I observed in 9.6, much of social life is already organised simply on the basis of human cooperation and negotiation. One can build on this.

One might think to put trades unions in this group of currently existing cooperatives. And on their first formation in the 19th century, they certainly did fulfill this function. However, they have long since ceased to behave in this way—notwithstanding the significant good that they still do. They have developed into groups with their own top-down power structures. Moreover, they have been domesticated by capital. Generally speaking, where they are tolerated, they have been incorporated into the capitalist system. Unions are allowed to try to improve the conditions of the workers they represent to a limited extent, as long as their action does not challenge the overall structure, for example, by organising political strikes, notably general strikes. The *quid pro quo* is that unions function to keep workers under control, making sure that their collective actions are limited to things which are marginal to the whole system.[27] As I noted above, history demonstrates just how progressive groups can be domesticated and diverted from their original organisational purposes.

None the less, it remains the case that there are already in existence things which amount to SOCs, and one might hope that these, and things of a similar kind, would form the germ of a post-capitalist structure. What one can envisage is that these nascent SOCs would gradually solidify, multiply, and join forces into SSOCs, perhaps absorbing original but suitably reformed

---

25. Indeed, a 2014 report for the United Nations Department of Economic and Social Affairs estimated that one in every six people in the world is already a member or client of a cooperative venture. See Dave Grace and Associates (2014).

26. Metcalf (2015), p. 4. For a discussion of a number of bottom-up institutions, see ch. 4. In this regard, see also Hopkins (2014).

27. For a discussion—polemical but insightful—of the complicity of trades unions, see Berkman (2003), ch. 10. Even given that unions play this role, capital in general would obviously prefer to have no unions. So, when it feels strong enough, it acts to destroy unions. Thus, in the last 30 years we have seen massive efforts by capitalist governments in the UK, the US, and elsewhere, both by legislation and policy, to destroy unions and any power they have.

top-down structures, until a new kind of society is formed. Lebowitz puts it as follows:[28]

> The solidarian society develops organically by beginning at the neighbor-hood and community level, but it continues only by building solidarity directly between rich and poor communities—both within and between individual nations.

Or as Gare says, with bolder vision:[29]

> The challenge is to create a network of mutually supporting partially autonomous alternative local economic systems which can function as stepping stones for transforming the whole of society and eventually for participating in the creation of an ecologically sustainable world civilization.

One would not expect the process envisaged here to be uniform, in space or time. In different places, things will happen in different ways and at different rates. Indeed, developments are not going to happen in a uniform fashion, but will depend on contingencies of time and place. Schweickart puts the point this way:[30]

> A [post-capitalist theory] will also emphasize the need for diverse strategies and diverse aims. The transition to a genuinely democratic socialism will likely vary, depending on whether the country is rich or poor, on whether the country has undergone a socialist revolution in the past, and on various other historical and cultural contingencies. Although there will be commonalities of vision, there will be differences as well—of tactics, transitional strategies and ultimate goals. Unlike the program of neo-liberal capitalism, one size does not fit all. The counter-project does not envisage all nations aiming for the same patterns of development, or adopting the same technologies, values, and consumption habits. The counter-project calls for a halt to the McDonaldization of the world.

Such is exactly to be expected if organisation is distributed and bottom-up.

However, successful action at some places will encourage action of a similar kind at other places.[31] Perhaps one might expect those places where the

---

28. Lebowitz (2010), p. 148.
29. Gare (2014), p. 36.
30. Schweickart (2011), p. 15.
31. 'Society is composed of smaller institutions or organizations that are subject to change. Activists |can| work to create new institutions, one at a time—each one building on the last, each new institution opening up possibilities for further change' (Metcalf (2015), pp. 6, 5).

exploitation of workers is most evident to take the lead in the process. That is, the global South. However, there is nothing inevitable about such processes. What happens in various places depends very much on local conditions and events. History reminds us that the first real workers' revolution—though it did not remain that for long—happened in Russia, an essentially peasant economy, and not in the advanced capitalist countries of Britain or Germany, as might have been expected.

But whatever the exact historical contingencies, the new society can grow bottom-up in organic fashion. And it should be remembered that much of it does not have to be invented *de novo*. Old institutions that are worth preserving can be revised and restructured in a bottom-up and democratic fashion.

Finally, let us note the following possible objection. Change requires organisation; organisation requires power. Hence there is no change without power. So if there is change, there will be a power structure, and a power structure, once formed, will—as we have noted—start to operate in the interests of those in power. Hence, one might think, there is a Catch-22 situation. Without power, change is impossible; with power, it is be ill-fated. However, the argument is invalid. The point about power functioning in the interests of those in power applies to *top-down* power structures; and the power structure required for organisation does not have to be of this kind.

10.3.2.1 Collegial Decision-Making

As I have stressed, decisions in any bottom-up organisation need to be taken collegially. Let me now discuss this in more detail.

A collegially made decision is one taken collectively by the group after informed discussion. In collegial decision-making, consensus can often be achieved without a formal vote, but the process can certainly include some formal voting procedure, the result of which all agree to abide by.[32]

Collegial decision-making has many virtues; most obviously, it gives people control over the decisions which affect them. In 9.2.3 I noted Mansbridge's point that collegial decision-making generally results in better decisions as well. She adds to this virtue others, noting that[33]

> consensus protects the minority from being "trashed" by allowing it to command sufficient attention from the majority to make its positions understood. Consensus guarantees respect and listening, by right.

32. Mansbridge (1983), p. 32, defines consensual decision-making as one 'in which, after discussion, one or more members of the assembly sums up prevailing sentiment, and if no objections are voiced, this becomes agreed policy'. All the examples of such decision-making she examines have provision for formal voting procedure where necessary, however. So this doesn't quite get it.
33. Mansbridge (1983), p. 253.

Further:[34]

the rule of consensus seems not only to reflect empathy but to create it.

Metcalf reiterates these points:[35]

> Those of us who believe in deliberation have several different reasons: we think the process will result in better decisions—more informed, more aware of the distinct interests of different people, more fully thought through; and we believe the process of deliberation is potentially transformative for the people who do it—and that it nurtures qualities of empathy and understanding, that in some sense it raises consciousness.

Collegial decision-making is, then, beneficial on many levels.

It may not come naturally to those who are used simply to being told what to do, however. So here are some helpful thoughts formulated by the UK-based workers' co-op and advocacy group *Seeds for Change*:[36]

- If you don't understand something, don't be afraid to ask.
- Be willing to work towards the solution that's best for everyone, not just what's best for you. Be flexible, and willing to give something up to reach agreement.
- Help to create a respectful and trusting atmosphere. Nobody should be afraid to express their opinions. Remember that we all have different values, backgrounds and behaviour, and we get upset by different things.
- Explain your own position clearly. Be open and honest about the reasons for your view points. Express your concerns early on in the process so that they can be taken into account in any proposals.
- Listen actively to what people are trying to say. Make an effort to understand someone's position and their underlying needs, concerns and emotions. Give everyone space to finish, and take time to consider their point of view.
- Think before you speak, listen before you object. Listen to other members' reactions and consider them carefully before pressing your point. Self-restraint is essential in consensus—sometimes the biggest obstacle to progress is an individual's attachment to one idea. If another proposal is good, don't complicate matters by opposing it just because it isn't your favourite idea! Ask yourself 'Does this idea work for the group, even if I don't like it the best?' or 'Does it matter which one we choose?

---

34. Mansbridge (1983), p. 256.
35. Metcalf (2015), p. 39.
36. Quoted in Kinna (2019), pp. 234–5. In this context, one might also help to be aware of the techniques of what is sometimes called non-violent or compassionate communication. See Center for Non-Violent Communication (2007).

- Don't be afraid of disagreement. Consensus isn't about us all thinking the same thing. Differences of opinion are natural and to be expected. Disagreements can help a group's decision, because with a wide range of information and opinions, there is greater chance the group will find good solutions. Easily reached consensus may cover up the fact that some people don't feel safe or confident enough to express their disagreements.

Meaningful collegial decision-making of course requires people to be well informed, and so educated about the matters in question. There will be more to be said about such matters in due course; but this will do for the present.

10.3.2.2 Collegial Leadership

Collegiality obviously raises the question of what leadership could be in such a context. Clearly, there can be no change without political action, and political action requires leadership of some kind. It can be leadership of a temporary and moving kind, but there must be people who can see where things should be going, who can persuade others that this is so, and who can motivate them to act so as to achieve this end. How should this be done? Obviously one does not do this by going in and telling people what to do, taking it for granted that one knows best—as the global North has so often done with the global South.[37] What does leadership mean in a collegial context?

It means that the individuals in question should work as part of the group, helping to explain, educate, organise, motivate, all in a cooperative and collective spirit. Working together, not competition, is the order of the day. The Brazilian educationalist Paulo Freire puts matters concerning those who lead ('help') change in a community thus:[38]

> Authentic help means that all who are involved help each other mutually, growing together in their common effort to understand the reality they seek to transform. Only through such praxis—in which those who help and those who are being helped help each other simultaneously—can the act of helping become free from the distortion in which the helper dominates the helped.

As Freire emphasises, leadership of this kind means listening to others, understanding their points of view, and learning from them, as well as offering insights, suggesting guidelines, and so on. Such leadership is, then, an interactive form of interdependence.

37. See, e.g., Madeley (1995), Penz et al. (2011), and Munk (2014).
38. This is quoted in hooks (1994), p. 54. The quotation appears to come from Freire's *Pedagogy in Process*, but no further details are given.

We may add some Buddhist thoughts to the picture as well. As Slott puts them:[39]

> In a radical political organization, the activist with Buddhist sensibility can attempt to interact with others more on the basis of mindfulness and loving kindness; thus facilitating more respect and compassionate interactions among the group's members. He/she can also help the group avoid actions that are primarily rooted in ego-driven rage and fear. Finally, he/she can help the group to envisage and make changes in organizational functioning that facilitate communication, democracy, and mutual respect.
>
> Within Buddhist Centres or organizations, the radical political activist can, in a mindful, non-hectoring, way draw attention to the social structural dimension of suffering. He or she can encourage his/her fellow Buddhists to expand their understanding of harm, skillful actions, and other key Buddhist notions. The activist can propose forms of political engagement based on this broader understanding.

And of course, in settings that are neither of these things, the person can do both.

10.3.3   Putting the Two Pieces Together

I have now discussed a two-pronged strategy of radical action. The prongs are:

1. Emaciate top-down power/organisation structures.
2. Develop bottom-up power/organisation structures.

Step 1 works to render the top-down power structures of government and capital less able to enforce their woeful effects. Step 2 works to grow the grassroots decision-making processes to replace these. Top-down power structures are inimical to bottom-up decision-making processes. Those at the top wish to retain their power, and will therefore work to remove or undercut contravalent tendencies. (I will return to this matter in 11.4.) Hence, step 1 will make it easier for step 2 to proceed. Conversely, introducing collective decision-making procedures makes it harder for top-down power structures to be effective. Thus, success in step 2 not only starts to build a more rational and humane society, but also makes top-down resistance harder. The two prongs of the strategy are not, then, independent; and working on the two fronts simultaneously may provide a success that each on its own cannot achieve. (Of course, I am not suggesting

---

39. Slott (2011), p. 359. Note that 'loving kindness' is a standard translation of the Buddhist virtue *maitrī*. See 2.3.3.

that everyone or every group does everything. Different groups may focus on different things—hopefully with increasing cooperation and coordination.)

Thus, there will be no silver bullet for moving to a more rational and humane society, no magic trick that changes everything—which is not to say that there will be no moments of sudden change. Indeed, as is well known a gradual increase of pressure can result in very sudden change, such as the collapse of a physical structure to which it is applied. We will have to work on many fronts at once. And of course, as Buddhist philosophy notes, these are interconnected. So one change is liable to occasion others. What we may then hope for is a network of interdependent changes, growing together organically—as one might put it.

In the end, of course, nothing will happen unless each person makes an individual start. As Gibbs says:[40]

> the revolution might begin with our refusals as individuals and as communities to participate in some of the worst aspects of the system. In other words, to stop contributing harm. This is what people in progressive social movements around the world are attempting to do by constructing community alternatives, by defending the rights of humans and other animals, by working in solidarity with communities around the world who share their values (including the liberation from oppressions of race, gender and sexuality) and, in the short term, by lobbying governments and international institutions to implement change.

You don't have to wait for others. And recall, as the *Dao De Jing* puts it, a journey of a thousand *li* begins with a first step.[41]

10.4 Conclusion

In this chapter I have discussed how one might attempt to move towards a more rational and humane society; that is, the steps one might take towards getting there. In particular, I have discussed how one might move in the direction a society organised in a more bottom-up fashion, including how one might take on the top-down power of the capitalist state.

In the process of this, it may well feel as though we are fighting a battle against some alien force. But we are not. The state is *us*. Power is no more a self-subsistent thing than is capital. Like capital, it is just something that is encoded in a set of social relations. The German anarchist Gustav Landauer (1870–1919) wisely reminds us:[42]

40. Gibbs (2017), pp. 182 f.
41. Ames and Hall (2003), ch. 64.
42. Quoted in Ward (2004), p. 8.

The state is not something which can be destroyed by a revolution, but is a condition, a certain relationship between human beings, a mode of human behaviour; we destroy it by contracting other relationships, by behaving differently.

In the end, then, we are both the source of the problem and the potential for its solution.

Many of the pieces of the story of this part of the book are now in place. But I have alluded to two further very big pieces. The first concerns ideology and related matters, notably consciousness and education. The second concerns changing ourselves. I will take up these topics in the next two chapters, in that order.

11

IDEOLOGY, CONSCIOUSNESS, EDUCATION

11.1 Introduction

At the end of the last chapter I noted that questions concerning ideology and related issues are central to matters at hand. This chapter addresses those. We will start by having a look at what ideology is, and how it functions in a capitalist society. We will then turn to the question of how its effects are to be neutralised. This will take us into questions of consciousness and education.

11.2 The Power of Ideology

But first let us see why ideology is such an important issue.

As I noted in Chapter 8, top-down power structures generally operate for the benefit of those in power. Now, those in power need not be in a minority. In matters of racism they are often a majority; and in matters of gender the proportion of males to females in the world is roughly equal. However, in many top-down power structures, those in power are a minority. This is certainly the case in matters of class in a capitalist society. Those who merely work for capital vastly outnumber those who own/manage it. Now, as Hume thoughtfully ponders, how is it possible for a minority to make a majority submit to their power? He writes:[1]

> Nothing appears more surprising to those, who consider human affairs
> with a philosophical eye, than the easiness with which the many are governed
> by the few; and the implicit submission, with which men resign

1. From 'On the First Principles of Government'. Miller (1985), p. 32.

DOI: 10.4324/9781003195146-13

their own sentiments and passions to those of their rulers. When we enquire by what means this wonder is effected, we shall find, that, as Force is always on the side of the governed, the governors have nothing to support them but opinion. It is therefore, on opinion only that government is founded; and this maxim extends to the most despotic and most military governments, as well as to the most free and most popular.

Sometimes—despite what Hume says about force—it is indeed violence that is used to keep a majority subjugated. That was the case, for example, in apartheid South Africa. There, the black and coloured population was much larger than the white population. The white population kept the non-whites in subjugation by ruthless police and military violence, as became clear to the rest of the world—if it was not so before—in the proceedings of the Truth and Reconciliation Commission set up after the fall of apartheid.

However, it is a striking fact that violence is not normally necessary to keep control in a capitalist class structure. (Which is not to say that there is not structural violence within the system.) Violence may be used, and sometimes is, when other measures fail. Violence may be used to "keep order". But occasions when this is required are relatively rare: it is not normally necessary. As Schweickart puts it:[2]

> Capitalist societies tend to be "tolerant" societies—unless the basic institutions of capitalism are threatened. Then the gloves come off, and we get death squads, military coups, and fascism. At least, that has been the historical record to date.

And lest one think he is exaggerating, he lists (pp. 160–2) 19 well-acknowledged US attacks on democracies and cases of support for repressive dictatorships in the last 100 years. The list of covert actions is, of course much, much longer than this.

But, when the gloves do not need to come off, how does the minority keep control of the majority? Not by controlling their bodies, but by controlling their minds—'opinion', as Hume puts it. Ideology controls the way that people think, and, because of this, they do not challenge the *status quo*. Thus, Ward says:[3]

> The power of a government, even the most absolute dictatorship, depends on the agreement of the governed. Why do people consent to be ruled? It isn't only fear; what have millions of people to fear from a

2. Schweickart (2011), p. 158.
3. Ward (1996), p. 19.

small group of professional politicians and their paid strong-arm men? It is because they subscribe to the same values as their governors. Rulers and ruled alike believe in the principle of authority, of hierarchy, of power. They even feel themselves privileged when, as happens in a small part of the globe, they can choose between alternative labels on the ruling elite. And yet, in their ordinary lives they keep society going by voluntary association and mutual aid.

Loy puts it more pithily:[4]

> Dictatorships control people with violence and the threat of it, to restrain what they do. Modern democracies control people with sophisticated propaganda, by manipulating what they think. The title of one of Noam Chomsky's books sums it up well: *Manufacturing Consent*. We worry about weapons of mass destruction, but we should be concerned with weapons of mass deception.

What, then, is capitalist ideology, how does it work, and how may it be challenged? Understanding such matters is essential if one wishes to move to a civilised post-capitalist society.[5] So let us turn to these questions.

11.3   So What Is Ideology?

The word 'ideology' is often thrown around in a somewhat indeterminate way. Initially, it meant no more than something like the science (study) of ideas. It is now rarely used that way. More commonly, it means something more like 'a system of beliefs'. It is clear that it is often used with pejorative overtones, however, to mean a system of beliefs with which the speaker has no sympathy. The pejorative overtones of the word derive, I suspect, from Marx' use of the word. For Marx—at least in his later writings—an ideology is a system of beliefs that obscures or covers up the real nature of reality.[6] This is the sense in which I will use the term here.[7]

In this sense, an ideology has a number of defining features. First, it is a system of beliefs, or concepts and practices which inform these. Second, the beliefs are not true, or if they are literally true, they do not tell the

4. Loy (2008), p. 100.
5. 'Capitalism is regarded as [a legitimate system under which to organize society] by millions of people around the world. Therefore it is important to examine the hegemonic processes that ensure a social system that is genocidal manages not only to perpetuate itself, but also to be celebrated. The hegemonic discourse of capitalism is perpetuated through the media, education, and culture to preserve the dominant paradigm' (Leech (2012), pp. 7 f.).
6. See Mills (2003), ch. 1, and Bottomore (1983), pp. 219–23.
7. It is close to the one endorsed by Carroll (1998), ch. 6.

whole truth, and so imply what is not true. Third, these things are not only not true: they are deceptive. They cover up the way that things really are—and in the case of a political ideology, hide the way that the political and economic system actually functions. They are the way that those in power wish matters to be seen. Marx puts it this way:[8]

> The ideas of the ruling class are in every epoch the ruling ideas, i.e. the class which is the ruling material force of society, is at the same time its ruling intellectual force. The class which has the means of material production at its disposal, has control at the same time over the means of mental production, so that thereby, generally speaking, the ideas of those who lack the means of mental production are subject to it. The ruling ideas are nothing more than the ideal expression of the dominant material relationships, the dominant material relationships grasped as ideas.

In Marx' own terms, they serve to mystify the system. Thus, for capitalism:[9]

> in this economic trinity [capital-interest, land-rent, labour-wage] represented as the connection between the component parts of value and wealth in general and its sources, we have the complete mystification of the capitalist mode of production, the conversion of social relations into things, the direct coalescence of the material production relations with their historical and social determinations. It is an enchanted, perverted, topsy-turvy world in which Monsieur le Capital and Madame le Terre do their ghost walking as social characters and at the same time directly as mere things.

Finally, in virtue of obscuring the truth, the ideology protects the system from critical challenge. If you can't see what's wrong with things, you won't object to them. And of course, people are for the most part unaware of the functioning of ideology. Ideology works its effects below the level of awareness. In this way, it, itself, can avoid challenge, to which it would be all too open once brought to the surface.

As is clear, I am taking it for granted that there is such a thing as truth, and that about many things we can have a grasp of what that truth is—albeit a fallible and revisable one—and so, in particular, we have the ability to weed out ideological elements of our own beliefs. Fashionable—well, perhaps not so fashionable any more—so-called postmodernism denies these claims. However, this is not the place to take on this view. Suffice it here to say

---

8. *German Ideology*, McLellan (2000), p. 192.
9. *Capital*, Vol. 3. McLellan (2000), pp. 542 f.

that those who hold these views refute themselves every time they have their usual breakfast believing that the food is nourishing (that is, that such is true), and are justified in so believing.[10]

11.4 Capitalist Ideology

Turning specifically to capitalist ideology, this has many strands. Some of the most important of these are as follows.

People Are Social Atoms. First, in the form of the social contract theory, to be found in Locke and Hobbes, and as embedded, for example, in the US Constitution, it tells a story about human beings and the society which they form. Human beings are essentially social atoms. A person may be thought of as fully formed with interests and abilities quite independently of those of any other person. Persons then come together to form a society, perhaps giving up some of those interests, in order to form a society with a government (sovereign, state) which protects and enforces some of the most important ones, such as life, liberty, and the pursuit of happiness—and, of course, capitalist property.

As I noted in 2.3.2, this picture is both socially and metaphysically absurd. People are essentially interdependent from birth. Society is not a configuration formed to enforce pre-existing interests, but a pre-existing matrix, which forms such interests and provides for the needs of its members. In other words, this aspect of the ideology serves to cover over the essential interconnectedness of people. Hence it can deliver those *us/them* attitudes which undermine solidarity.[11] Indeed, since capitalism involves competition, part of the ideology of capitalism is that competition is always good. This is absurd, as we noted in 3.7. None the less it delivers a very general strategy for setting people against each other, in this strategy of divide-and-conquer.

Quite generally, top-down power structures are wont to destroy communal solidarity and collegiality, since these provide a source of resistance to such top-down power. This is well documented (though somewhat archaically) by Kropotkin in his 1902 book *Mutual Aid*,[12] and at much greater length by Rocker in his monumental *Nationalism and Culture*.[13] Further, as the Harvard economist Marglin argues,[14] contemporary economics—the handmaiden of capitalist ideology—itself destroys communal structure and solidarity:[15]

10. On the matter, see, for example, Boghossian (2006).
11. Thus, for example, as Leech (2012), p. 118, notes, workers in wealthy capitalist nations often side with capital against immigrant labour to defend what they think to be their own interests.
12. Bookchin (2008).
13. Rocker (1998).
14. Marglin (2008).
15. Marglin (2008), pp. 4, 27. The way that contemporary economic theory fallaciously promotes a pernicious individualism is explained in detail in ch. 4.

In arguing for the market, economics legitimizes the destruction of community and thus helps to construct a world in which community struggles to survive. ...

Indeed, we may have good reason to dismantle the engine of growth—not because growth is a threat to our relationship with nature, but because it is a threat to our relationships with one another.

By promoting market relationships, economics undermines reciprocity, altruism, and mutual obligation, and therewith the necessity of community. The very foundations of economics, by justifying the expansion of markets, lead inexorably to the weakening of community.

The Free Exchange of Labour Power. Next, as part of this story of coming together, people, it is said, confront each other as owners of property, and make voluntary agreements about how this is to be used. In particular, the agent of a quantity of capital confronts people who have none of it, save their ability to work—their labour power, in Marx' terms. The two then freely agree to exchange labour power (on the part of the worker) for money (on the part of capital). Since this a free exchange, it is perfectly just. However, this free exchange and its supposed justice is an illusion. As Marx cuttingly puts it:[16]

> The contract by which he [GP: the wage labourer] sold his labour power to the capitalist proved in black and white, so to speak, that he was free to dispose of himself. But when the transaction was concluded, it was discovered that he was no "free agent", that the period of time for which he is free to sell his labour power is the period of time for which he is forced to sell it.

The capitalist does not have to employ the worker. They can employ someone else—perhaps from the global South. Or they can—indeed will—move their capital elsewhere if it can make a greater profit. The worker has no choice. They must sell their labour or become destitute. True, they may sell it to the "highest bidder", but sell it they must. This is no more a free exchange than giving away your wallet at gunpoint.

The Capitalist Has Earned It. Another ideological claim is that the agent of capital is entitled to use it in this way because they have earned it by their own efforts, and so may dispose of it as they wish. Generally speaking, they have not. Their wealth comes from an accident of birth: the time, place, and family into which they were born. Those who own great wealth have usually inherited a large amount of it. True, they may have used it to make more, but this is standardly done by investing the money, the returns of

16. Fowkes (1976), p. 415.

which clearly depend on the labour of others (and its exploitation). In other words, the money is not obtained by the person's "own efforts".

In occasional cases, it can certainly happen that someone who starts with nothing on paper can amass a lot of money, say by forming a "startup". Most successful startups are soon sold to or bought out by larger companies. So the founder can indeed make a lot of money. But where does that money come from? The profits of the large company, obtained, again from the labour of others.

There is a particularly American version of this bit of ideology: *anyone* can make it if they work hard enough. Corollary: those who do not make it are lazy. This is completely false. Those who come from poorer sections of society have the odds stacked against them from the start—in terms of education, resources, opportunities. And the single mother who holds down two jobs to bring up a couple of kids in a poor neighborhood of New York or London works much harder than a broker who plays the stock market. Moreover, *anyone can make it* does not imply *everyone can make it*, any more than the fact that anyone who plays a fair game can win it implies that everyone who plays the game can win it. It is conceptually impossible for everyone to get rich by exploiting everybody else.

And in any case, the paper wealth that a person starts with is only a minute fragment of the capital they mobilise. Whoever they are, they freely use amassed social capital, in the form of previous technological developments, social infrastructure, education and research, none of which has been earned by their own efforts. Stiglitz sums up as follows:[17]

> A simple thought experiment should induce a note of humility: What would I have achieved if I had been born to parents in a remote village of Papua New Guinea or in the Congo? Every American business benefits from the rule of law, the infrastructure, and the technology that has been created over centuries. Steve Jobs could not have created the iPhone if there had not been the multitude of inventions that went into it, much of it based on publicly funded research over the preceding half century.

Indeed, it needs to be remembered that much of the social capital of the global North is the result of violence, robbery, and exploitation of people in the countries of the global South.[18]

Everyone Benefits. Next is the view that in a capitalist free-market system everyone benefits. The "invisible hand of the market" functions for the

---

17. Stiglitz (2019), p. 139.
18. See, e.g., McKelvey (2018), ch. 1.

benefit of all. In a much noted passage from *Wealth of Nations*, Adam Smith says:[19]

> As every individual ... endeavours as much as he can both to employ his capital in the support of domestic industry, and so to direct that industry that its produce may be of the greatest value, every individual necessarily labours to render the annual revenue of the society as great as he can. He generally, indeed, neither intends to promote the public interest, nor knows how much he is promoting it. By preferring the support of domestic to that of foreign industry, he intends only his own security; and by directing that industry in such a manner as its produce may be of the greatest value, he intends only his own gain, and he is in this, as in many other cases, led by an invisible hand to promote an end which was no part of his intention. Nor is it always the worse for the society that it was not part of it. By pursuing his own interest he frequently promotes that of the society more effectually than when he really intends to promote it. I have never known much good done by those who affected to trade for the public good. It is an affectation, indeed, not very common among merchants, and very few words need be employed in dissuading them from it.

Now, as often as this claim is parroted by capitalist ideologues, it is well known to be false, as is recognised by at least some economists. Here, for example, is Stiglitz:[20]

> The idea that markets are a powerful way of organizing production of goods and services has been deeply influential. It has provided the intellectual underpinnings of capitalism. But two centuries of research have now brought us to a better understanding of why Adam Smith's invisible hand can't be seen: because it isn't there.

Smith's claim is refuted by some simple examples from game theory (of which, living in the 18th century, he had no knowledge). These show that if two or more people act in such a way as to each promote their own interests, the result is sub-optimal for both.

One kind of example which demonstrates this is usually called the *Prisoners' Dilemma*, since it may be illustrated by the following sort of example.[21] Archie and Bettie have committed a crime, and been arrested on suspicion. The magistrate, Maggie, needs a confession. Maggie puts the two in separate cells (so

19. Cannan (1937), p. 423.
20. Stiglitz (2019), p. 76.
21. See, e.g., Osbourne (2009), ch. 2.

that they cannot communicate) and tells them each the following. If neither of you confesses, you will both get 1 year. If both of you confess, you will both get 5 years. *But* … if one of you confesses (and turns state's evidence) and the other does not, the one who confesses will get off (0 years) and the other will get 10 years. The information may be displayed as follows.

		Archie	
		Confess	*Don't*
Bettie	*Confess*	5 5	10 0
	Don't	0 10	1 1

Maggie then leaves the two to ruminate. Archie reflects as follows. Bettie will either confess or she won't. Suppose she confesses. I'm better off if I confess (5 years) than if I don't (10 years). Suppose she doesn't. Again, I'm better off if I confess (0 years) than if I don't (1 year). So in either case, I'm better off confessing. Bettie reasons in exactly the same way. So both confess. By acting in terms of self-interest, then, each of the pair gets 5 years. This is sub-optimal, since they could have got away with 1 year each.

Note, also, that what Smith actually says is that if every person works so as to promote their own interest, the result is the promotion of the public interest. What exactly, he means by 'public interest' is not explained; but I presume that he means that the *total* social wealth is increased. Even if this claim were true, it hardly implies that *most* people benefit from this, however, as Smith himself later points out concerning the division of labour enforced by a free market. In a much less noted passage from *Wealth of Nations*, he says:[22]

> [t]he man whose life is spent in performing a few simple operations, of which the effects are, perhaps, always the same, or very nearly the same, has no occasion to exercise his understanding, or to exercise his invention in finding out expedients for removing difficulties which never occur. He naturally loses, therefore, the habit of such exertion, and generally becomes as stupid and ignorant as it is possible for a human creature to become. The torpor of his mind renders him, not only incapable of relishing or bearing a part of rational conversations, but of conceiving any generous, noble, or tender sentiment, and consequently of forming any just judgment concerning many even of the ordinary duties of private life.

22. Cannan (1937), pp. 734 f.

It is those who are most adept in exploiting their fellow human beings that benefit from unbridled competition. The fact that a capitalist free market system, to the extent that there is one,[23] results in the concentration of wealth in a few hands means that those who have poor sanitation, education, health care, do *not* benefit from it, as they could if wealth were used more equitably, in a humane and compassionate way.

Possession Brings Happiness. Another aspect of ideology is that people can be happy, or happier, if they possess more.[24] It thus generates a never-ending sequence of *tṛṣṇa* which is itself a cause of unhappiness. Sivaraksa puts matters as follows:[25]

> According to Buddhism, there are three poisons: greed, hatred, and delusion. All three are manifestations of unhappiness, and the presence of any one poison breeds more of the same. Capitalism and consumerism are driven by these three poisons. Our greed is cultivated from a young age. We are told that our desires will be satisfied by buying things, but of course, consuming one thing just arouses us to want more. We all have these seeds of greed within our selves, and consumerism encourages them to sprout and grow.

The desire to possess more is not a path to happiness. It is a path to the opposite.

Capitalism Cannot Be Changed. Finally, there is the old saw that capitalism is the only game in town—or at least, that it is so, now that we have it. Thus, any attempts to radically change the system will cause a dysfunctional chaos. I have already pointed out why this is not true (3.7).

Marx famously called religion—by which he meant Christianity—the opium of the people.[26] Religion combines elements of hope and fear, an effective way of keeping people in their place. One might well see capitalist ideology—as Amber Carpenter pointed out to me—as having exactly the same combination of properties, with exactly the same effect. The fear of change plus the lure of possessing more make one prey to the capitalist game.

---

23. In fact, we have never really seen a free market, since markets in "liberal democracies" are always gerrymandered by governments and by capital manipulation itself. As Stiglitz (2019), p. 47, writes: 'Standard economics textbooks—and much political rhetoric—focus on the importance of competition. Over the past four decades, economic theory and evidence have laid waste to the claims that most markets are by and large competitive and the belief that some variant of the "competitive model" provides a good, or even adequate, description of our economy'.

24. And as Gibbs (2017), p. 90, notes, so powerful is the emotion this can generate, that one may well feel it, even when one knows the view to be false.

25. Sivaraksa (1992), p. 8.

26. The remark is made at the beginning of *Contribution to the Critique of Hegel's Philosophy of Law*, Marx and Engels (1975), p. 175.

Freire summarises many of these aspects of capitalist ideology as follows—and bear in mind that he is not talking just about capitalism in the global North; capitalism in the global South is very much in his sights:[27]

> It is necessary for the oppressors to approach the people in order, via subjugation, to keep them passive. This approximation, however, does not involve *being with* the people, or require true communication. It is accomplished in the oppressors' depositing of myths indispensable to the preservation of the status quo: for example, the myth that the oppressive order is a "free society"; the myth that all persons are free to work where they wish, that if they don't like their boss they can leave him and look for another job; the myth that order respects human rights and is therefore worthy of esteem; the myth that anyone who is industrious can become an entrepreneur—worse yet, the myth that the street vendor is as much an entrepreneur as as the owner of a large factory; the myth of the universal right of education ...; the myth of equality of all individuals ...; the myth of the charity and generosity of the elites, when what they really do as a class is to foster selective "good deeds" (subsequently embodied into the myth of "disinterested aim" ...); the myth that the dominant elites "recognizing their duties", promote the advancement of the people, so that the people, in a gesture of gratitude, should accept the words of the elites and be comforted by them ...; the myth of private property as fundamental to human development (so long as oppressors are the only true human beings); the myth of the industriousness of the oppressors and the laziness and dishonesty of the oppressed, as well as the myth of the natural inferiority of the latter and the superiority of the former.

In short, the ideology of capitalism does not tell the truth about how capitalism functions. It paints a picture of capitalism as just, beneficial for everyone, and inevitable. No wonder that if people believe this they will not be motivated to take action to contest the system.

11.5 The Propagation of Ideology: How?

Let us turn to the question is how this manifestly false ideology is inculcated in people. Since it does not stand up to rational inspection, this has to be done by techniques of propaganda. Propaganda, as the term is now standardly used, comprises techniques whose point is to get people to believe something or do something, by non-rational means. Thus:[28]

27. Freire (1970), pp. 112 f.
28. Marlin (2013), p. 91.

propaganda is an organized attempt to affect a given audience's beliefs and actions through communications that circumvent or suppress an individual's ability to judge adequately the truth of what is conveyed.

Of course, propaganda, so understood, can be used for things other than propagating ideology. Thus, it is used heavily in advertising, simply to sell things—and often the techniques of psychological manipulation are at their most overt there. Be that as it may, propaganda is certainly used for propagating ideology.[29]

The techniques of propaganda are various.[30] The most obvious is simply repeating something again and again. Think of how a TV advert may be used repeatedly in a short space of time, or of how often one hears members of the capitalist class extolling the virtues of capitalism. As Lewis Carroll quipped: what I tell thee three times is true.[31]

Then there is not just what is said or shown, but what is implied by what is said or shown. Thus, an advertiser may show a picture of a trendy-looking and fashionable person driving a car. The implication is that if you drive the car shown you will be such a person. In racist political propaganda, footage is shown of a black person being violent or being imprisoned. What is implied by the context is that black people are more violent and more criminal than white people.[32]

Then there is the appeal to emotion. Desire and fear are strong human motivators. If something can be depicted in a way which shows it to be desirable, people will incline to it. Conversely, if something is depicted in a way that generates fear, people will be inclined against it. Hence we find the use of emotive and rhetorical language in propaganda. A politician will claim to 'make America great again'. People are not asylum seekers; they are 'illegal immigrants'. Politicians will use pictures of themselves in which they appear in a handsome patriotic context. Their opponents will use pictures of them in which they appear ugly or ridiculous.

The flip side of this is that unpalatable truths about a situation are redescribed in patently inverted terms. Thus, firing someone is called *giving them their freedom*. Government departments which manage military aggression are called *defence departments*. In his book *1984*, Orwell darkly satirises the Ministry of Truth (= Ministry for the Propagating of Lies), whose slogans are: *war is peace, freedom is slavery, ignorance is strength.*

---

29. Thus Bernays (2005) explains how it may be used for both purposes, though he calls the latter 'political leadership'.
30. An analysis of many of these can be found in Marlin (2013), ch. 3.
31. *Hunting of the Sark*, second quatrain.
32. When the overt message is innocent, but the covert message is clearly understood by the intended target audience, this political technique has become known as dog-whistling. See Saul (2018).

Then, there is a technique that is often overlooked: what is *not* said. As the old adage goes: don't do things which put ideas in people's minds. In particular, in the ideological case, don't give any "breathing space" to anything which suggests that the system is fundamentally wrong. The thought may then not occur to people. And if it does, they are likely to put it quickly out of their minds. If no one is talking about it, it must be because it is a silly idea.

All these techniques are pretty obvious once one has seen them. Why are they not commonly pointed out? For exactly the last reason that we noted: keeping quiet about them is a way of making them invisible.

11.6 The Propagation of Ideology: Who?

So much for the *how*. Next, the *who*. Who are the purveyors of capitalist ideological propaganda? There are many. Those concerned may do it wittingly or unwittingly; they may lie or be sincere. These things are irrelevant. What is relevant is not the intention; it is the effect.

The most obvious agents of capitalist propaganda are politicians, but we may group with these other "leaders of society", such as CEOs, bankers, and perhaps in some societies religious leaders: all the other people whose views are given much public airing. Anyone who takes the time to work through what is said by such people, or what is shown in advertisements on their behalf, will find numerous examples of the techniques I have enumerated in the last section.

Then there are the popular news media, such as the *Sun* in the UK and Fox News in the US. Again, if one looks at publications such as these, one does not have to be Sherlock Holmes to see all the techniques I have just enumerated.

It might be thought that the "quality press" is a different kettle of fish. And so in many ways it is. One will not find there emotive language, fear-mongering, and sensationalism of the same order of magnitude as is to be found in the mass new media. But the propagation of ideology is found there none the less. How so is well documented by Herman and Chomsky (1988, chap. 1). In a series of detailed case studies they show how the press (including the "quality press") runs a pro-state—and therefore pro-capital—line. They explain this in terms of five factors (filters) which control what is printed. They enumerate these as follows (p. 2):

- Size, concentration of ownership, owner wealth, and profit orientation of the dominant mass media firms.

The press is dominated by a relatively small number of organisations, the role of each of which is to make a profit.

- Advertising as the primary income source of mass-media firms.

The primary source of income is advertising. Those who advertise (primarily, capitalist institutions) are therefore able to control content.

- The reliance of the media on information provided by the government, business, and "experts" funded and approved by these primary sources and agents of power.

Because independent journalism is time (and money) intensive, presses are heavily dependent on what is fed to them by the powers that be. One should not forget, in the context, "access journalism" whereby the state gives to journalists privileged access in such a way that it can control them—such as "embedding" journalists with troops engaged in action.

- "Flak" as a means of disciplining the media.

Complaints, formal or informal, legal or political, by powerful groups and individuals concerning material they do not like, affect what is printed.

- "Anti-communism" as a national religion and control mechanism.

Fear-mongering is used in support of policies of the powers that be. *Anti-communism* is a feature of the time the book was published. One might now substitute *anti-terror* or *anti-migrants*.

These techniques control what is said, and, just as significantly, what is not said. By the choice of what to publish and what not to publish, the quality press is able to control public discourse—all the more so, since it tends to be what is read by the more thoughtful elements of society.

While we are on the media, one should not forget all the rest of it: novels, films, and so on. These are themselves capable of, and often used for, the propagation of ideology.[33] To see this, think only of how a film can glorify a war and its imperialistic cause, or how it can justify genocide in the cause of imperialist expansion—consider an old-fashioned "Western".

This kind of media—increasingly in the hands of a few powerful capitalist mega-organisations[34]—also has a less obvious role in controlling the public mind. A large chunk of the contemporary (especially US) film industry is devoted to making fantasy films. Such films function—as well, of course, as to make large profits—to divert public interest from more important political

---

33. See Carroll (1998), ch. 6.
34. Thus, as of 2015, 90% of the US mainstream media was owned by six corporations: General Electric, News Corp., Disney, Viacom, Time Warner, and CBS, as shown by a report of the Canadian Centre for Research on Globalization (Bishop (2015)). General Electric, incidentally, is also the twelfth-largest US military defence contractor.

matters. One is reminded of the old Roman adage of *bread and circuses*. The *circuses* keep people amused and their attention diverted from more important things. As Loy cuttingly puts it:[35]

> As the earth begins to burn, as ecosystems start to collapse, the media focus our collective attention on the things that really matter: the Superbowl, the price of gas, the latest murder or sex scandal.

While we are on the topic of the media, it is worth saying a word about the internet. This is a way of distributing views, information, lies, and so forth. To this extent, it functions in a way that the media have always functioned, ever since the invention of the printing press. However, the internet functions with a speed and outreach that no medium of this kind has ever had before, which gives it an unprecedented power. One kind of phenomenon is particularly worth noting in this context: conspiracy theories and other false and deceptive theories. Such things may well have a "grassroots" origin, not driven by any obvious top-down power group—though of course it can be used by such groups, in the way that Trump and his administration did. The internet, then, is a very powerful engine of what one might call "popular" propaganda.

The importance of education in immunising people against "fake news" is well recognised. Finland was rated the European country most resistent to material of this kind in 2020, due to the implementation in Finnish schools of relevant programs of critical thinking.[36] This is just another example of the importance of an appropriate education—more of which in a minute.

The next item on our list of the purveyors of ideology is, of course, advertising. As noted, this uses the techniques of propaganda, and these may just be deployed for selling commodities. But advertising can be used to sell political ideology as well. The father of modern advertising and propaganda, Edward Bernays, was himself instrumental in advertising campaigns to promote capitalism in the US.[37] So a major propagator of ideology are the advertising companies whose services are employed exactly to do this.

Let us turn to systems of education. These can be used to inculcate and reinforce class attitudes explicitly. That was (and is) how the British public (= private, for non-British readers) school system functioned to maintain the British class system, teaching its students of their "elite" place in society.[38]

35. Loy (2008), p. 101.
36. See Madahwi (2021).
37. See, e.g., Tye (2002).
38. Thus, in the 2019 election for the leader of the British Conservative Party (and so the prime minister), four of the six candidates had been schooled at Eton.

However, in a capitalist society, a major aim of a mass education system is simply to provide the skills required to produce the workforce that capital requires. Nothing more. Gibbs notes:[39]

> Building on a long tradition of scholars that identify the role of education in capitalist societies, sociologist David Nibert[40] suggests that the content of education is creating an 'indoctrinated, disciplined and docile workforce' that tends to reflect and reinforce what is present in the mainstream media. He notes that 'the history of women, humans of colour, humans with disabilities, and other devalued groups have been told primarily from the vantage point of the privileged. Even with the current day's increased emphasis on multiculturalism, schools rarely address, or address seriously, the role of capitalism in creating and perpetuating prejudice and social ills'.

Putting the matter in explicitly Buddhist terms, Sivaraksa notes that the three "poisons" of Buddhism—greed, hatred, and ignorance—operate on a social level as well as on a personal level, as we noted in 5.4; and on the social form of the third of these, he says:[41]

> ignorance … is caused mainly by centralized education. Students are taught not to think holistically, but to compartmentalize their thinking, to memorize, and to abide by the existing norms. … Often times, students are trained and equipped just with the skills to become employees for multi-national companies, to exploit their fellow nationals and nature.

Again, what is *not* said plays a central role in education. Critiques of the capitalist system are given no significant "air time". The job of education is not to scrutinise the system critically; it is just to train people so that they can get a job.

Whilst on the subject of education, note also that most educational institutions are highly authoritarian. Students are disciplined to accept often arbitrarily exercised top-down power. In this way, they are conditioned into accepting a top-down power hierarchy.

And so we come to the "dismal science" of economics (as Carlyle put it). Contemporary economics is not a value-free science, like physics. It is based on many dubious (to say the least) value judgements—most notably that capitalism and its economic growth are a good. These values are virtually never subjected to scrutiny, but are presented as uncontested truths. The usual way

39. Gibbs (2017), p. 23.
40. Nibert (2002), p. 214.
41. Sivaraksa (2006), pp. 288–9.

in which economics is presented—in the public discussions, in economics courses, and so on—just, then, covers over these dogmas.

Finally, and ironically, one should not forget the well-known phenomenon of those who are kept down by a power system internalising the ideology of their oppressors—seeing themselves in the way their oppressors do.[42]

Such internalisation may be called *false consciousness*, or in Buddhist terms, *moha* (delusion/confusion). Thus, oppression is not seen as a social construction, but just as the way that things are. Marx puts it thus:[43]

> It is not enough that the conditions of labour are concentrated at one pole of society in the shape of capital, while at the other pole are grouped masses of men who have nothing to sell but their labour-power. Nor is it enough that they are compelled to sell themselves voluntarily. The advance of capitalist production develops a working class which by education, tradition and habit, looks upon the requirements of that mode of production as self-evident natural laws. The organisation of the capitalist process of production, once it is fully developed, breaks down all resistance.

Such internalisation both maintains and reinforces the ideology. It may also transmit it. Thus, working-class parents and school teachers may teach their children, explicitly or implicitly, to "know their place in society".

The phenomenon of false consciousness has been subjected to scrutiny in some detail in matters concerning gender and race.[44] For example, it is standard fare in gender theory to note that it is women themselves who play a major role in the socialisation of girls.[45]

The phenomenon of internalisation concerning class has been analysed, perhaps most notably, by Freire.[46] He describes it in the following way (pp. 22, 37):

> The oppressed suffer from the duality which has established itself in their innermost being. They discover that without freedom they cannot exist authentically. Yet although they desire authentic existence, they fear it. They are at one and the same time themselves and the oppressor whose consciousness they have internalized.
>
> Self depreciation is another characterization of the oppressed, which

---

42. The way that a power structure can engender this kind of subjectivity is analysed by Foucault in a number of places, perhaps most acutely Foucault (1977).

43. *Capital*, Vol. 1. Fowkes (1976), p. 899.

44. See, e.g., David (2014). For a discussion of this phenomenon as it concerns gender, see, e.g., Bartky (1990), esp. chs. 2, 5.

45. See, e.g., Bartky (1990), p. 36.

46. Freire (1970), esp. ch. 1.

derives from their internalization of the opinion the oppressors hold of them. So often are they … [told so] that in the end they become convinced of their own unfitness. 'The peasant feels inferior to the boss because the boss seems to be the only one who knows things and is able to run things'.[47]

The victim of ideology becomes complicit in their own victimisation.

11.7   Base and Superstructure

It is clear from what I have said that if the capitalist power structure is to be changed—as it must be if we are to move to a better post-capitalist society—its ideological machinery must be attacked and dismantled. The question is, then, how to do this.

Part of the answer is that people's consciousness may be changed by changing the conditions of their material production. Thus, forming collective decision-making procedures in neighborhoods, communities, and workplaces is likely to do this. Marx and Engels were, of course, well aware of this. Indeed, they insist that it is changes in these material conditions which determine changes in people's consciousness. They draw a distinction between the base and the superstructure of society. The base comprises the means and relations of production; the superstructure comprises the consciousness of people. And the base determines the superstructure. As they put it in *The German Ideology*:[48]

> The phantoms formed in the human brain are also, necessarily, sublimates of their material life-process, which is empirically verifiable and bound to material premises. Morality, religion, metaphysics, all the rest of ideology and their corresponding forms of consciousness, thus no longer retain their semblance of independence. They have no history, no development; but men, developing their material intercourse, alter, along with this, their real existence, their thinking and the products of their thinking.

The view is, frankly, incredible. It is clear that ideas can themselves have an enormous impact on people. Merely consider the effects of the teachings of Christ, Mohammed, or the Buddha, and their disciples. Moreover, such ideas can have an enormous impact on the economic base itself. To see this, one has to look no further than the ideas of Marx and Engels themselves. These helped to shape the political economy—whether in a way that Marx

47. Words of a peasant during an interview with the author.
48. McLellan (2000), pp. 180 f. We met the whole quote in 5.2.

and Engels intended or not—of both the Soviet Union and China after Mao's revolution.[49]

It is unsurprising, then, to find Engels, at least, later backtracking. In a letter of 1890 to Bloch, he writes:[50]

> According to the materialist conception of history, the production and reproduction of real life constitutes *in the last instance* the determining factor of history. Neither Marx nor I ever maintained more. Now when someone comes along and distorts this to mean that the economic factor is the *sole* determining factor, he is converting the proposition into a meaningless, abstract phrase. The economic situation is the basis but the various factors of the superstructure—the political forms of the class struggle and its results—constitutions, etc., established by the victorious classes after hard-won battles—legal forms, and even the reflexes of all the real struggles in the brain of the participants, political, juridical, philosophical theories, religious conceptions and their further developments into religious dogmas—all these exercise an influence on the course of historical struggles, and in many cases determine for the most part their *form*. There is a reciprocity between all these factors in which, finally, through the endless array of contingencies (i.e., those things and events whose inner connections with one another is so remote, or so incapable of proof, that we may neglect it, regarding it as non-existent) the economic movement asserts itself as necessary.

Engels is clearly prevaricating. He says that the base determines the superstructure 'in the last instance', but he has no explanation of what that means. Indeed, in the last sentence, it becomes the banality that the economic activity is necessary for whatever else is to happen. He even states clearly the mutual effect ('reciprocity') of the base and the superstructure.

Why did Marx and Engels run this line? I presume that it was because they wanted to distance themselves from the views of the most influential German philosopher of their day, Hegel. For him, the motor of history is not people and their society, but thought, in the form of the cogitations of *Geist*—something like the mind of the cosmos. As *Geist* goes through its dialectical reflections, the reality in which it is embodied goes through corresponding changes.[51] Under the influence of Feuerbach, Marx and Engels came to the conclusion that this was all mystification.[52] The actions of people were the real driving influence of history. *Geist* (or God, as it could be seen) was just a projection of this onto a

---

49. A trenchant critique of determinism by the base can be found in ch. 1 of Rocker (1998). As he shows, power and ideology both play significant roles in determining what happens.
50. Engels (1934).
51. For details of all this, see, e.g., Redding (2015).
52. On Feuerbach, see, e.g., Gooch (2015).

fiction. Thus, they determined to "stand Hegel on his head",[53] so arriving at the view of determination by the base.

But the reversal goes too far. To reject the view that the superstructure determines the base, one does not have to hold that the base determines the superstructure. One has to hold only that there is inter-determination. And this is a much more plausible view. Indeed, it is exactly the view that a more thoroughgoing dialectics would deliver. For dialectics tells us that opposite poles, like base and superstructure, mutually interact.

One finds this view essentially in Gramsci, who discusses and endorses a more dialectical view of the relationship between the base and the superstructure. These form an integrated block, whose elements are interdependent:[54]

> Structure and superstructure form a 'historic block'. That is to say the complex, contradictory and discordant ensemble of the superstructure is the reflection of the ensemble of the social relations of production. ...
> This reasoning is based on the necessary reciprocity between structure and superstructure, a reciprocity which is nothing other than the real dialectical process.

Given, then, that we have a dialectical understanding of the relationship between base and superstructure, it follows that to attack the hegemony of a capitalist structure, one must attack both the base and the superstructure simultaneously. Indeed, these things must go hand in hand.

11.8   Dismantling the Ideological System

So how does one go about attacking that part of the capitalist structure which is its ideology directly?

For a start, Marlin has some useful suggestions as to how to do this on an individual level. When one is supposedly informed of things, one can ask oneself:[55]

- What is the source of the (supposed) information?
- What, exactly, is it saying or suggesting?

53. 'The mystification which the dialectic suffers in Hegel's hands by no means prevents him from being the first to present its general forms of motion in a comprehensive and conscious manner. With him it is standing on its head. It must be inverted, in order to discover the rational kernel within the mystical shell' (Fowkes (1976), p. 103).
54. Forgacs (1988), pp. 192 f. The word 'reflection' might suggest the epiphenomenal nature of the superstructure; but the context makes clear that 'reflect' has its literal meaning: bend back on.
55. Marlin (2013), ch. 3.

- Who stands to gain by getting the message across?
- What techniques of communication are being used?
- What is not being said? Why?

That's good as far as it goes, but much more can be done.

For a start, news media must be taken out of capitalist control. News should tell people what happens in the world—and, by all means, give them a variety (a *real* variety) of opinions on this. It should not be used just to make profit for some quantity of capital, or to shape people in such a way that they conform to the views of capital and its agents.

To a certain extent, this can be done by the production of non-capitalist publications, though, given the capitalist market, such publications have always faced the problem of distribution. Distribution is now easier, given the internet. As noted before (8.4), however, given the quantity of information on the net, the question of *effective* access is now crucial. And if this is in the hands of capitalist organisations—such as Google and Facebook—and their algorithms, it is easy enough for distribution to be manipulated.[56]

There is also a more brute-force method: for parliament, or whoever the central political authority is, to take the news media out of the hands of capital. Of course, this is not going to happen while this power is in the thrall of capital. So it requires making inroads into the political structure. As noted in the previous chapter, this process is itself fraught with danger. And of course, to take the news media out of the hands of capital, and place it directly under the control of politics to deliver a "state-run" news service has obvious dangers of its own, as is clear from the way that such state-run news services operate in countries where there is no "free press". What is required is some arrangement to prevent the press becoming simply a voice of power: capital or political. The BBC in the UK (and the ABC/SBS in Australia) provide one such model; public radio in the US another.

The provision of information is an important aspect of a good education, one that must be embedded in a more general education system—though not of the traditional kind, but of the kind envisaged by Freire.[57] In this, people are encouraged to discuss openly their economic and political views and problems. Doing so exposes ideological assumptions, which can then be put under the microscope, as well as delivering a sense of solidarity, as people see the commonality of their situation and experiences.

Such groups are, in fact, well known in a different context: the women's movement. In the 1970s and 1980s it was common in a number of countries for women to organise "consciousness-raising" groups. In these, groups of

---

56. For a few examples of internet control—commercial and political—see Etter (2017), Grasseger and Krogerus (2017), Lewis (2018), Miller (2015).
57. See Freire (1970), ch. 3.

women came together to discuss their experiences as women, rendering clear the patriarchal power structure they faced and the ideological assumptions that helped to enforce it.[58] The idea of consciousness-raising groups, and even the terminology itself, has now gone out of fashion. But the terminology was, in fact, a good one; and so was the strategy. The aim of such groups was precisely to change the consciousness of people: to make them see how their consciousness had been shaped by ideological forces beyond their control, and so confront them. And it often did just this.

Indeed, an anti-capitalist movement has much to learn from the women's movement. My mother was born in the UK in 1911; my daughter was born in the UK in 1976. And when I compare the life conditions of each, there is really no comparison. The conditions of education, employment, opportunity, and the social and sexual expectations of women which my daughter faces are entirely different from those my mother faced. And the changes are *much* for the better. Much of the old machinery of patriarchy has been dismantled; and considering the thousands of years it has lasted in the UK (and of course in nearly every other country), in an amazingly short period of time: a mere 60 years.

How has this been achieved? By a whole combination of things, none of which would have been sufficient on its own. There was action within the parliamentary system, changing laws. There was extra-parliamentary action, such as the protests by the suffragettes. There was grassroots pressure on employers, such as universities and other institutions, to change their employment and hiring practices to make them gender-neutral. There were books, and articles in the press and learned journals. There were public campaigns, such as the *MeToo* movement. There were, as noted, consciousness-raising groups. And then there were just individual women showing individual men that some of their attitudes to women were unthinkingly patriarchal.[59]

I am by no means saying that the women's movement has achieved its goal: the irrelevance of gender in education, employment, the professions, the home, and so on. It has not. Even in those countries where these changes have occurred, a good deal remains to be done. And in most regions of the world, the women's movement has as yet had little effect (India, much of Africa, most Islamic countries, parts of Latin America). Women are as much subjugated by patriarchy in those places as ever they were.

The point is simply that action on a number of disparate fronts, many of these bottom-up, can make highly significant changes in an historically relatively short time. There are lessons for an anti-capitalist movement here.

58. See Bartky (1990), p. 12.
59. This is a comment from personal (though by no means unique) experience. I owe a personal debt to some of the women in my life.

And, to return to the matter of ideology, the effect of consciousness-raising groups in attacking ideology is one of these. Such groups can be formed by any group of people, friends, work colleagues, or professional groups. And if such a group is formed on the basis of a group of employees, a neighbour-hood group, or even a group such as an environmental group, it is not without the bounds of possibility that it could morph into an SOC.[60]

11.9   Education and Ideology

Let us now return to the general question of the importance of education in dismantling ideology.

The first of the octet of the Fourth Noble Truths is *Right View*. To act effec-tively in the world, one must understand how it works—and how it does not work. This is the role of education: not just the education where people are trained in the skills required for earning a living, but an education which shows the many ways in which the world and its parts are interconnected: human, sociological, historical, geographical, ecological. In Buddhist terms, one needs to eliminate *avidyā* (ignorance) concerning *pratītyasamutpāda* (inderdependence).

For a start, people need to understand how we have got to where we are now. History is important. People need to know how in Europe in the 18th century workers were driven off the land to provide an urban workforce, and how similar things happened—and are still happening—in the global South. They need to know how the riches of the global South were appropri-ated by capitalist-driven imperialism. People need to know of the support of repressive dictatorships in the Middle East and South America by capitalist countries; the role they have played in producing the current geography and politics of the Middle East, including the development of militant Islam; the role that these things have played in the production of refugees and migration.

People need to know how societies work now. They need to understand the geography of the world, and the conditions of people in other parts of the world. They need to know how the capitalist system affects people. They need to know how their own actions, individual and collective, affect other people. They need to know how the environment works in producing the food they eat and the clothes they wear. They need to know the conse-quences of their actions on that environment.

People also need to understand where present tendencies are taking us. They need to know that we are presently heading for a world where wealth and power are—even more than presently—largely in the possession of a very

---

60. How this might happen is discussed in Bookchin (2004), pp. 152 ff.; and an actual example is the community scheme, *Every One, Every Day*, recently pioneered by the London Borough of Barking and Dagenham. See Monbiot (2019a).

small few; that the drive for capital growth is currently trashing our natural world; that the collection of large data and its analysis by techniques of artificial intelligence are taking us to a world where profit-making enterprises monitor and fashion our activities.

People need to know and understand all these things, and doubtlessly many others. Despite good things that some educational systems in some places do, and the fact that many educationalists are undoubtedly well-intentioned concerning their students, education systems cannot be said to be performing well in this regard.

Nor, when I talk of education, am I talking of something simply for the young. The education of adults is even more important. Not only is our understanding of the world constantly changing, but as people grow and their understanding of the world deepens, they are in a position to offer the wisdom of their understanding to others.

Moreover, although there needs to be people who have the knowledge to impart the information required, education should not be one person simply feeding others facts. That is just a way of producing a new top-down power structure: the authority of knowledge—what Freire calls *the banking conception of education*.[61] By way of critique of this, he says:[62]

> The correct method for a revolutionary leadership to employ in the task of liberation is … *not* "libertarian propaganda". Nor can leadership merely "implant" in the oppressed a belief in freedom, thus thinking to win their trust. The correct method lies in dialogue. The conviction of the oppressed that they must fight for their liberation is not a gift bestowed by the revolutionary leadership, but a result of their own *conscientização*.

People should form communities that think, challenge, disagree, investigate, together. Moreover, as Freire notes,[63] dialogue cannot exist without humility and the preparedness to listen to others—the "leader" of a group as much as anyone else. And it is important that members of the group feel free to challenge the thoughts of others, including any "leader". We are back to collegial leadership, as I discussed in 10.3.2.2.

The educational fora required by this sort of education are not exactly consciousness-raising groups, but they are not entirely disjoint from them either. Both serve to help people see the world aright.

---

61. Freire (1970), ch. 2.
62. Freire (1970), p. 41. The term *conscientização* might be translated as something like 'consciousness raising'.
63. Freire (1970), p. 63.

11.10 Education in General

Education, then, is crucial in attacking ideology. But as I have noted at many places in this book, the importance of education is much more general than this. It helps people to understand the world in which they live and its many inter-related parts. It helps to overcome bigotry and xenophobia. It makes it harder for people to have the wool pulled over their eyes. It empowers people to think critically, and to take considered actions. It is the basis of making informed collective decisions, and of creating a sense of collegiality and solidarity. It is fundamental to any true democracy. It is, hence, essential both in moving towards a better society and in making it work.

Of course, I'm not talking about what Freire calls the banking system of education, where people are just told what to think; but education as a collective enterprise which involves communal discussion, the sharing of views, airing and exploring disagreements, hearing from the experts on a subject and learning to interrogate them. How best to organise and structure this kind of education is an important question. Various "progressive" systems of education are well known. But it is hardly likely that there is a one-size-fits-all model; and as ever, experience will have to guide the development of ideas and practices.[64]

It is not to be expected that people will all be of a like mind in such discussions, nor is this desirable. As Mill emphasised in *On Liberty*, disagreement fills many essential educational functions.[65] In particular, people come to understand their own views better, and may even come to see some of these views as misguided. Naturally, it may be difficult to bring those who hold their views dogmatically into an open-minded dialogue, but little by little it may work.

People are a work in progress, and education of the right kind is an essential part of helping to bring it about that that change really is *progress*.

11.11 Conclusion

In this chapter we have been discussing ideology and how it functions—particularly in a capitalist society. We have also seen that changing the way that people think and how they produce are mutually dependent. Both are necessary for moving to a better society. We then looked at some of the things that can work to change people's consciousness directly. The importance of education of an appropriate kind in the process was also noted—an importance which continues even after any transition to a more bottom-up society: education is part of making us better people.

That brings us squarely to the matter of changing ourselves for the better, and how one might do this. I turn to this topic in the next chapter.

---

64. For some relevant contemporary developments, see O'Brien and Howard (2020).
65. See Gray (1991), esp. ch. 2 of the essay. See also Macleod (2016), §4.5.

12

CHANGING ONESELF

12.1 Introduction

In the feminist movement of the 1970s there was a saying: the personal is polit-ical.[1] This would make an appropriate title for this chapter as well. The sense would be slightly different, though. In the feminist movement, it meant some-thing like: personal relations are part of the politics of power. Here, it would mean that structural changes in the socio-political cannot be divorced from changes in people themselves.

Marx would, of course, have agreed with this. Changes in the relations of production are going to affect what people do, how they think, and how they behave with respect to others. This is little more than the effect of the base on the superstructure. However, as I argued in the last chapter, the rela-tionship between base and superstructure is dialectical. For as much as changing society can change people, changing people can change society. In particular, if people acquire more of a sense of their mutual interdependence, and so become more compassionate, they may come to reject those social elements, be they economic or political, which are rebarbative to this sense. In political jargon, one might say that they will develop a spirit of solidarity. Transforming the per-sonal will, thus, take matters beyond the merely personal.

Indeed, just changing the means of production and hoping that everything else will fall into place seems wishful thinking. As Ray worries:[2]

---

1. See, e.g., Hanische (2000).
2. Ray (2006), p. 67.

DOI: 10.4324/9781003195146-14

The desire to change the world is a very good thing. However, if you don't work on yourself first, you'll bring all your personal paranoia, arrogance, aggression, and preconceptions along, and you'll just get in a fight with whomever you're trying to change.

In this chapter we will look at how appropriate changes might be effected. This will take us through a discussion of the cultivation of appropriate ethical virtues, mindfulness, and moral phenomenology.

An appendix to the chapter discusses something which may seem odd initially: a training in *karatedō*. However, it serves to illustrate and underline many points made in the chapter and elsewhere in the book.

12.2 Praxis and Cultivating Virtues

Let us start the discussion with quite general matters.

People are complex organisms. For evolutionary reasons, we have both aggressive and cooperative tendencies. As the evolutionary biologist Stephen Gould says:[3]

> Violence, sexism, and general nastiness are biological since they represent one subset of a possible range of behaviors. But peacefulness, equality, and kindness are just as biological—and we may see their influence increase if we can create social structures that permit them to flourish.

Putting a Buddhist spin on matters, Sivarksa says:[4]

> In Buddhist psychology, it is taught that each of us carries inside us many different seeds, which can be likened to potentialities, and they manifest from time to time as actions and feelings: love, anger, compassion, greed, and so on. Depending on how we live our lives, different seeds are watered. When we are in conflict, the seeds of anger can easily sprout and come to the surface. When we are calm and at peace, the seeds of happiness come forth.
>
> Some people doubt that an individual can have much impact on society. But each of us is a seed for the whole of society. When we are angry and violent, we encourage violence in others. If we are mindful, we encourage mindfulness throughout society. In today's world, the dominant ethics of consumerism and materialism water the seeds of everyone's greed, hatred, and delusion. Our modern culture glorifies our worst capabilities. A change in our life-styles and our ethics is increasingly urgent.

3. Gould (1977), p. 257.
4. Sivaraksa (1992), p. xv.

As Gould and Sivaraka say, then, different social structures may bring out the different tendencies in us. In particular, as noted in 3.4 and 11.4, a capitalist social structure and its ideology tends to bring out selfish, non-compassionate, tendencies. And conversely, more cooperative social structures may bring about the opposite. So, Metcalf:[5]

> [O]ne of the great virtues of alternative institutions [is] that by providing participants with a different lived experience, they can begin to resocialize people into new ways of behaving.

Indeed, even much smaller-scale contexts can bring out different tendencies in people. Thus, the appalling behaviour of the guards at the notorious Abu Ghraib prison[6] was due to the circumstances in which they found themselves—and, of course, the encouragement and legitimisation from above.[7] Conversely, a sense of solidarity in a group can bring out practical concern for the welfare of others in the group, and the resultant altruistic behaviour. Thus, on the abortive Scott expedition of 1910–1913 to the South Pole, one of the team, Captain Lawrence Oates, famously decided to commit suicide because he felt that his condition was holding up the others, which seriously lessened their chances of survival.[8] It is thus a good idea to put oneself in situations that elicit compassionate responses—perhaps, for example, by working with disadvantaged groups. Conversely, it is a good idea to keep out of situations which encourage aggressive actions, such as hostile confrontations (though of course, such may be unavoidable sometimes in working for change).

But how does one go about enhancing compassion and decreasing self-centred tendencies *directly*? It is hardly a secret that we can train ourselves into our dispositions. Thus, by repeated practice, a musician can engender the disposition of responding to dots on a page in a certain way. Similarly, a sports person can engender the disposition of reacting physically in a certain way.

As we noted in Chapter 4, and as both Buddhist and Marxist philosophy recognise, there is no fixed self. What we are is an indefinitely ongoing work in progress. Thus, as Marx himself noted, when we labour, we

---

5. Metcalf (2015), p. 33.
6. Hirsh (2004).
7. In this context, and with reference to Chapter 8, it is worth remembering, also, the notorious Stanford Prison Experiment (see McLeod (2018)). In this, very ordinary people administered what they believed to be excruciating electric shocks to subjects—albeit very reluctantly—when they were told by a person they believed to be in a position of power that it was perfectly fine to do so. People are socialised into taking commands from those above them in a top-down power structure.
8. See, e.g., Smith (2006).

produce not just external goods (commodities, in a capitalist society), we produce ourselves. He says:[9]

> The worker produces capital, capital produces him—hence he produces himself, and man as *worker*, as a *commodity*, is the product of this entire cycle.

Our practices create us. In Marxist thought, the idea was taken up most notably by the Yugoslav Praxis School of Marxism.[10] One of its leading figures, Petrović, puts it thus:[11]

> Praxis is a universal-creative self-creative activity by which man transforms and creates his world and himself.

And Lebowitz concludes correctly:[12]

> Regardless of any differences of path, *all* paths to socialism necessarily must create the conditions by which people transform themselves through their activity.

Moreover, it is not just physical dispositions that can be trained into us; moral dispositions can be. Aristotle notes that:[13]

> by doing the acts that we do in our transactions with other men we become just or unjust, and by doing the acts that we do in the presence of danger, and being habituated to feel fear or confidence, we become brave or cowardly. The same is true of appetites and feelings of anger; some men become temperate or good-tempered, others self-indulgent and irascible, by behaving in one way or the other in appropriate circumstances. … It makes no small difference, then, whether we form habits of one kind or of another from our very youth; it makes a very great difference, or rather *all* the difference.

So what kind of practices are effective in the present context? This is what the Noble Eightfold Path is all about. And of central concern here is the triple: Right Action, Right Speech, Right Livelihood. Do not make a livelihood by

---

9. *Economic and Philosophical Manuscripts*, 2nd ms. Marx and Engels (1975), p. 283. Further on the dialectical interaction between a person and their socio-economic matrix with respect to Marx, see Sztompka (1991), ch. 3.
10. On the school, see Marković and Cohen (1975).
11. Petrović (1967), pp. 77 f.
12. Lebowitz (2010), p. 130.
13. *Nichomachean Ethics*, bk. 2, ch. 1. Barnes (1984), p. 1743.

something which makes you used to exploiting others; make a practice of not lying to or denigrating others; make a practice of not stealing from or in other ways of hurting others.

12.3   Mindfulness Within

Of course, there is more to the Eightfold Path than this. Right Mindfulness is another of the octet of the Path, and we noted in 2.2.3.3 how important this is. Let us consider it further.

As I noted there, mindfulness is the ability to hold an object in mind, allowing the application of cognition to it—including ethical appraisal—so that this can be taken to heart. To bring about appropriate changes one should be mindful, in this sense, of what is going on in one's mind—no, this isn't a pleonasm, as we shall see in a moment. One has little hope of bringing the mind, and the actions consequent on its state, under control (or of shaping subsequent states of mind), if one is unaware of what is going on there. In his poem *Bodhisattvacaryāvatāra*, Śāntideva makes the point with the following striking metaphor:[14]

> A crazy, untamed elephant in this world
> Cannot inflict so much harm
> As the sufferings of the deepest hell
> Caused by the rampaging elephant of the mind.
> But if the elephant of our mind
> Is bound tightly on all sides by the rope of mindfulness,
> All fears will cease to exist
> And all virtues will fall into our hands.

So how is such mindfulness to be achieved? Śāntideva recommends a number of practices. One of these is a simple reality check on one's mental state:[15]

> Whenever I wish to move my body
> Or to utter any words,
> I should first examine my mind
> And then steadfastly act in an appropriate way.
>
> Whenever there arises in my mind
> The desire to become attached or angry,
> I should not do or say anything
> But remain as impassive as wood.
>
> Whenever I am pretentious, mocking,
> Arrogant, or self-important;

14. *BCA* V: 2–3. Elliot (2002), p. 47.
15. *BCA* V: 47–53. Elliot (2002), pp. 54 f. There are a few more verses, but you get the picture.

Whenever I develop the intention to speak of others' faults,
Or think of profiteering or deceiving;

Or whenever I start to solicit praise,
Deprecate others,
Or use harmful or divisive speech,
I should remain as impassive as a block of wood.

Whenever I desire wealth, honour, or fame,
Or the attention of a circle of admirers;
Or whenever my mind wishes for veneration,
I should remain as impassive as a block of wood.

We can cut Śāntideva some poetic slack here. If one stopped and thought before one did *everything*, one would do very little. The point, I take it, is that it is good to reflect on one's state of mind, motives, and emotions, before one undertakes at least important things. Similarly, I do not think that when he uses the words 'remain as impassive as a block of wood' Śāntideva intends us simply to freeze: after all, as he himself says, this contemplation is a guide as to what to *do*, not what *not* to do. Rather, the point is that such reflection will act to check the negative actions engendered by unwholesome mental states. Or as Śāntideva later summarises matters:[16]

The defining characteristic of guarding alertness
Is to examine again and again
The state of our body, speech, and mind,
And to understand whether our actions are correct or not.

Śāntideva's advice is sound: reflecting on one's own emotions and motives for acting is a good practice into which to train oneself.

A more contemporary Buddhist underlines the effects of such mindfulness in a social context as follows:[17]

The more I am motivated by greed, ill will, and delusion, the more I must manipulate the world to get what I want, and consequently, the more alienated I feel and the more alienated others feel when they see they have been manipulated. This mutual distrust encourages both sides to manipulate more. On the other side, the more my actions are generated by generosity, loving-kindness, and the wisdom of interdependence, the more I can relax and open up to the world. The more I feel part of the world and genuinely connected with others, the less I will be inclined to use others, and consequently the more inclined they will be to

16. *BCA* V: 108. Elliot (2002), p. 64.
17. Loy (2008), p. 63.

trust and open up to me. In such ways, transforming my own motivations not only transforms my own life; it also affects those around me, since what I am is not separate from what they are.

12.4   The Psychology of Power Revisited

This takes us back to the matter of 10.2, of the lure of power and the way that this can corrupt action within a top-down power structure. In 8.3 we looked at the Buddhist analysis of what drives the desire for power. At its root are a number of unhealthy motives (unhealthy, if for no other reason, than that they are self-defeating). A way to attack the lure is to be aware of these motives and their pernicious effects; and mindfulness is a way of doing this. As Slott notes, concerning Buddhist ethical virtues more generally:[18]

> If one looks at the development of radical political parties and radical rev-olutionary movements from a historical perspective, there is a pervasive tendency for idealism and solidarity to be increasingly replaced by authoritarianism and unethical behaviour. Certainly, establishing and maintaining democratic structures that ensure accountability of leaders and due process can help to constrain degenerative organizational ten-dencies. Just as important, however, a Buddhist-inspired sense of loving-kindness and non-attachment would provide additional support for egalitarian modes of action. If our actions within an organisation are less determined by ego-based desire, anger, and delusion, we are more likely to make a productive contribution and to treat others with greater respect and dignity.

It might be thought that developing Buddhist virtues, with their accompa-nying peace of mind, would make one a less effective political actor. But this is not at all the case. As I observed in 2.2.4, it is the opposite. A mind clouded by fear and aggression does not operate efficiently. Slott again:[19]

> the cultivation of non-attachment and loving kindness, core components of the Buddhist tradition, can help activists be more effective and sustain long-term commitment to social change. One might argue that recogniz-ing the impermanence of things and events, as well as feeling a powerful compassion for other beings, would weaken or dilute an activist's passion and lead to a devaluation of politics. In fact, I think the opposite is true. When activism is less fueled by rage and aggression, we can better con-front exploitative social structures and those in power. Our ability to

18. Slott (2011), p. 357.
19. Slott (2011), pp. 356 f.

develop workable strategies will be increased insofar as we 'keep our eyes on the prize', rather than have a vision clouded by aversion and anger linked to the needs of our ego.

Developing Buddhist virtues is, then, not only desirable for engendering a saner society, it makes one more effective in bringing this about.

Finally on this topic, could it be the case that when enough people have overcome the lures of power, genuinely compassionate top-down political power structures are a possibility? Perhaps. We do not know what future possibilities will emerge. Clearly, though, we are presently nowhere near this possibility, if ever we will be.

12.5   Exchanging Self and Other

Let us return to the subject of mindfulness itself. Śāntideva also has another useful technique for this, called *exchanging self for other*. At its most basic, to exchange self for other is simply to put oneself in another person's shoes, and so see the world as they see it. Clearly, understanding and experiencing how another sees the world is an empathy-inducing practice. I think that most of us have experienced this at some time or other.

Śāntideva gives the idea a special twist, though, which is to see *oneself* from the perspective of the other. Notice that in the following, the *he* that is being talked about is actually *oneself*:[20]

> He is honoured, but I am not.
> I do not have the wealth he has.
> He is praised, but I am despised.
> He is happy, but I suffer.
>
> I have much heavy work to do,
> While he remains comfortably at rest.
> His reputation has spread throughout the world,
> But all I am known for is my lack of good qualities.
>
> But what do you mean, "I have no good qualities?"
> I have many such qualities.
> In comparison with many, he is inferior,
> While there are many to whom I am superior.
>
> My morals, views, and so on degenerate
> Though the force of my delusions, not because I want them to.
> You, Bodhisattva, should help us regenerate them in any way that you can,
> And willingly forbear any hardship you might encounter doing so.

20. *BCA* VIII: 140–154. Elliot (2002), pp. 136 f.

But he does nothing to help us,
So why does he make us feel so insignificant?
What use are his so called good qualities to us?
He never uses them for our benefit!

What Śāntideva is asking us to do is choose someone whom we know and who
knows us, and put ourselves in their place, to see how they see us. This is certainly a good exercise for puncturing any inflated conception one has of
oneself, and seeing one's own failings.

But then Śāntideva makes a remarkable turn:

I will proclaim my own good qualities to the whole world
By whatever means I can,
But I will make sure that no one ever hears
Of any good qualities he might possess.

I will hide my own faults but make his known.
I will be venerated by others but ensure that he is not.
I will acquire a great deal of material wealth
And encourage others to honour me, not him.

For a long time, I will take pleasure
In seeing him humiliated.
I will make him the laughing stock of all
And an object of ridicule and blame.

(The passage goes on in this way for several more verses.) Śāntideva's other is
not a very nice person. So why is he getting us to think about this rather
unpleasant character? Simply because, in this exercise, we come to see what
effect we have on others. The things we do to people can actually make
them worse people. Of course, Śāntideva's other has a rather extreme reaction,
and when we choose someone we know, and who knows us, it is somewhat
unlikely that they would have such a reaction. But the point of the exercise
is to see what effects we are having on others. They may not be the beneficial
effects in which we wish to pride ourselves; they may actually be detrimental.[21]

The exercises Śāntideva suggests are thus exercises in seeing ourselves better,
of stripping away some of the illusions we may cherish about ourselves, and
understanding the effects of our actions on others.

21. Many commentaries interpret the passage rather differently. We have now changed to a different other. The first other was someone taken to be inferior to oneself. The second other
is someone taken to be superior. Śāntideva is asking us to see ourselves in the eyes of
someone who has contempt for us so that we can appreciate the corrosive character of our
own contempt. I find this a less plausible interprtation of the text, since we have given up
seeing ourselves through the eyes of another (v. 140). However, I am sure that this interpre-
tation delivers a useful exercise too!

12.6 Mindfulness Without

Another important aspect of mindfulness is not mindfulness of one's own attitudes, but mindfulness of the interconnectedness of things, and of one's own actions in this interconnectedness. One needs to see one's role in the chains of dependencies.

In *Why the Dalai Lama Is a Socialist*, Gibbs describes an interesting fantasy (her word) that she has. Clearly, the thought experiment is aimed at consumers in the global North, but the point is, in fact, a quite general one. Anyone, anywhere, can work at being aware of the consequences of their choices, and owning them. I quote at length:[22]

> Pondering [the fact that our actions have consequences, often far beyond our understanding] led me to imagine the concept of a warning system that I rather gruesomely labelled as the 'bodies in the basement' approach. For example, we would immediately at point-of-purchase see the entanglement of the cell phone purchase with the fate of the children engaged in coltan mining in the Congo who are facing violence, the rape of their mothers, and not being able to attend school; or as we stood in line to order a Big Mac we would reflect on the fact that due to our heavily meat-based diet we are dependent upon a system of raising livestock that is the single largest contributor of greenhouse gas emission globally; or we would witness the working conditions of the Bangladeshi sweatshop workers as we were about to purchase a new shirt; or as we turned our heating system on we had a vision of the skin problems and respiratory diseases afflicting communities living on or near land owned by multinational coal-mining companies; or as we pulled out our credit card to buy new cotton pants we realized that over 200,000 unsubsidized Indian farmers had committed suicide because they couldn't compete with the heavily subsidized cotton growers in wealthy nations; or looking at the menu in a restaurant we would witness the mental health problems of slaughterhouse workers, and so on.
>
> I envisioned that people, after seriously reflecting on these gruesome realities that are currently hidden from them (i.e., bodies in the basement), would have to choose which of two buttons to push before making their purchase. The first button would declare, 'Yes, I know what this means, but I'm still going to do it'. The second button would state, 'No, I guess I don't really need to buy or eat this thing or do this activity'. In other words, it would require people to act mindfully to understand the consequences of their actions.

---

22. Gibbs (2017), pp. 122 ff.

Without getting bogged down about the practicalities—or impracticalities—of such an approach to addressing structural violence, imagine how it would impact the world if we did this in some form or another as individuals, as parents, as workers, as communities, as countries?

Of course, when the object in question is purchased, the events leading up to its availability are passed, and there is nothing one can do to change them. The point, rather, is this. These are ongoing practices; and if enough people ceased to practice, those running the show would cease to do so, since they would no longer make a profit—or, at least, make enough profit.

Now, Gibbs' scenario, requiring as it does near omniscience, is indeed a fantasy. However, one does not need to know *everything* for such mindfulness to have an effect. A weekend's reading on the realities of global production would provide quite enough knowledge. And bearing such matters in mind in our acts of consumption would, I am sure, affect our actions and practices, as Gibbs suggests.

We may, of course, choose to ignore all these interconnections, consoling ourselves that we are not *deliberately* doing anything which has these damaging knock-on effects. But as Gibbs later says:[23]

> even if we don't *do* anything, if we live on autopilot, we are still reinforcing a specific set of values, but they might not be the ones that we want to reinforce.

The consequences of your actions are those very consequences, whether you choose to pay attention to them or not.

And—to come back to the main point—being mindful of one's locus in such chains of events is a good practice for changing one's actions for the better. Gibbs, again, puts it this way:[24]

> as we gain an understanding of our interdependence with others, rather than continuing on autopilot, we act with intention to remove suffering. It may be useful here to borrow from the Four Stages of Competency model developed by psychologists in the 1970s. According to this model, we move from 'unconsciously incompetent' to 'consciously incompetent' to 'consciously competent' and, finally, to 'unconsciously competent'. In terms of compassion, this may at first take practice—as we work with 'conscious competence'—but eventually we become 'unconsciously competent', at which point, compassion is expressed instinctually rather than as a conscious act.

23. Gibbs (2017), p. 215.
24. Gibbs (2017), p. 52.

Appropriate practices can make our moral dispositions spontaneous, just as much as a musician's or a martial artist's practices can make their bodily dispositions spontaneous. (Recall the discussion of spontaneity in 2.6.)

12.7   Moral Phenomenology

Let us now turn to the related subject of phenomenology. The word 'phenomenology' gets used in a number of rather different ways; but, essentially, phenomenology concerns the way the world appears to us. That, itself, is ambiguous. The sense of 'appear' here is not 'appears, as opposed to really is', as in 'the police appeared honest, but in reality were very corrupt'. The sense is about how reality shows itself, as in 'the measles became evident when the rash appeared'. And how the world shows itself to us is deeply connected with our understanding of it and of our actions in it—as well as vice versa.

Phenomenology in this sense is integral to Buddhist thought, as Garfield notes:[25]

> Phenomenology is central to Buddhist thought, because, in the end, Buddhism is about the transformation of the way we experience the world. ... The whole point of ... [the Buddhist analysis of phenomenology] is to conclude with an account of how ... [cognitive and intentional structures] can be transformed so as to enable us to experience the world without engendering suffering.

The way the world appears to us depends heavily on our understanding of it, and the categories which we deploy to express this understanding. Thus, one might say, 'Halley's Comet appears on Earth every 75 years'. This clearly depends on an understanding of celestial phenomena and time. Or one might say, 'The world appears to be heading for an ecological catastrophe'. This depends on an understanding of the concept of ecology and the nature of the connectedness of Earth's biosystems which informs this.

Buddhist phenomenology is informed by the categories of Buddhist thought, such as attachment and compassion—and, crucially, the interconnectedness of things: people to each other, people to the environment, the environment to people, and the elements of the environment to each other. Someone who sees the world in these terms will experience it in ways different from those in which it is experienced by someone without those concepts—or someone with those concepts, though they have never taken them to heart. For example, through capitalist categories, an interaction with someone else may appear one of competition and confrontation; whilst through Buddhist

---

25. Garfield (2015), p. 179. As should become clear, what follows is heavily indebted to ch. 9 of this.

categories, it may appear one of cooperation and mutual benefit. Garfield describes appearances through Buddhist categories as follows:[26]

> The bodhisattva path is motivated in part by the realization that not to experience the suffering of others as one's own, and not to take the welfare of others as one's own, is to suffer even more deeply from profound existential alienation born of a failure to appreciate one's own situation as a member of an inter-dependent community. Our joys are social joys; our sorrows are social sorrows; our identity is social identity; the bounds of our society are indefinite. We either suffer and rejoice together in recognition of our bonds to one another, or we languish in self-imposed solitary confinement, afflicted both by the cell we construct, and by the ignorance that motivates its construction.

12.8   Perception

As is clear from some of the previous examples, the appearances involved in phenomenology need not be visual appearance.[27] But they often are. Such phenomenology is to do with the way one literally sees the world.

The world does not appear to us visually simply as a melange of colours and shapes.[28] We *interpret* the world we see. Thus, seeing is always *seeing as*.[29] We see the object as a chair, or a weapon, or a work of art. We see the object as a tree, or an elm, or a resource to be cut down and sold for profit. And of course, as these examples make clear, these perceptions are heavily conceptually loaded.

The conceptual dependence of vision is well known in the philosophy of science.[30] And the conceptually loaded perception may well depend on the scientific training that the perceiver has undergone. Thus, if most of us look at an X-ray, we see a confusing array of black and white patches; but a radiologist may see a liver with a tumor in it. Or when I look at a forest, I just see a bunch of trees (I know very little about trees); but a trained biologist may see the different species, the disease on some of them, and so on.

The visual phenomenology of someone who is trained in Buddhist understandings and practices may well be very different from that of someone who has not undertaken those practices. Thus, one person may see a dirty old

---

26. Garfield (2015), p. 296. He is not referring specifically to the Marxist notion of alienation, but this should not be forgotten either.
27. Or appearances pertaining to other sensory modalities. I will talk of vision in what follows, but the same considerations apply to the others as well.
28. Well, perhaps one can be trained to see it in this way, but this is not easy to do; neither is it our normal visual engagement with the world.
29. As Wittgenstein discusses in much of Part 2 of his *Philosophical Investigations*.
30. There, it is usually called the *theory-dependence* of observation, because scientific concepts are usually embedded in theories. See, e.g., Hanson (1958), Kuhn (1962), Chalmers (2013), ch. 2.

homeless person on the street; whilst another sees someone who is suffering, perhaps from a mental illness, and who could use help. Or one person may see an object in a junk shop as an opportunity to purchase it and sell it at a profit; whilst another may see it as a beautiful piece of sculpture; and so on. So, Garfield again:[31]

> When we engage perceptually, we categorize. We see others as colleagues, adversaries, friends, family members, or strangers, superiors or subordinates, white, black, male, female, and so forth. And of course, often these categories are far from morally neutral, and their moral valence may vary considerably with context. But perception is impossible without ascertainment of this kind. And once again, this ascertainment process is one that while present in any moment as a kind of perceptual reflex, is also malleable. We develop skills of ascertainment constantly in daily life, as when we learn to recognize kinds of flowers, genres of art, or the work of particular composers. But we can also hone our skills in moral ascertainment. Indeed, we used to have a term for this—*consciousness raising*.

And such perception is indeed integral to the way we see the world *morally*. Thus, one person may see the homeless person as lazy and morally despicable; whereas another may see an unfortunate person whom society has thrown on the scrapheap. Or, at the border, one person may see a bunch of refugees as a menace and a threat to the integrity of their country; whereas another may see people who are trying to escape violence and oppression in their own country, and who are doing their best to make a better life for their children. Garfield, one more time:[32]

> Each of our perceptual encounters, whether with other people or with the animate or inanimate objects around us, involves hedonic or affective tone. We may find ourselves averse to people who don't look like us, or attracted to objects that lend us status, for instance. And every morally charged interaction begins with a perceptual encounter. The affective sets are neither morally neutral nor fixed. Changing the affective dimensions of our perceptual experience is both possible, and can lead us to be better (or worse) people, can lead us to experience and to create more or less suffering. This is part of the work of ethical development.

In other words, we literally see the world in moral terms, the terms are provided by our moral understanding and practices, and can be changed by these.[33]

31. Garfield (2015), p. 288.
32. Garfield (2015), p. 287.
33. On the connection between affect and perception, see also Wright (2017), chs. 7, 11.

And of course, how a person sees the world affects how they act. Someone who sees another person as a physical threat is likely to avoid them or attack them. Someone who sees another person as having money they can be swindled out of is likely to exploit them. Someone who sees a suffering person they can help is likely to help them.

12.9   Being in the World and Interbeing

We are no mere passive spectators of the world in which we live. We are, and cannot but be, actively engaged with it. As Heidegger puts it in *Being and Time*, we are *thrown* into the world. We thus have no option but to act, interact, and operate, with the world and others in it. Again as Heidegger puts it, we have a certain *being in the world*. Moreover, our phenomenology, the way we see and understand the world, informs the way we are in it. Phenomenology is at the basis of our being in the world.[34]

The phenomenology informed by the understanding provided by Buddhist philosophy, and its practices such as those of mindfulness and patience, deliver a distinctive way of being in the world—though this may certainly be a work in progress. The world appears as a totality of interconnected parts, many of which are sentient, and who can therefore suffer. One sees the need for compassion. And one sees that such compassion aids the well-being of others and of oneself. Following Thich Nhat Hanh, one may call this form of being in the world *inter-being*. As he puts matters, commenting on mindfulness:[35]

> Studying and practicing the mindfulness trainings can help us to understand the true nature of interbeing—we cannot just be ourselves alone; we can only inter-be with everyone and everything else. To practice these trainings is to become aware of what is going on in our bodies, our minds, and the world. With awareness, we can live our lives happily, fully present in each moment we are alive, intelligently seeking solutions to the problems we face, and working for peace in large and small ways.

In other words, the full import of *pratītyasamutpāda* and *karuṇā*, both personal and social, are realised.

12.10   Conclusion

In this chapter, we have seen how changing to a more humane and rational society goes hand in hand with changing the kind of people we are. Ideas

---

34. For Heidegger's discussion of the matter, see Wheeler (2011), §2.2.
35. Edelglass (2009), p. 427.

from Buddhist moral psychology provide the way. Of course, following the practices involved may not be easy. The sixth of the octet of the Eightfold Noble Path is, after all, Right Effort. And one might well wonder why one would undertake these practices. One has to be persuaded of the philosophical views which inform them. In other words, one has to have taken on the first of the octet as well: Right View. Conversely, of course, understanding the world aright can motivate one to act. The elements of the Eightfold Path interact and mutually condition each other, as do all the other parts of the world—and this book.

12.11   Appendix: *Karatedō*—An Illustration

The topic of this chapter is that of practices for changing oneself—and changing oneself for the better. I have discussed several such. There are many more that people may find useful; and indeed, different things may work for different people. Some people may find certain forms of meditation, or yoga, a martial art, calligraphy, or even cooking in certain ways, have this effect. One can but try them, and monitor their effect. In this appendix I want to discuss one that has been significant for me, personally: a training in *karatedō*.[36] The discussion will, in fact, serve to further illustrate many of the points in this chapter, and, indeed, in the book.[37]

12.11.1   Karatedō *and Buddhism*

Since most readers of the book will have nothing but a very superficial knowledge of *karatedō*, let me begin with a little history of the subject and its connection with Buddhism.

Karatedō developed in Okinawa from a fusion of an old Okinawan martial art, *te* (hand), and Chinese *wushu* (martial) techniques. Indeed, 'karate' originally meant 'China-hand', until its meaning was changed to 'empty-hand' in the 20th century, under the influence of Japanese nationalism.[38] Though it is hard to tie down exactly, there is, in fact, an intimate connection between *karatedō* and the other Japanese martial arts, on the one hand, and Buddhism, especially Zen Buddhism, on the other.

Legend has it that the first patriarch of Zen Buddhism was Bodhidharma, an Indian missionary who took up residence at the Shaolin Temple. Legend has it

---

36. A few autobiographical details may be relevant. I practiced (learned and taught) *karatedō* for about 25 years. I am a fourth dan in *Shitoryu*, and a third dan in *Shobukai*. I have trained in a number of different countries, including extended periods in Japan. Before I left Australia, I was a National Referee and Kata Judge.
37. In what follows, I draw on Priest (2013) and Garfield and Priest (2020).
38. Because there is no written docummantation before the 20th century, objective and reliable histories of *karatedō* are hard to find. Bishop (1999) is one of the most authoritative I know.

that the same Bodhidharma was the founder of the Shaolin *wushu*. Whatever the history, the Shaolin Temple is famous for producing Chan (Zen) Buddhist monks who are also *wushu* practitioners. The connection goes far beyond this, though. Many samurai, such as the legendary Musashi Miamoto (who also practiced Zen calligraphy), were Buddhists, and saw their Buddhism and their martial practice as deeply connected.[39] The Zen Buddhist monk Takuan Sōhō is well known for having written letters to martial practitioners giving them Zen advice.[40] Indeed, in traditional *dōjō*, training sessions begin and end with short *zazen* (kneeling meditation) sessions. The Buddhist connection is also evident in popular martial arts books,[41] and Buddhist ideas are evident in the thought of many great karate masters.[42]

Given this connection, it is hardly surprising that there are illuminating connections between Buddhist theory/practice and training in *karatedō*.

12.11.2   *Training in* Karatedō

So let us turn to this training. Whatever else it is, *karatedō* is a practice of self-defence. Sometimes the best form (and even the only form) of self-defence is attack. So *karatedō* skills teach one to neutralise attacks using techniques, some of which can cause the attacker serious injury, and perhaps even death.

Two standard parts of training are *kata* and *kumite*.[43] *Kata* are series of movements. These are something like a dictionary of techniques. They need to be mastered, and their applications understood. *Kata* vary from the very simple to the very complex. They are repeated over and over again until they can be done without thought, though with acute psychological focus. That is, one does not have to think about what to do next. It just happens.

Moreover, a *kata* done well is performed with complete focus and concentration. When one performs a move of the *kata*, that and only that is where one's being is. In other words, there is deep, one-pointed concentration. One might think of *kata* performance as a kind of moving meditation. As I noted (2.2.3.3), in Buddhist traditions, meditation does not have to be done kneeling, or sitting on a cushion.

Kumite is sparring. Again, this can be of many kinds, from simple pre-arranged exercises, to free sparring, where both people can attack or defend in any way they like (though always with control). For many people, this is the hardest

---

39. See King (1993). On Musashi specifically, see the last chapter of his *Book of Five Rings* (Cleary (1993)), 'The Book of Emptiness'.
40. See Cleary (2005).
41. Such as Herrigel (1981) and Hyams (1982).
42. See, e.g., Funakoshi (2003).
43. Increasingly, karate is coming to be seen as a sport, where one's aim is simply to win a prize by scoring points in a certain way. However, competition was not a part of traditional *karatedō*, but started only around the middle of the 20th century. With the emphasis on sports training, a number of the more traditional aspects of *karatedō* are, in fact, being lost.

part of the training. Being attacked by someone (often someone who is better than you) naturally brings out fear, and aggression naturally comes in its wake. One must learn to conquer these—if only because fear and aggression make one much less efficient in performing: they slow down one's reactions, and make one's techniques wild and inefficient.

What one must learn to do is to empty the mind of all thoughts and emotions, and react purely spontaneously (a spontaneity based, of course, on routines hard-wired in by constant repetition). This is what Buddhists call *mushin* (no mind) and Daoists call *wuwei* (no—premeditated—action). One thing that can go in the process is any sense of self. Perhaps for evolutionary reasons, in a situation where one has to fight, one's sense of self is particularly strong. If it can be over-come in this particularly stressful situation, it is much easier to overcome it in more mundane situations.

The aim of both *kata* and *kumite* is to develop the skill of self-defence which, if it is deployed, is completely spontaneous and natural (in the sense of being unforced). One does not think about what to do, one just reacts appropriately to the situation.

Another thing that a good *karatedō* training develops is awareness. In the first instance, this is an awareness of one's opponent. One learns to read them instinctively. But the awareness carries over to one's environment quite gener-ally. One learns how not to put oneself (or others) in harm's way. So, for example, one may see when an interaction with someone (perhaps in a pub) could turn nasty, and take action to defuse the situation. Or when walking, one might perceive possible trouble ahead (perhaps a group of people who could mean no good), and just walk another way. And if trouble does loom, one becomes mindful of exit opportunities, things that might serve as a weapon of self-defence, and so on. In short, one's training affects how one per-ceives one's environment.

From the discussion so far, it might seem that *karatedō* is simply about the use and avoidance of violence; but when it is taught with a certain (and traditional) spirit it can be much more than this.[44] *Karatedō* is a *dō*, that is, a way. All the Japanese *dō*—*iaidō* (swordsmanship), *shodō* (calligraphy), *chadō* (tea service)—can be seen as practices which inform and develop a way of being in the world. Most of the great *karatedō* masters saw their practices in this way. Not that these things are usually taught explicitly in the *dōjō*. It is the practice itself which develops the appropriate virtues. A good training in *karatedō* devel-ops, amongst other things, perseverance, self-discipline, mindfulness, patience.

Thus, much effort and self-discipline are required in training. For example, these things are necessary in exercises that build up strength and stamina.

---

44. I note, however, that karate is not always taught in such a way. Some martial arts clubs are quite prepared, for example, to turn out bouncers who are only too happy to apply their martial skills.

Training routines also have to be repeated many times until they become reflexive. And one learns the self-discipline of patience. For many things (such as the results of grading exams) one just has to wait. This discipline, in turn, generates a certain kind of non-attachment. In the *dōjō*, things will often happen that you don't like: you get hit in sparring, you make a mistake in a *kata* when everyone is watching, you fail a grading exam. You have to learn to shrug this off, put it behind you—to just carry on and focus on whatever comes next. If not, you will not do this next thing as well as you could.

One also learns ethical virtues, such as a respect for others, a respect for oneself, an awareness of what one owes to others, and of what one can give to others. Though these things are rarely discussed in a *dōjō*, a good training embeds in people crucial ethical values. Thus, for example, one bows with respect on entering and leaving a *dōjō*, at the beginning and the end of a *kata* performance, and of training with a partner. One comes to have respect for one's teacher and the senior students from whom one learns, and for those who one teaches.[45]

We might also add to the list of virtues non-violence. This may seem a rather odd thing, given that *karatedō* is undoubtedly a training in violence. However, a good *karatedō* training should engender a peaceful attitude.[46] Its techniques are only ever to be used for defensive purposes, and then only as a last resort. One should use no more violence than necessary; and it is better to use none at all, simply by avoiding situations where it might be required. Thus, there is a traditional saying: *karate ni sente nashi* (in karate there is no first strike).[47]

I might add that though one learns all these things in the *dōjō*, one does not leave them behind when one leaves the *dōjō*. One takes them out into the world beyond.

12.11.3 The Import of This

Let us now turn to how these things illustrate various matters of the book. First, and perhaps most obviously, the topic reinforces what I have said about violence. Buddhism is not opposed to violence, but it should be used only when absolutely necessary. (See 10.3.1.2.)

Next, the material in the last sub-section helps to underline many of the points in this chapter:

• That one trains oneself into one's virtues by constant repetition of the practice.

45. On the importance of respect in the martial arts, see Young (2009).
46. And can well do so. See, e.g., Layton (1988), (1990), Nosanchuck (1981), Nosanchuck and MacNeil (1989), Rothpearl (1980).
47. See, e.g., Funakoshi (2003).

- That when one has done so, the virtues become reflexive and so spontaneous, and therefore much more effective.
- That an appropriate training may make one more aware of one's actions, other people, and the world in which one lives. That is, it makes one more mindful.
- That it may change the way one perceives the world and those in it. That is, it changes one's phenomenology.
- That it may change, also, one's ethical attitudes to oneself and other people.

Third, it underlines the importance of a number of matters discussed in other parts of the book, such as:

- The importance of effort and self-discipline. (See 2.2.3.1, 2.2.4.)
- The efficacy and effect of concentration. (See 2.2.3.3.)
- The importance of patience. (See 2.3.3, 7.5.)
- The importance and efficacy of non-attachment. (See 2.2.4, 10.2.2.)

Finally, a word on education. A training in *karatedō* is obviously an education of some sort. Clearly, it is quite different from the sort of education discussed in 11.9 and 11.10. An appropriate learning of techniques (*knowing how*) tends to be very different from an appropriate learning of cognitive attitudes (*knowing that*). One does not discuss with a teacher of *karatedō*, or of the violin, or of mathematics, the best way to go about things—at least until one is a very advanced student. One assumes that the teacher knows best, and just does (or attempts to do) what they say. This requires one to trust the teacher; but with good teachers the trust pays off because one's techniques improve.

Of course, the teacher must, in return, merit the trust: they must have the interests of the student at heart, rather as a good parent does for their child. And it must be said that, unfortunately, not all teachers of *karatedō*—or the violin, or mathematics—are good teachers. And I do not just mean that they are not good at developing the right technical skills; I mean that they do not live up to what is required of them morally. The student must, then, monitor, not just how their techniques are improving, but what other, less tangible, things they are learning from the teacher: what kind of person the teacher is making them. If this is not good, they need to go and find a better teacher.

13
MATTERS ARISING

13.1 Introduction

The main aim of the book is now complete. We have looked at the need to replace the current capitalist socio-economic system with something more rational and humane, what that replacement might be like, and how one might go about getting there. Of course, there is much more to be said about all of these matters. If the present book achieves anything, it will only be to start a discussion, not to finish it.

In the the previous chapters I have touched on a number of other matters. Each of these deserve a book in its own right, but this is not it. What I have said is not without implications for these matters, however, and I should at least point some of these things out. That is the function of this chapter. Think of this chapter, if you wish, as noting a few corollaries of what has gone before. In particular, I will discuss some points concerning matters of race and gender, religion, war and nationalism, the environment, the treatment of animals, and people who are just nasty.

An appendix deals with the 2020 Covid-19 pandemic and its relationship to matters in this book.

13.2 Race and Gender

Let us start with race and gender. Capitalism causes economic oppression. But oppression is also caused by other power structures—notably, those of these.

As I argued in 3.6, such power structures are, in principle, independent of economic power structure, and one would not expect them to disappear

DOI: 10.4324/9781003195146-15

simply because economic oppression disappeared. As noted by Arruzza in the case of gender oppression:[1]

> To have thought that the class struggle alone could resolve this question [GP: of the power structure within the traditional family], magically dissolving family ties and radically changing its character without an adequate analysis of the problem, without challenging sexual roles and without a specific politicization of women is in the best case to be blindly optimistic, and in the worst case to show utter bad faith.

Exactly the same point could be made about race.

As should hardly need saying by this point in the book, getting rid of such forms of oppression is important—and for exactly the same reason that getting rid of economic oppression is: they are cause of much *duḥkha*. However, the concern of this book has been socio-economic oppression. I fixed on this for two reasons. First, we have at least some understanding of what a modern society without discrimination by race and gender would be like. It is a society where these factors play no role whatever in education, opportunity, employment (in and out of the home), and so on. We have no real understanding of what a society without economic oppression would be like. Moreover, as I have already remarked, significant progress has been made—at least in some countries, and some sections of the populations in those countries—in dismantling gender oppression; and to a certain extent, the same is true of race. (This is *not* to say that there is not a great deal more to be done, even in these relatively more enlightened parts of the globe.) By contrast, virtually nothing has been done to dismantle economic oppression. Indeed, with the growth of capital, such oppression increases.

Of course, working to get rid of economic oppression does not mean *not* working to get rid of the others as well. These power structures interact. And just because of this interaction, attacking specifically economic oppression will at least weaken some of the elements of the other two. Thus, capitalism wishes to minimise wages. If there are already disempowered sections of the society, be they women or a racial group—capitalism will exploit this fact to keep down their income (or in the case of domestic labour, to ensure none at all).[2] Nor will a capitalist structure be inclined to put money into improving the lot of such groups, with better education, health care, and so on—unless it is needed to make a profit. A society which is not driven by profit, but where all have an equal say in the distribution of resources, will not have these features. Conversely, attacking the other forms of oppression may at least weaken economic oppression. For example, getting rid of racism may strengthen the solidarity between workers and other groups fighting capitalism,

1. Arruzza (2013), p. 89.
2. For aspects of how capitalism has, and continues to, exploit race, see Fraser (2019).

making it harder for them to be exploited. Similarly, removing the repression of women—say in the global South—could unleash a powerful voice of socio-economic criticism. Thoughtful progressive action requires one to be aware of, and act on, these things. An understanding of this kind of interdependence would certainly benefit from careful consideration in the light of matters in this book.[3]

Next, at the basis of all systems of oppression, there is a question of power. And some of the subjective factors behind the wielding of power in such systems work quite generally. For a start, there is ignorance by those in power of the effects of their actions. One does not see oppression when one is a member of a dominant group; one comes to understand this only from below. With respect to economic power Freire puts it as follows:[4]

> The oppressors do not perceive their monopoly of *having more* as a privilege which dehumanizes others and themselves. ... For them, *having more* is an inalienable right, a right they acquire with their own "effort," with their "courage to take risks". If others do not have more, it is because they are incompetent or lazy, and worst of all is their unjustifiable ingratitude towards the "generous gestures" of the dominant class.

The importance of education in making these things clear to those on the top-side of any top-down power structure is crucial—another aspect of the general importance of education, which I stressed in 11.10.

There is also the ego-addictive nature of power itself, which I discussed in 8.3. Power, be it economic, gender, or racial, is something that people—at least unenlightened people—want, want to retain, and want to maximise, in the (forlorn) hope it will make them happier. In Chapter 12 I discussed ways to eliminate, or at least diminish, this ego drive. These are applicable to power structures quite generally.

A number of the points made in the book about dismantling economic power therefore apply to dismantling power in race and gender as well.

13.3   Religion

It is clear that oppression can occur on the basis of religion as well. One hardly needs a very detailed knowledge of the world (both historical or contemporary) to know that the power structures of one religion have often oppressed members of a different religion: Christians and Muslims, Muslims and Christians, Christians and Jews, Jews and Muslims, Hindus and Muslims, Muslims and Hindus, and so on. The same is true of groups within one religion:

---

3. For some thoughts on such interdependence, see Yates (2019).
4. Freire (1970), p. 33.

Catholics and Protestants, Protestants and Catholics, Sunni and Shia, Shia and Sunni, and so on.

There is no particular reason why one religious group has to oppress another in this way. Most world religions can exist and have existed in multi-cultural and relatively tolerant communities—Spain and India, at some times in their histories; and currently New Zealand is doing a pretty good job, given the substantial multi-cultural response to the 2019 Christchurch mosque shootings. Matters go awry when religion gets mixed up with matters of power.

The power in question may be religious power itself, such as when one religious group wishes to force another group to subscribe to its own view.[5] Or it may be power of a non-religious kind, as when, in 20th-century Northern Ireland, the different sides of a political dispute became lined up with different religious groups.[6] Quite generally, one should note the intersectionality between political/capital power and religious power. Thus, Sivaraksa notes correctly:[7]

> Over the past two centuries, in all the world's religions … [most] churches support the political *status quo*, no matter how oppressive the regimes may be. Their religious hierarchies have become entrenched and their vision static. Since the rise of capitalism, all the world's great faiths have catered to the rich, even if their leaders pay lip service to the poor.

It is hard to disagree.

All this brings us back to the matter of power itself; and what I said about this in the last section is equally applicable here.

I note that there is no reason why an SOC should not have a generally agreed religion if it so wishes. Nor is there any reason why all the SOCs in an SSOC should have the same religion, or any at all. The important thing is tolerance. Each group should show the other groups the same tolerance they would wish themselves to be shown. Intolerance is hardly an act of compassion; and compassion is a virtue endorsed by all the major world religions.

Of course, nearly all religions or sub-religions have their own top-down power structures, with their typical pernicious effects. In particular, they are often wielded to stop people thinking for themselves. Such is incompatible with the spirit of genuine education. Perhaps those in power might try to justify this with an appeal to a misguided paternalism; but clamping down on people's freedom of thought is not in their best interests—and in any case, such repression is liable to be counterproductive in the long term.

---

5. This hardly needs a reference.
6. See, e.g., Mitchell (2013).
7. Sivaraksa (1992), p. 59. Nor is Buddhism to be exempted from this. See Victoria (2006).

There has always been and may always be hypocrisy. To note just one small example: two recent prime ministers of Australia, Tony Abbott and Scott Morrison, are self-ascribed devout Christians. Yet, quite contrary to the Christian imperative of compassion, they have allowed many asylum seekers to languish in offshore concentration camps, when they could have allowed these people to enter Australia and be processed in a civilised fashion for much less money.[8] Moreover, they have deliberately tried to hide what goes on in the camps from public scrutiny, and fought to stymie attempts at humanitarian aid for those in the camps. Their actions have been guided, not by compassion, but by political expediency, and in particular the retention of power. Hypocrisy of this kind should be resolutely criticised. Another lesson in taking on the abuse of top-down power.[9]

Again, let me stress the importance of education here. The more people know about the cultures and religions of other parts of the world, the more they will realise that they have a *choice* about what to believe. Most people who have a religious belief have it simply because they were brought up in a community which held that belief. If the pope had been born in Saudi Arabia, he would have been a Muslim; and if Osama bin Laden had been born in Italy, he would have been a Catholic. You hardly need to be a deep thinker to see that your religious beliefs should not be hostage to the random fact of where you were born. Whatever one's religious beliefs (including none), these should be held because of open minded consideration of all possibilities. Blind faith is not a virtue. It is simply gullibility.

Let me also say that I do not exempt Buddhism from these considerations. Indeed, there are a number of religious Buddhists who would agree with me. Thich Nhat Hanh says:[10]

> *Aware of the suffering created by fanaticism and intolerance*, we are determined not to be idolatrous about or bound to any doctrine, theory, or ideology, even Buddhist ones. Buddhist teachings are guiding means to help us learn to look deeply and to develop our understanding and compassion. They are not doctrines to fight, kill, or die for.

8. See, for example, Cave (2019) and Refugee Council of Australia (2020). Incidentally, the term 'concentration camp' is now most often associated with the Nazi extermination camps, but the *Cambridge Dictionary* defines the term as 'a place where large numbers of people are kept as prisoners in extremely bad conditions, especially for political reasons' (https://dictionary.cambridge.org/us/dictionary/english/concentration-camp). Concentration camps were, incidentally, invented by the British in the Boer War.

9. Nor is hyprocrisy limited to the famous and powerful. There are plenty of Evangelical Christians in the US who support capital punishment, oppose asylum seekers, and clearly are not acting out of compassion.

10. Edelglass (2009), pp. 421 f.

And Sivaraksa:[11]

> It is not a Buddhist approach to say that if everyone practiced Buddhism, the world would be a better place. Wars and oppression begin from this kind of thinking.

If people subscribe to Buddhist views, this should be because these stand up to inspection, not because of blind faith.[12]

And let me make this absolutely plain again: I have endorsed many aspects of Buddhist philosophy in this book. This is not an endorsement of Buddhist religion (such as its soteriology, rites, cosmologies, power structures, and so on). That is a different matter entirely. I am most certainly not arguing that we should all be religious Buddhists.

13.4 War and Nationalism

Whilst on the matter of things which cause suffering, let us turn to the obvious subject of war. As I observed in 6.3, capitalism has been behind many wars in the capitalist epoch. With the demise of capitalism, one would then see the disappearance of one of the main drivers of contemporary war, and so of many wars themselves.

Of course, there were wars long before there was capitalism. So many other factors produce wars, and one would not expect the demise of capitalism to itself stop all wars. That would be too much to hope for.

One of the other main drivers of war is nationalism (or tribalism of some other form). In the end, the only way to get rid of nationalism is to get rid of nations. Nations are not built into SSOCs. We just have lots of different communities cooperating with one another. Any SSOC may be cooperating with many different other SSOCs about different issues. And some of this cooperation may well cut across geographical boundaries. Perhaps there might be a highest-level global coordinating committee. Perhaps not. There might need to be one to coordinate activity on ecological sustainability; but there is no obvious reason why the same committee should have to coordinate activity on other matters, for example. At any rate, moving towards a world with the structure of an SSOC may eliminate nations, and so nationalism.

---

11. Sivaraksa (1992), p. 68.
12. Indeed, as the Buddha himself says in the *Kālāma Sūtra*: 'Don't go by reports, by legends, by traditions, by scripture, by logical conjecture, by inference, by analogies, by agreement through pondering views, by probability, or by the thought, "This contemplative is our teacher". When you know for yourselves that, "These qualities are unskillful; these qualities are blameworthy; these qualities are criticized by the wise; these qualities, when adopted and carried out, lead to harm and to suffering"—then you should abandon them'. https://www.accesstoinsight.org/tipitaka/an/an03/an03.065.than.html

Indeed, moving to something like a global SSOC requires getting rid of nation states. The simple reason is that a nation state is, almost by definition, a top-down power structure. Such is incompatible with an SSOC. Of course there could still be parts of it with different cultural, ethnic, or religious identities. As I have said already, an SSOC does not have to be a one-size-fits-all matter. But such things do not have to be states, any more than, in Britain, Cornwall and County Durham are nation states, though they have different cultural identities, and even linguistic dialects. And all may benefit from a knowledge of the fact that the world contains many different cultures and traditions. For a start, a knowledge of these helps to put one's own culture and tradition in perspective, and gives one a wider frame of reference for thoughtful decisions.

One needs to bear in mind, also, that any structure of SSOCs that is not global is liable to be under stress. While some nation states remain, one might well expect them to feel threatened by political entities that are not of this nature, and so move against them.

Another main driver of war, historically, has been religion—well, perhaps more accurately, religion has been appealed to in an attempt to justify a war undertaken for some other purpose involving power. Indeed, ultimately, what war is about is the desire for power, whether this manifests itself as religious power, economic power, national power, or power of some other kind. Thus, in *Roots of War*, Winter says:[13]

> Whatever the particular circumstances, issues, or adversaries—in theory or history—talk of war is talk of power.

In the end, then, the best way to remove war is to change the kind of people we are, so that we are not driven by the desire for power and other forms of *tṛṣna*—which takes us back to the previous chapter.

Neither is this utopian. People—at least in the "civilised" world—are now generally revolted by, for example, the thought of public executions or torture, though these were once commonplace. Or again, people in the capitalist world are now more prone to individualistic consumerism than they used to be. In Buddhist terms, this is simply *pratītyasamutpāda*: these things are brought about by certain causes, and can be changed by the appropriate causes.

13.5   The Environment

Let us move on to the subject of the environment.

13. Winter (2018), p. 93. See ch. 3, 'Power', for a discussion of a number of aspects of the relationship between war and power.

Some Buddhist writers have taken interdependence to entail an environmental ethics, where one has a duty to maintain the environment and its species.[14] It does not. As I have observed (2.4), *pratītyasamutpāda* is a purely descriptive claim. Moral consequences require (extra) moral premises; in particular, in our case, that one should act to mitigate suffering.

Nothing follows from these things about maintaining the environment. Indeed, it follows that we *should* change the environment. Humans have been changing the environment since there have been humans—with the development of farming practices, urbanisation, and so on. The question is only how to change it for the better. Thus, we should eliminate, as far as possible, those species which occasion suffering, such as malaria-carrying mosquitos, human parasites, and bacteria and viruses which cause human suffering. Such things are not sentient, and so causing them suffering is not an issue.

This does not mean that we can do anything we like to the environment. Because of *pratītyasamutpāda*, any changes we make to the environment will have knock-on effects, and we need to be very clear about what these are likely to be. As I discussed in 3.9, the changes that human action is currently bringing about to the environment are ones which will cause much suffering: the disruption of arable land, the fishing-out of the seas, and so consequent food shortages; rising sea levels and forced mass forced migration; and so on. This kind of environmental change needs to be brought under control before the whole house of cards comes tumbling down.

Buddhist ethics is about the elimination of *duḥkha*, and that is not just the *duḥkha* of current sentient beings. It includes ones that do not yet exist, but will: future generations. (We cannot do much about the *duḥkha* of past generations.) We should show compassion for those to whom we bequeath the environment.

13.6 The Treatment of Non-human Animals

And while we are talking about sentient beings, one should remember that there are creatures other than humans that suffer. How far down the evolutionary scale sentience goes is unclear, but, certainly, animals of many non-human species feel pain. Destroying their environment will doubtless cause them to do so, so we need to take care to preserve their environments too. Of course, animals make other animals suffer. There must be pain when a zebra is torn apart by a pack of lionesses. That, one can do little about. However, it does not follow that because some animals do this to each other, we should also do it to them. We are humans, and we have control over what we do, in a way that (other) animals do not.

14. See Keown (2005), ch. 3.

And so we come to the subject of what we eat.[15] The current farming practices are clearly inhumane—to put it mildly.[16] Much farming is driven by large agro-businesses, whose aim is solely to make a profit. If increasing profit means increasing the suffering of animals, this just goes along for the ride. Clearly, these practices should be eliminated.

One should also bear in mind that the farming of mammals causes a major part of the greenhouse gasses that we are currently producing.[17] Another reason to desist in the practice. Add to this the fact that meat production is a highly inefficient and wasteful form of protein production. It takes something like 7 kg of human-usable vegetable protein to produce 1 kg of human-usable animal protein.[18] The production of animal protein is very much driven by the affluent consumer-oriented part of the world. Our resources of food production are already quite adequate to provide a good diet for everyone in the world. (Or currently in the world. With the growing world population, it is unclear how long this will continue to be the case. This is just one of the major reasons to stop the growth of the world population.) Our farming practices should therefore be taken out of the hands of profit-making organisations, and adjusted to ones which can produce enough for everyone in a sustainable fashion. None of this mandates a strict vegetarianism, but it does mandate a radical restructuring of our diet and how it is produced. Vegetarianism is certainly a sensible part of the picture.[19]

13.7   Negative Emotions

The causes of suffering I have discussed in the previous sections of this chapter are all institutional in some sense, in that they have to do with a structural feature of a society, be it racism, nationalism, or dietary practices. There are, of course, causes which are not structural, but purely personal. There are people, who, for particular individual reasons (not connected with motivations generated by structural factors), cause others to suffer. It would be utopian to suppose that one could ever eliminate such entirely. We are never going to create a world of saints—Buddhist or otherwise. However, the things I have already discussed do bear on this matter. Let me explain how.

Ask why it is that people make others suffer. Unless one is dealing with the kind of psychopath who is totally impervious to the suffering of others, the answer would seem to be that such action is typically motivated by hate, anger, jealously, revenge, insecurity, the lust for personal power, or similar

15. On which, see also Gibbs (2017), ch. 5.
16. See, e.g., Harrison (2013), Faruqi (2015), Nibert (2002), (2017).
17. Food and Agriculture Organization of the United Nations (2020).
18. See, e.g., Brown (2006), ch. 9.
19. See Peter Singer's classic *Animal Liberation* (2015). Though this is written from the ethical perspective of utilitarianism, there is much here with which a Buddhist ethics will agree.

negative emotions. Such emotions are inherently unpleasant, paradigm cases of *duḥkha*. And, if there is less of the cause, there will be less of the effect.

One way to see that what causes people to make others suffer is their own *duḥkha* is this. *Duḥkha* comprises various forms of suffering. One might call these, collectively, forms of dis-ease. Of course, there is a flip side to this. The word 'ease' does not exactly capture it. Much closer is *peace of mind*, or *upekṣa* as I discussed in 2.6. Peace of mind is mental equanimity, a tranquility that cannot be shattered by the brickbats thrown by life.

Now, it is indeed hard to see how or why someone who is in a peaceful state of mind should knowingly wish to cause another to suffer. The desire to inflict emotional or physical violence, that is, aggression, hardly seems to be compatible with inner peace. Indeed, as is well known, a prime cause of aggression is fear; and this is certainly not compatible with peace of mind. When the mind is at peace, there is an absence of fear, and so of one of the major drivers of the infliction of suffering.

The Dalai Lama sums up the whole matter as follows:[20]

> Another result of spiritual development, most useful in day-to-day life, is that it gives a calmness and presence of mind. Our lives are in a constant state of flux, bringing many difficulties. When faced with a calm and clear mind, problems can be successfully resolved. When, instead, we lose control of our minds, through hatred, selfishness, jealousy, and anger, we lose our sense of judgment. Our minds are blinded and at those wild moments anything can happen, including war.

Things go awry when *duḥkha* destroys calmness of mind.

That an agent causing others to suffer is caused by their own suffering is, incidentally, why it is appropriate to have compassion for those who make others suffer—as well as those who they make suffer, of course (and this most certainly does not mean that one should allow them to continue to make others suffer). Indeed, understanding the causes operative here, and how we ourselves could have been subject to those causes, can help engender more of a sense of compassion for those who make others suffer. Indeed, which of us has not hurt others because of these negative emotions sometimes? A simple act of exchanging self for other (see 12.4) is an excellent exercise here.[21]

13.8 Conclusion

The aim of this book has been to address one central issue: the problems and dangers that capitalism poses for the contemporary world, and how to move

---

20. Tenzin Gyatso (2006), p. 21.
21. See Thich Nhat Hanh's essay, 'Please Call Me by My True Names', Hanh (2019).

the world to a saner post-capitalist society. Of course, as I have noted, doing so will hardly solve all the world's problems; and I would not pretend otherwise. However, as I also noted, because of the way that capitalism aids and reinforces these other structures, removing it will at least *help* to eradicate some of these and their pernicious effects. We have also seen that there are lessons concerning education and power which are quite generally applicable to these matters. However, this is not the place to go into any of these issues further. Replacing capitalism is an important and tough enough problem for one book.

It remains only to draw together some of the central threads of the book, to which I will turn in its Epilogue.

13.9   Untimely Appendix: The Covid-19 Pandemic

Anyone who reads this book in the foreseeable future will have lived through the Covid-19 pandemic which brought much of the world to a halt in 2020. Though the matters of this book will still, I am sure, be highly relevant to the world when the pandemic has faded in memory, it will naturally occur to most to wonder how the two relate to each other. This appendix addresses the matter.[22]

13.9.1   *Preparedness*

It is clear that world governments were taken by surprise by the pandemic. Hospitals and medical resources have been stretched to their limit—indeed, well beyond their limit in a number of places. Many people have died, and many times more have lost their source of income and their livelihood. We will have an economic recession at least as deep as that of the Great Depression of 1929 and the 1930s. How long this will last is unclear.

True, there has not been a pandemic like the present one since the 1918/1920 flu pandemic. Yet medical bodies like the World Health Organization have often enough warned that a pandemic of this kind was on the cards. Governments were, nevertheless, not prepared for the situation and have been scrambling around to deal with it. Indeed, once it came to power in 2016, the Trump administration in the US systematically dismantled government and national organisations that were required to cope with the present situation, for reasons that were clearly ideological and focussed on short-term political interests.

22. The appendix was drafted when I was locked down just outside New York City in May 2020. Some of it—though not the socio-political material—is already a little dated. The pandemic and its consequences are still unfolding as I produce the final draft of the book, and will doubt-less continue to do so for some time; so this is likely to be true of anything I say. Hence I decided to leave what I had written. Think of it, if you will, as a sort of—somewhat US-centric—time capsule.

So the first lesson of the pandemic is that you do not wait till your house burns down to take precautions in case of a bush fire. A relatively small amount of money spent on medical and other measures could have saved not only many lives, but the large amount of money that the depression will cost the world.

It is now too late, of course, to do anything about that in the present case. But, one might hope, the world will be better prepared to deal with both the medical and economic effects of the next pandemic (whenever that may be): effective national health care systems, a reserve of medical equipment—or at least the ability and preparedness to produce this very fast; the ability to care for all those that are in dire economic straits; the cooperation necessary for effective international action.

One might also hope that a similar lesson will be learned concerning the looming climate disaster and its consequences. As we well now know, these will impact upon the conditions of life in every country; though of course, they will hit the poorer countries of the world, who have done least to cause the situation, hardest. (Not that the more affluent countries are immune to the problems there: these will ricochet back into those countries because of the destruction of primary resources on which the affluent countries depend, forced migration, and so on.) If you close your eyes till a major crash happens, you have left it too late.

13.9.2 Interdependence

Another lesson that the present situation hammers home is the thoroughly interconnected nature of the world.

Because of world commerce and travel, nations are tightly connected with other nations. An insidious virus is bound to move from country to country rapidly. Of course, international connections have always been present, but in the modern world they are much more evident because of the speed with which they propagate.

Within nations, it is hard to see how anyone who has lived through the pandemic cannot have become more aware of their interconnectedness with other people: those they walk past in the street, those who maintain the food chain, transport, and other 'essential services', those health workers who fight the disease—and of course, those in governmental power who make financial and other decisions that affect us all. Indeed, it is an irony of the present situation that, for the most part, those who are deemed 'essential workers', and so are required to put themselves at high risk, are the lowest paid and economically most insecure.

I note also that, in the US at least, the pandemic puts many people who fall into the category of essential workers in a particularly vulnerable situation. Often their relative poverty has caused pre-existing health conditions which make the virus more dangerous. Moreover, their lack of health insurance and income support has stopped many seeking timely medical help. Not only is this obviously bad for them, it has aided the spread of the infection. I note also that, especially in big cities like New York and Detroit, because of the long-term effects of racism, the proportion of people in this category has been disproportionately black and Hispanic.

Finally on this topic, the wealthy countries have been so concerned with themselves that they have done little for the poorer parts of the world, such as countries in Africa, where medical resources are often pitiful. (And that situation could have been very different had there been very modest and appropriately directed financial help from wealthier countries over the last few decades—say, the cost of a handful of nuclear weapons.) Yet, the pandemic will not only hit our human colleagues in these countries particularly hard, such neglect is shortsighted, even for self-interested reasons. As I have noted, problems from those countries bleed back into the wealthier countries. In the case at hand, because the pandemic is only starting to hit these countries now, it will be going full-blast there when it is starting to pass in richer countries. This is liable to produce a resurgence of the virus, possibly mutated, in the richer countries themselves. (The 1918/1920 flu pandemic killed even more people on its second time around.)

13.9.3   Capital, Politics, and the Pandemic

The next thing to consider is what the current situation tells us about the economic and political situation of the world in which we live.

First, capital is behaving as you would expect it to behave: putting itself before people. There are many large capitals that are using the present situation to reap large amounts of profit—indeed they are profiteering. These include manufacturers of medical equipment in short supply, and of drugs that may or may not aid treatment; companies searching for a vaccine which they can patent and then use to hold governments and health systems to ransom; IT companies like Google and Zoom, and online delivery companies like Amazon, to whose services we have all become hostage.

Of course, many companies are in deep financial trouble, especially those in travel, service, and entertainment industries. Where this is so, most companies in question are doing everything possible to shed their labour force, with little regard for the financial hardship of their employees—with all that this entails. Some businesses will collapse entirely. But even this is good news for financial corporations with deep pockets. They will buy up the collapsed companies at rock-bottom prices, claiming the losses as tax deductions. They will therefore accumulate valuable capital assets, and ordinary taxpayers will pay for these.

Some politicians, it must be said, have been genuinely concerned with the suffering of people. (In the US, Bernie Sanders and Alexandria Ocasio-Cortez come to mind.) But by and large, politicians have also been more concerned with capital than people. Many have been prepared to let the virus spread, in the (somewhat forlorn) hope that capital is not damaged, even though people die in the process. Of course, a number of governments have shelled out large amounts of money, and some of this has gone to those who have lost their livelihood; but governments know well the Keynsian lesson that a slump in demand deepens a recession, so the money is given for economic reasons, not humanitarian ones. Naturally, also, the governments have their eye on the next election. But the amount of money that has gone to ordinary workers is small compared with the vast amount that has gone to capital enterprises—often in the US to the large capital enterprises that have the deepest reserves, not to the small ones. The reason? These have the greatest political clout.

We have also seen right-wing governments (such as those of Trump, Bolsonaro, Orban, Modi, Erdogan, Putin, and others) taking advantage of the situation to push through their political agendas, such as increasing their own power, racist policies, the destruction of environmental regulations, and so on.

On a small, positive note, we have seen a rise in human solidarity: an increase in support for, and appreciation of, health workers; a genuine concern for those who cannot pay their rent; a feeling that "we are all in this together"—and some countries, such as Cuba, have been sending doctors and other medical help to nations where medical resources were severely stretched. On the other hand, we have also seen a rise in racist, nationalist, and libertarian (read: self-centred) tendencies amongst sections of the population, driven not only by right-wing politicians but by far-right activist groups, who can use the situation to manipulate people's emotions, such as fear and hatred.

13.9.4   How Matters Might Have Been Handled in an SSOC

The next question is whether things would have been better handled in an SSOC. The short answer is that there is every reason to believe so, since the effects of capital and top-down power, and the nationalist and racist strategies promoted by these, would not be operative.

The long answer is, of course, much more complicated. First, what would be required is a good public health-care system. In an SOC, a community might have its own health-care system; but more likely, a health-care system would have to be organised at a higher level of an SSOC, since individual communities are unlikely to have the resources necessary to support a complex modern system. Next, it would need the ability to deliver a short term economic redirection necessary for the production of essential resources, such as those of medicine and food. Third, it would require the ability to provide for those in short-term economic need. (Hopefully, it would already have been providing for those with long-term needs, such as the elderly and disabled.)

Clearly, these things need to be organised at reasonably high levels of cooperation—not necessarily all by the same body. But the potential for such is present in an SSOC: the appropriate bodies just need to have been set up in a bottom-up fashion. And it might well be hoped that this *would* have been done in a society where people are better educated, and so understand the inter-connectedness of people. Naturally, some measures would have to be taken without the time necessary for fully democratic consultation. But thoughtful constitutions should specify standing procedures for handling such emergencies; and those implementing them would need to be held accountable for their actions in the appropriate fashion as soon as it is possible to do so.

All actions of this kind could, in theory, be taken by a pure top-down power structure. However, as we have seen, they have not been—even in China, where they would have been much easier to organise than in so-called liberal democracies. Why? Such top-down power structures are not characterised by the sense of solidarity one would hope to find in an SSOC. Could things have been better handled in a capitalist liberal democracy? Yes, of course. New Zealand handled the situation more effectively than many countries in Europe and the Americas. However, capitalism, its competitive mechanisms which set people against each other, and its putting capital before people, will always render the measures required less effective.

13.9.5   Consequences of the Present Situation

Finally, what is the likelihood of the present situation moving us in the direction of a more rational and humane society?

There is room here for some hope. Many will have come to understand what social isolation means, how much social creatures we are, and how much social interaction is important. Some people may have found virtual interaction some kind of substitute for face-to-face interaction. But again, it takes only a moment's reflection to understand what things would have been like without the possibility of virtual communication—and how much this is the result of human cooperation.

Many will reflect on the current situation, how it has been (mis-)handled by national governments, and how it could all have been done a lot better. This could (and hopefully will) lead to a change in national government policies. More perceptive people will understand, however, that the fundamental problems are not a result of the particular actions of this or that government, but of general institutional features concerning capitalism and top-down power structures.

The present situation may also help people to start to see through the ideological illusion that capitalism and its political entourage really function in the best interest of all—and not merely those who own/manage capital. In other words, it might go some way toward breaking the ideology of capitalism. Such an understanding might be aided by appropriate educational measures, such as discussion groups, consciousness-raising groups, internet material, and so on.

And, it might be hoped, these developments could draw on whatever increased sense of solidarity there is—though I fear that this increased sense will soon evaporate after the immediate health emergency is over. The propaganda machines of capitalist ideology will doubtless be ramped up to help destroy this.

Of course, it doesn't have to be like this. Capitalism and its top-down power structure may simply adapt, and even strengthen in doing so—as, historically, it has shown itself very capable of doing. Probably, some things will not go back to being what they were before. More will be done online, now that people have seen that this *can* be so done. International travel may decrease. Many small businesses may well have gone for ever, swelling the ranks of the "working class"—though large and powerful capitals, such as Google and Amazon, will increase in power and size as a result of this. But nothing fundamental to the capitalist socio-economic system may change.

Indeed, matters could become even worse. Authoritarian right-wing political parties and groups may be strengthened as a result of what is happening. And these may well be backed by large capital—and the data harvesting and utilisation techniques which they have at their disposal, and which have been greatly increased by the present situation—just as large capitalists in Germany fell in behind Hitler in the 1930s. So we could well see a lurch towards fascist or some other kind of totalitarian states.

Nothing in all this is inevitable. What actually happens will depend on what we (collectively) do. As Marx said, it is people who make history. They do not make history in circumstances of their choice. The current pandemic brings this home vividly. But it is people who make history, none the less. And both capitalism and political power structures are ensembles of human relationships, that is, the relationships we all bear to one another. Perhaps the best thing that could come out of the pandemic is a more widespread and profound awareness of these social interconnections between people—all people.

No one has the right to be indifferent to the suffering of others. No one has the right to lose faith in the future of humanity.

Fidel Castro[23]

---

23. Quoted in McKelvey (2018), p. 96.

EPILOGUE

In this book I have drawn on three areas of philosophical thought. One consists of certain aspects of Marxist philosophy; another consists of certain aspects of Buddhist philosophy; a third consists of certain aspects of anarchist philosophy. I have explained, defended, and developed each of the three.

In the first part of the book I employed the first and second of these to articulate an analysis of the unhappy socio-economic condition of the world in which we find ourselves at the beginning of the 21st century. Drawing on this analysis, in the second part of the book, I employed the second and third of them to discuss the much more important question of the possible shape of a better world, and how one might get there. That, as we have seen, is a much more complex matter.

Let me end the book by underlining a few things. First, the aim of this book is not to design a utopia. It would be impossible to suppose, people being what they are, that any system we might ever manage to achieve will be without problems. What we certainly can do, however, is to improve the world in which we live, so that it is better for the people in it (and other sentient creatures, to the extent that we are a cause of their suffering).

Moreover, a utopia is a single system. In our world, there is such variety of histories, traditions, cultures, that one would not expect a one-size-fits-all model. Indeed, to achieve a one-size-fits-all model in anything like the foreseeable future would require the imposition of a centralised top-down power structure, which, for reasons we have seen, is not going to deliver what is required. What we might hope to move towards, though, is a federation, or federation of federations—or federation of federations of federations, and so on—each part of which is self-regulating, though it cooperates with other parts in matters of mutual interest.

Next, the path to such a structure will not be a one-size-fits-all matter either. Every group of people can but start from where it is, and—global though capitalism is—people find themselves in radically different circumstances in Australia, China, Iran, Brazil, Nigeria, and so on. What might happen, though, is that groups of people take on the responsibility for self-management, from a basis of which they can cooperate with other groups. Such change may both draw on and produce a sense of solidarity. The solidarity may also be engendered by an understanding of the fact that we are all mutually dependent, and that the best way for us to flourish is collectively.

Thus, if change is to be successful, the major impulse must be bottom-up—though of course one may take advantage of any top-down power structure in the process if it is possible to do so, at the same time as working to undermine it. And this will mean many different groups working on many different things simultaneously—though, of course, each may be informed of what others are doing, be encouraged by them, and learn from them. As Ward puts it:[1]

> Revolution does not need conveyor belt organization. It needs hundreds, thousands, and finally millions of people meeting in groups with informal contacts with each other. It needs mass consciousness. If one group takes an initiative that is valuable, others will take it up. The methods must be tailored to the society [each group] live[s] in.

Indeed, learning, quite generally, will be important. People, economies, and societies, are complex systems. We can hardly claim to have a detailed understanding of how each works as a stand-alone system, let alone how each interacts with the others. Change must therefore proceed critically; things must be reviewed and possibly revised in the light of new and better understandings.

Further, as we have seen, moving to a saner, more compassionate society poses a number of problems; and the answers to many of these are far from obvious. We will have to work out solutions to these as we go along. In the end, the first step in the solving such problems is to be aware of them. One cannot solve a problem of which one is unaware.

These things, in turn, entail the importance of education. Education of the appropriate kind is central to breaking the hold that ideology has on our thinking. And people are not going to make intelligent decisions if they are not informed and educated about their situation, the situations of others, the likely effects of their actions, and so on. But an appropriate education is, as we have seen, itself a collective activity. It involves not just listening, but also sharing and discussing ideas, perspectives, and so on.

1. Ward (1996), p. 57.

We have also seen that changing the society in which we live must go hand in hand with changing ourselves. We are all works in progress. In particular, people have the ability to work on themselves: each person can work to make themself less subject to the desires for power and possessions, more aware of the interdependence of things, and more compassionate.

The three areas of philosophical thought I mentioned in the first paragraph interact with each other. Each informs the other two, both reinforcing their major ideas, and providing aspects of the overall picture on which the other two say little. This is clearly a case of interdependence. Indeed, since interdependence appeared in Chapter 2, it has played an increasing visible role as the book has gone on. We have seen how people are dependent on each other; people are dependent on their society, and vice versa; people are dependent on their natural environment, and vice versa; inanimate elements of the natural environment are dependent on each other. Moreover, a number of these dependences are of a dialectical kind, where the dependence involves opposites: base and superstructure, oppressor and oppressed, social and individual, personal and political, top-down and bottom-up power/organisation.

We are dealing with systems that are deeply entangled, causally, spatially, temporally, conceptually. For this reason, action is required on many fronts: education and consciousness-raising, reorganising local communities and workplaces, using top-down power structures in place, and creating new bottom-up ones, changing society to reshape ourselves and changing ourselves to reshape society. Because of the web of *pratītasamutpāda*, all of these things are interconnected.

The complexity of *pratītasamutpāda* is also a reason why thoughtful action is difficult: consequences can ramify widely. This should not lead to skeptical paralysis, however. In many cases we know what the most significant consequences of our actions will be. I know, for example, that voting for a right-wing political party will promote the interests of capital: those in the party are not going to have a magical change of heart after the election. What the realisation of interconnectedness *should* lead to, however, is a humble realisation of our fallibility.

It should also lead to a realisation of the importance of collective action—solidarity, in political terms. No one is going to change the system on their own. Change will always be grounded in collective action. And solidarity works for the benefit of the group and each member of it. In Buddhist terms, this is *karuṇā*, care. Solidarity and care, then, form the basis of the actions that can drive change in our world to make it a more humane and rational place.

The lotus is a creature of beauty which emerges from the muck and mire of a dirty pond. In Buddhism it is a symbol of the way that enlightenment may emerge from *saṃsāra*—the world of the three poisons: greed, hatred, and delusion. Let us hope that it may also symbolise the emergence of a better society from the muck and mire of capitalism.

BIBLIOGRAPHY

Albert, M., and Hahnel, R. (1991), *Looking Forward: Participatory Economics for the Twenty First Century*, Boston, MA: South End Press.

Al-Rhodin, N. (2014), 'The Neurochemistry of Power Has Implications for Political Change', *The Conversation*, 2/2014, http://theconversation.com/the-neurochemistry-of-power-has-implications-for-political-change-23844.

Alston, P. (2020), 'Covid-19 Has Revealed a Pre-Existing Pandemic of Poverty That Benefits the Rich', *The Guardian*, 11/7/2020, https://www.theguardian.com/global-development/2020/jul/11/covid-19-has-revealed-apre-existing-pandemic-of-poverty-that-benefits-the-rich?CMP=Share_iOSApp_Other.

Althusser, L., and Balibar, E. (1956), *Reading Capital*, London: Verso.

Amadeo, K. (2018), 'Why Trickle Down Economics Works in Theory but Not in Fact', *The Balance*, 3/1/2018, https://www.thebalance.com/trickle-down-economics-theory-effect-does-it-work-3305572.

Ames, R., and Hall, D. (eds. and trs.) (2003), *Dao De Jing: A Philosophical Translation*, New York, NY: Ballantine Books.

Arendt, H. (1963), *Eichmann in Jerusalem: A Report on the Banality of Evil*, New York, NY: Viking Press.

Arruzza, C. (2013), *Dangerous Liaisons: The Marriage and Divorce of Marxism and Feminism*, Pontypool: Resistance Books and IIRE.

Aryiaratne, A. T. (1982), *In Search of Development: The Sarvodya Movement's Efforts to Harmonize Tradition with Change*, Moratuwa, Sri Lanka: Sarvodya Press.

Baer, H. A. (2018), *Democratic Eco-socialism as Real Utopia: Transitioning to an Alternative World System*, Oxford: Berghahn.

Barnes, H. (tr.) (1956), *Being and Nothingness*, New York, NY: Washington Square Press.

Barnes, J. (ed.) (1984), *The Complete Works of Aristotle*, Princeton NY: Princeton University Press.

Bartky. S. (1990), *Femininity and Domination: Studies in the Phenomenology of Oppression*, London: Routledge.

Bauman, Y., and Rose, E. (2011), 'Selection or Indoctrination: Why Do Economics Students Donate Less Than the Rest?', *Journal of Economic Behavior and Organization* 79: 318–27.

Berkman, A. (2003), *What Is Anarchism?*, Oakland, CA: AK Press.

Bernays, E. (2005), *Propaganda*, New York, NY: Ig Publishing.

Bishop, M. (1999), *Okinawan Karate*, revised edn, Boston, MA: Tuttle Publishing.

Bishop, V. (2015), *The Illusion of Choice: Ninety Percent of American Media Controlled by Six Corporations*, Montreal, QC: Centre for Research on Globalisation.

Bodhi, Bhikkhu (1998), 'Toward a Threshold of Understanding', *BPS Newsletter*, cover essays nos. 30 & 31; accessed 15 Jan. 2007 from 'Access to Insight', http://www.accesstoinsight.org/lib/authors/bodhi/bps-essay_30.html.

Bodhi, Bhikkhu (2009), 'Socially Engaged Buddhism and the Trajectory of Buddhist Ethical Consciousness', *Religion East and West* 9: 1–23.

Bodhi, Bhikkhu (2012), 'A Buddhist Perspective on Occupy Wall St. Part 2', https://www.youtube.com/watch?v=sz76o34QRcY.

Boghossian, P. (2006), *Fear of Knowledge: Against Relativism and Constructivism*, Oxford: Oxford University Press.

Bookchin, M. (2004), *Post-Scarcity Anarchism*, 3rd edn, Oakland, CA: AK Press.

Bookchin, M. (ed.) (2008), *Mutual Aid*, London: Penguin.

Bookchin, M. (2015), *The Next Revolution: Popular Assemblies and the Promise of Direct Democracy*, London: Verso.

Bottomore, T. (ed.) (1983), *A Dictionary of Marxist Thought*, Oxford: Blackwell.

Brandmeir, K., Grim, M., Heise, M., and Hozhauseen, A. (2015), *Allianz Global Wealth Report 2015*, Munich: Allianz.

Brien, K. M. (2004), 'Buddhism and Marxism: Ironic Affinities', *Dialogue and Universalism* 14: 35–59.

Brook, A., and Raymont, P. (2017), 'The Unity of Consciousness', in E. Zalta (ed.), *Stanford Encyclopedia of Philosophy*, https://plato.stanford.edu/entries/consciousness-unity/.

Brown, C. (2017), *Buddhist Economics: An Enlightened Approach to the Dismal Science*, New York, NY: Bloomsbury Press.

Brown, L. (2006), *Plan B 2.0: Rescuing a Planet Under Stress and a Civilization in Trouble*, New York, NY: W. W. Norton & Co.

Burnheim, J. (2006), *Is Democracy Possible? The Alternative to Electoral Democracy*, new edn, Sydney: Sydney University Press.

Callicot, J. B. (2010), 'The Metaphysical Implications of Ecology', pp. 400–8 of D. R. Keller (ed.), *Environmental Ethics: The Big Questions*, Oxford: Wiley-Blackwell.

Cannan, E. (ed.) (1937), *An Inquiry into the Wealth of Nations*, New York, NY: The Modern Library.

Carpenter, A. (2014), *Indian Buddhist Philosophy*, Durham: Acumen.

Carroll, N. (1998), *The Philosophy of Mass Art*, New York, NY: Oxford University Press.

Cave, N. (2019), 'A Timeline of Despair in Australia's Off-Shore Detention Centers', *New York Times*, 24/6/2019, https://www.nytimes.com/2019/06/26/world/australia/australia-manus-suicide.html.

Center for Non-Violent Communication (2007), 'An Introduction to Non-Violent Communication', http://www.schooltransformation.com/wp-content/uploads/2012/06/Kendrick_NVC_Materials.pdf.

Chalmers, A. (2013), *What Is This Thing Called Science?*, 4th edn, Brisbane: Queensland University Press.

Charbit, Y. (2009), *Economic, Social, and Demographic Thought of the XIXth Century*, Dordrecht: Springer.

Chomsky, N. (1976), 'The Relevance of Anarcho-Syndicalism', interview, https://www.youtube.com/watch?v=h_x0Y3FqkEI.

Chomsky, N. (1999), *Profit over People: Neoliberalism and Global Order*, New York, NY: Seven Stories Press.

Chomsky, N. (2013a), *On Anarchism*, New York, NY: The New Press.

Chomsky, N. (2013b), 'What Is Anarchism?', lecture, https://www.youtube.com/watch?v=oB9rp_SAp2U.

Cleary, T. (tr.) (1993), *The Book of Five Rings*, Boston: Shambhala.

Cleary, T. (tr.) (2005), *Soul of the Samurai*, North Clarendon, VT: Tuttle Publications.

Cohn, A., Fehr, E., and Maréchal, M. (2014), 'Business Culture and Dishonesty in the Banking Industry', *Nature* 516: 86–9.

Comparative Constitution Project (2019), *Cuban Constitution 2019* (English Translation), https://www.constituteproject.org/constitution/Cuba_2019D.pdf?lang=en.

Compassion (2020), 'Poverty Around the World', https://www.compassion.com/poverty/poverty-around-the-world.htm.

Cowherds, The (2015), *Moonpaths: Ethics and Emptiness*, New York, NY: Oxford University Press.

Crenshaw, K. (2005), 'Intersectionality and Identity Politics: Learning from Violence against Women of Color', ch. 92 of W. K. Kolmar and F. Bartowski (eds.), *Feminist Theory: A Reader*, 2nd edn, New York, NY: McGraw-Hill.

Crosthwaite, J., and Priest, G. (1996), 'The Definition of Sexual Harassment', *Australasian Journal of Philosophy* 74: 66–82; reprinted in G. L. Bowie and M. Michaels (eds.), *13 Questions in Ethics and Social Philosophy*, 2nd edn, San Diego, CA: Harcourt, Brace, Jovanovich, 1997.

Dabla-Norris, E., Kochhar, K., Ricka, F., Nujin Suphaphiphat, N., and Tsounta, E. (2015), 'Causes and Consequences of Income Inequality: A Global Perspective', *International Monetary Fund Discussion Note*, https://www.imf.org/en/Publications/Staff-Discussion-Notes/Issues/2016/12/31/Causes-and-Consequences-of-Income-Inequality-A-Global-Perspective-42986.

Dancy, J. (2017), 'Moral Particularism', in E. Zalta (ed.), *Stanford Encyclopedia of Philosophy*, https://plato.stanford.edu/entries/moral-particularism/.

Dave Grace and Associates (2014), 'Measuring the Size and Scope of the Cooperative Economy', https://www.un.org/esa/socdev/documents/2014/coopsegm/grace.pdf.

David, E. J., (ed.) (2014), *Internalized Oppression: the Psychology of Marginalized Groups*, New York, NY: Springer Publishing Co.

Deguchi, Y., Garfield, J., Priest, G., Sharf, R. (2021), *What Can't Be Said: Paradox and Contradiction in East Asian Thought*, New York, NY: Oxford University Press.

Dennett, D. (1993), *Consciousness Explained*, London: Penguin Books.

Desilver, D. (2018), 'For Most U.S. Workers, Real Wages have Barely Budged in Decades', Pew Research Institute, https://www.pewresearch.org/fact-tank/2018/08/07/for-most-us-workers-real-wages-have-barely-budged-for-decades/.

Dietz, R., and O'Neil, D. (2013), *Enough is Enough*, San Francisco, CA: Berrett-Koehler Publishers.

Dolgoff, S. (ed.) (1974), *The Anarchist Collectives: Workers' Self-Management in the Spanish Revolution 1936–1939*, New York, NY: Free Life Editions.

Draper, H. (1987), '*The Dictatorship of the Proletariat' from Marx to Lenin*, New York, NY: Monthly Review Press.

Dreyfus, G. (2013), 'Is Mindfulness Present-Centred and Non-Judgmental? A Discussion of the Cognitive Dimensions of Mindfulness', pp. 41–54 of J. Mark, G. Williams, and J. Kabat-Zinn (eds.), *Mindfulness: Diverse Perspectives on its Meaning, Origins, and Applications*, Abingdon: Routledge.

Duerlinger, J. (tr.) (2003), *Indian Buddhist Theories of Persons*, London: Routledge.

Eberth, J., Sedlmeier, P., Schäfer, T. (2019), 'Promise: A Model of Insight and Equanimity as the Key Effects of Mindfulness Meditation', *Frontiers in Psychology* 10: 1–16.

Edelglass, W. (ed.) (2009), 'Thich Nhat Hanh's *Interbeing: Fourteen Guidelines for Engaged Buddhism*', pp. 419–27 of W. Edelglass and J. Garfield (eds.), *Buddhist Philosophy: Essential Readings*, New York, NY: Oxford University Press.

Elliot, N. (tr.) (2002), *Guide to the Bodhisattva's Way of Life*, Ulverston: Tharpa Publications.

Emmanuel, S. (2013), *A Companion to Buddhist Philosophy*, Chichester: Wiley-Blackwell.

Engels, F. (1934), 'Engels on Historical Materialism', *New International* 1: 81–5.

Engels, F. (1939), *Herr Eugen Dühring's Revolution in Science*, New York, NY: International Publishers.

Etter, L. (2017), 'What Happens when the Government Uses Facebook as a Weapon?', *Economic Times*, 11/12/2017, https://economictimes.indiatimes.com/small-biz/startups/newsbuzz/what-happens-when-the-government-uses-facebook-as-a-weapon/articleshow/62016172.cms.

Faruqi, S. (2015), *Project Animal Farm: an Accidental Journey into the Secret World of Farming and the Truth about Our Food*, New York, NY: Pegasus Books.

Faubion, J. (ed.) (1994), *Michel Foucault: Power*, New York, NY: The New Press.

Fiala, A. (2017), 'Anarchism', in E. Zalta (ed.), *Stanford Encyclopedia of Philosophy*, https://plato.stanford.edu/entries/anarchism/.

Figgis, J. N., and Laurence, R. V. (eds.) (1907), *Historical Essays and Studies*, London: Macmillan.

Fisher, M. (2012), 'Why Mental Health is a Political Issue', *The Guardian*, 16/7/2012, https://www.theguardian.com/commentisfree/2012/jul/16/mental-health-political-issue.

Fisk, S., and Dépret, E. (1996), 'Control, Interdependence and Power: Understanding Social Cognition in its Social Context', *European Review of Social Psychology* 7: 54–6.

Food and Agriculture Organization of the United Nations (2020), 'Key Facts and Findings', Food and Agriculture Organization of the United Nations, http://www.fao.org/news/story/en/item/197623/icode/.

Forgacs, D. (ed.), (1988), *The Antonio Gramsci Reader: Selected Writings 1916–1935*, New York, NY: New York University Press.

Foucault, M. (1977), *Discipline and Punish*, New York, NY: Pantheon Books

Foucault, M. (1988), 'Technologies of the Self', pp. 16–49 of L. H. Martin, H. Gutman, and P. H. Hutton (eds.), *Technologies of the Self*, Amherst: University of Massachusetts Press.

Fowkes, B. (tr.) (1976), *Capital*, Vol. 1, London: Penguin Books.

Fraser, N. (2013), *Fortunes of Feminism: From State-Managed Capitalism to Neoliberal Crisis*, London: Verso.

Fraser, N. (2019), 'Is Capitalism Necessarily Racist?', *Politics/Letters*, 20/5/2019, http://quarterly.politicsslashletters.org/about/.

Freire, P. (1970), *Pedagogy of the Oppressed*, London: Penguin Books.

Fulcher, J. (2015), *Capitalism: a Very Short Introduction*, 2nd edn, Oxford: Oxford University Press.

Funakoshi, G. (2003), *The Twenty Guiding Principles of Karate*, Tokyo: Kodansha International Ltd.

Gare, A. (2014), 'Creating an Ecological Socialist Future', *Capitalism, Nature, Socialism* 11: 23–40.

Garfield, J. (2015), *Engaging Buddhism*, New York, NY: Oxford University Press.

Garfield, J., Jenkins, S., and Priest, G. (2015), 'The Śāntideva Passage *Bodhicaryāvatāra* VIII: 90–103', pp. 55–76 of Cowherds (2015).

Garfield, J., and Priest, G. (2020), 'Skill and Virtuosity in Buddhist and Daoist Philosophy', ch. 1 of E. Fridland (ed.), *Routledge Handbook of Skill and Expertise*, Abingdon-on-Thames: Routledge.

Geras, N. (1983), *Marx and Human Nature: Refutation of a Legend*, London: Verso.

Gibbs, T. (2017), *Why the Dalai Lama is a Socialist*, London: Zed Books.

Gold, J. (2015), 'Vasubandhu', in E. Zalta (ed.), *Stanford Encyclopedia of Philosophy*, https://plato.stanford.edu/entries/vasubandhu/.

Goldman, E. (1923), *My Disillusionment in Russia*, Garden City, NY: Doubleday, Page & Co.

Gooch. T. (2015), 'Ludwig Andreas Feuerbach', in E. Zalta (ed.), *Stanford Encyclopedia of Philosophy*, https://plato.stanford.edu/entries/ludwig-feuerbach/.

Goodman, C. (2009), *Consequences of Compassion*, New York, NY: Oxford University Press.

Goodman, C. (2013), 'Buddhist Meditation: Theory and Practice', pp. 555–71 of Emmanuel (2013).

Goodman, C. (2016), 'Śāntideva', in E. Zalta (ed.), *Stanford Encyclopedia of Philosophy*, https://plato.stanford.edu/entries/shantideva/.

Gould, S. (1977), 'Biological Potential vs. Biological Determinism', ch. 32 of *Ever Since Darwin: Reflections on Natural History*, New York, NY: W. W. Norton.

Grasseger, H., and Krogerus, M. (2017), 'The Data That Turned the World Upside Down', *Motherboard*, https://motherboard.vice.com/en_us/article/mg9vvn/how-our-likes-helped-trump-win.

Gray, J. (ed.) (1991), *On Liberty and Other Essays*, Oxford: Oxford University Press.

Gross, R. (2013), 'Buddhist Perspectives on Gender Issues', pp. 663–74 of Emmanuel (2013).

Halkias, G. (2013), 'The Enlightened Sovereign: Buddhism and King-Ship in India and Tibet', pp. 491–511 of Emmanuel (2013).

Hanh, T. N. (1987), *Being Peace*, Berkeley, CA: Parallax Publishers.

Hanh, T. N. (2006), 'Compassion Is Our Best Protection', pp. 273–83 of McLeod (2006).

Hanh, T. N. (2019), 'Please Call Me by My True Names', pp. 113–20, 2nd edn, of Parallax Press (ed.), *True Peace Work: Essential Writings on Engaged Buddhism*, Berkeley, CA: Parallax Press.

Hahn, T. N., and Ann-Huong, N. (2019), *Walking Meditation: Easy Steps to Mindfulness*, Louisville, CO: Sounds True Inc.

Hanische, C. (2000), 'The Personal Is Political', pp. 113–7 of A. Crow (ed.), *Radical Feminism: A Documentary Reader*, New York: New York University Press.

Hansen, C. (2007), 'Daoism', in E. Zalta (ed.), *Stanford Encyclopedia of Philosophy*, https://plato.stanford.edu/entries/daoism.

Hanson, N. R. (1958), *Patterns of Discovery: An Inquiry into the Conceptual Foundations of Science*, Cambridge: Cambridge University Press.

Harrison, R. (2013), *Animal Machines*, Wallingford: CABI.

Hartmann, H. (1981), 'The Unhappy Marriage of Marxism and Feminism', pp. 1–42 of L. Sargent (ed.), *Women and Revolution: A Discussion of the Unhappy Marriage of Marxism and Feminism*, Boston, MA: South End Press.

Harvey, P. (2000), *An Introduction to Buddhist Ethics*, Cambridge: Cambridge University Press.

Herman, E., and Chomsky, N. (1988), *Manufacturing Consent*, New York, NY: Pantheon Books.

Herrigel, E. (1981), *Zen and the Art of Archery*, New York, NY: Random House.

Herzog, L. (2017), 'Markets', in E. Zalta (ed.), *Stanford Encyclopedia of Philosophy*, https://plato.stanford.edu/entries/markets/.

Hickel, J. (2019a), 'It's Not Thanks to Capitalism That We're Living Longer, but Progressive Politics', *The Guardian*, 22/11/2019, https://www.theguardian.com/commentis free/2019/nov/22/progressive-politics-capitalism-unions-healthcare-education? CMP=Share_iOSApp_Other.

Hickel, J. (2019b), 'Progress and Its Discontents', *New Inter-Nationalist*, 7/8/2019, https://newint.org/features/2019/07/01/long-read-progress-and-its-discontents.

Hirsh, S. (2004), 'Torture at Abu Ghraib, *New Yorker*, 10/5/2004, https://www.new yorker.com/magazine/2004/05/10/torture-at-abughraib.

hooks, b. (1994), *Teaching to Transgress: Education as the Practice of Freedom*, New York, NY: Routledge.

hooks, b. (2006), 'Buddhism and the Politics of Domination', pp. 57–62 of McLeod (2006).

Hope, D., and Limberg, J. (2020), 'The Economic Consequences of Major Tax Cuts for the Rich', Working Paper 55, London School of Economics, http://eprints.lse.ac. uk/107919/1/Hope_economic_consequences_of_major_tax_cuts_published.pdf.

Hopkins, J. (tr.) (2007), *Nagarjuna's Precious Garland*, Boulder, CO: Snow Lion Publications.

Hopkins, R. (2014), *The Transition Handbook: From Oil Dependence to Local Resilience*, Dartington: Green Books.

Hyams, J. (1982), *Zen in the Martial Arts*, New York, NY: Bantam Books.

Inwood, M. (ed.) (1992), *A Hegel Dictionary*, Oxford: Blackwell.

Irwin, T. (1989), *Classical Thought: A History of Western Philosophy, 1*, Oxford: Oxford University Press.

Jalata, A. (2013), 'The Impacts of English Colonial Terrorism and Genocide on Indigenous/ Black Australians', *SAGE Open*, 2013: 1–12, https://journals.sagepub.com/doi/pdf/ 10.1177/2158244013499143.

Jenkins, S. (2010), 'On the Auspiciousness of Compassionate Violence', *Journal of the International Association of Buddhist Studies* 33: 299–312.

Jenkins, S. (2013), 'Compassion and the Ethics of Violence', pp. 466–75 of Emmanuel (2013).

Jones, J-E. (2018), 'Locke on Real Essences', in E. Zalta (ed.), *Stanford Encyclopedia of Philosophy*, https://plato.stanford.edu/entries/real-essence/.

Jones, K. (2006), 'Four Noble Political Truths', pp. 111–2 of McLeod (2006).

Jones, T. (2010), 'Food Miles Fair Miles', Earth Institute, Columbia University, https:// blogs.ei.columbia.edu/2010/01/28/food-miles-fair-miles.

Kasulis, T. P. (1981), *Zen Action Zen Person*, Honolulu: University of Hawai'i Press.

Keller, J. (2015), 'The IMF Confirms That "Trickle Down Economics" Is, Indeed, a Joke', *Pacific Standard*, 18/6/2018, https://psmag.com/economics/trickle-down-economics-is-indeed-a-joke.

Keltner, D. (2016), 'Don't Let Power Corrupt You', *Harvard Business Review*, 10/2016, https://hbr.org/2016/10/dont-let-power-corrupt-you.

Keown, D. (2001), *The Nature of Buddhist Ethics*, New York, NY: Palgrave Macmillan.

Keown, D. (2003), *Dictionary of Buddhism*, Oxford: Oxford University Press.

Keown, D. (2005), *Buddhist Ethics: A Very Short Introduction*, Oxford: Oxford University Press.

King, S. (2005), *Being Benevolence: The Social Ethics of Engaged Buddhism*, Honolulu: University of Hawai'i Press.

King, W. (1993), *Zen and the Way of the Sword*, New York, NY: Oxford University Press.

Kinna, R. (2019), *The Government of No One: The Theory and Practice of Anarchism*, London: Pelican Books.

Klein, N. (2014), *This Changes Everything: Capitalism vs. the Climate*, London: Allen Lane.

Krugman, P. (2017), 'Zombies of Voodoo Economics', *New York Times*, 24/4/2017, https://www.nytimes.com/2017/04/24/opinion/zombiesof-voodoo-economics.html.

Kuhn, T. (1962), *The Structure of Scientific Revolutions*, Chicago: University of Chicago Press.

Lawson, M. (2016), 'It's Time to Demolish the Myth of Trickle-Down Economics', *World Economic Forum*, 19/7/2016, https://www.weforum.org/agenda/2016/07/it-s-time-to-demolish-the-myth-of-trickle-down-economics/.

Layman, E. (2015), 'Feeding Global Warming: Assessing the Impact of Agriculture on Climate Change', *PIT Journal*, 7/6/2009, https://planetsave.com/2009/06/07/global-warming-effects-and-causes-a-top-10-list/.

Layton, C. (1988), 'The Personality of Black-Belt and Non-Black-Belt Traditional Karateka', *Perceptual and Motor Skills* 67: 218.

Layton, C. (1990), 'Anxiety in Black-Belt and Non-Black-Belt Traditional Karateka', *Perceptual and Motor Skills* 71: 905–6.

Lebowitz, M. (2010), *The Socialist Alternative: Real Human Development*, New York: NY: Monthly Review Press.

Leech, G. (2012), *Capitalism: A Structural Genocide*, London: Zed Books.

Lehning, A. (ed.) (1973), *Michael Bakunin: Selected Writings*, London: Jonathan Cape.

Lewis, P. (2018), 'Fiction Is Outperforming Truth: How YouTube's Algorithm Distorts the Truth', *The Guardian*, 2/2/2018, https://www.theguardian.com/technology/2018/feb/02/how-youtubes-algorithm-distorts-truth?utm_source=esp&utm_medium=Email&utm_campaign=GU+

Long, W. (2019), *Tantric State: A Buddhist Approach to Democracy and Development in Bhutan*, New York, NY: Oxford University Press.

Lowey, M. (2006), 'Eco-Socialism and Democratic Planning', pp. 294–309 of L. Panitch and C. Leys (eds.), *Coming to Terms with Nature*, London: Merlin Press.

Loy, D. (2008), *Money, Sex, War, Karma*, Boston, MA: Wisdom Publications.

Luscombe, B. (2010), 'Do We Need $75,000 a Year to Be Happy?', *Time*, 6/9/2010, http://content.time.com/time/magazine/article/0,9171,2019628,00.html.

Maass, A. (2010), *The Case for Socialism*, Chicago: Haymarket Books.

Macleod, C. (2016), 'John Stuart Mill', in E. Zalta (ed.), *Stanford Encyclopedia of Philosophy*, https://plato.stanford.edu/entries/mill/.

Madahwi, A. (2021), 'How Many Anti-Vaxxers Does It Take to Misinform the World?', *The Guardian*, 31/3/2021, https://www.theguardian.com/commentisfree/2021/mar/30/how-many-anti-vaxxers-does-it-take-to-misinform-the-world-just-twelve.

Madeley, J. (1995), *When Aid Is No Help? How Projects Fail and How They Could Succeed*, London: Intermediate Technology Publications.

Maguire, J. (1972), *Marx's Paris Writings: An Analysis*, Dublin: Gill and Macmillan Ltd.

Mansbridge, J. (1983), *Beyond Adversarial Democracy*, Chicago: University of Chicago Press.

Mandel, E. (1976), 'Introduction', pp. 11–86 of Fowkes (1976).

Marcuse, H. (1964), *One Dimensional Man*, Milton Park: Routledge and Kegan Paul.

Marglin, S. (2008), *The Dismal Science: How Thinking Like an Economist Undermines Community*, Cambridge, MA: Harvard University Press.

Marković, M., and Cohen, R. (1975), *Yugoslavia: The Rise and Fall of Socialist Humanism: A History of the Praxis Group*, Nottingham: Spokesman Books.

Marlin, R. (2013), *Propaganda and the Ethics of Persuasion*, Toronto, ON: Broadview Press.

Marx, K. (1963), *The Poverty of Philosophy*, New York, NY: International Publishers.

Marx, K., and Engels, F. (1975), *Collected Works, Vol. 3, 1843–44*, New York, NY: International Publishers.

McEwan, J. D. (1963), 'Anarchism and the Cybernetics of Self-Organising Systems', *Anarchy* 31, https://libcom.org/library/anarchism-cybernetics-self-organising-systems.

McKelvey, C. (2018), *The Evolution and Significance of the Cuban Revolution: The Light in the Darkness*, London: Palgrave Macmillan.

McLellan, D. (ed.) (2000), *Karl Marx: Selected Writings*, 2nd edn, Oxford: Oxford University Press.

McLellan, D. (ed.) (2007), *Marxism after Marx*, 4th edn, New York, NY: Palgrave Macmillan.

McLeod, M. (ed.) (2006), *Mindful Politics: A Buddhist Guide to Making the World a Better Place*, Boston, MA: Wisdom Publications.

McLeod, S. (2018), 'The Stanford Experiment', *Simply Psychology*, https://www.simplypsychology.org/zimbardo.html.

Mental Health Today (2017), 'People Were Happier in 1957 Than They Are Today, According to Research', 23/1/2017, https://www.mentalhealthtoday.co.uk/people-were-happier-in-1957-than-today-according-to-research

Metcalf, G. (2015), *Democratic by Design*, New York, NY: St Martin's Press.

Miles, K. (2014), 'Next Time Someone Argues for "Trickle Down Economics", Show Them This', *Huffington Post*, 6/2/2014, https://www.huffingtonpost.com/2014/02/06/rich-richer_n_4731408.html.

Mill, J. S. (1920), *Principles of Political Economy with Some of Their Applications to Social Philosophy*, London: Longmans, Green and Co.

Miller, C. (2015), 'When Algorithms Discriminate', *New York Times*, 10/7/2015, https://www.nytimes.com/2015/07/10/upshot/when-algorithms-discriminate.html.

Miller, D., and Xu, X. (2015), 'A Fleeting Glory: Self-Serving Behaviour among Celebrated MBA CEOs', *Journal of Management Inquiries* 25: 286–300.

Miller, E. (ed.) (1985), *David Hume: Essays, Moral, Political, and Literary*, Indianapolis, IN: Liberty Classics.

Mills, C. (2003), *From Class to Race: Essays in White Marxism and Black Radicalism*, Lanham, MD: Rowman and Littlefield.

Mitchell, C. (2013), *Religion, Identity and Politics in Northern Ireland*, Farnham: Ashgate Publishing.

Mitchell, D. (2002), *Buddhism: Introduction to the Buddhist Experience*, Oxford: Oxford University Press.

Monbiot, G. (2019a), 'Could This Local Experiment Be the Start of a National Trans-formation?', *The Guardian*, 24/1/2019, https://www.theguardian.com/commentis-free/2019/jan/24/neighbourhood-project-barking-dagenham.

Monbiot, G. (2019b), 'For the Sake of Life on Earth, We Must Put a Limit on Wealth', *The Guardian*, 19/9/2019, https://www.theguardian.com/commentisfree/2019/sep/19/life-earth-wealth-megarich-spending-power-environmental-damage.

Monbiot, G. (2020), 'Extinction Rebellion as Showing What Real Democracy Is Like', *The Guardian*, 16/9/2020, https://www.theguardian.com/commentisfree/2020/sep/16/extinction-rebellion-britain-democracy-protest-westminster.

Montefiore, S. (2005), *Stalin: The Court of the Red Tsar*, New York, NY: Vintage Books.

Munk, N. (2014), *The Idealist: Jeffrey Sachs and the Quest to End Global Poverty*, New York, NY: Anchor Books.

Nibert, D. (2002), *Animal Rights/Human Rights: Entanglement of Oppression and Libera-tion*, Latham, MD: Rowman and Littlefield Publishers.

Nibert, D. (ed.) (2017), *Animal Oppression and Capitalism*, 2 Vols., Santa Barbara, CA: ABC-CIO, LLC.

Nicolaus, M. (tr.) (1973), *Karl Marx: Grundrisse*, London: Penguin.

Niggle, C. J. (1999), 'Business Cycle Theory', pp. 50–4, Vol. 1 of P. O'Hara (ed.), *Ency-clopedia of Political Economy*, London: Routledge.

Nightingale, J. (2015), *The Concept of Solidarity in Anarchist Thought*, PhD thesis, Lough-borough University, https://core.ac.uk/download/pdf/288371198.pdf.

Nosanchuck, T. (1981), 'The Way of the Warrior: The Effects of Traditional Martial Arts Training on Aggressiveness', *Human Relations* 34: 435–44.

Nosanchuck, T., and MacNeil, L. (1989), 'Examination of the Effects of Traditional and Modern Martial Arts Training on Aggressiveness', *Aggressive Behavior* 15: 153–9.

O'Brien, C., and Howard, P. (eds.) (2020), *Living Schools: Transforming Education*, Win-nipeg: University of Manitoba, ESWB Press.

O'Connor, T. (2018), 'Free Will', in E. Zalta (ed.), *Stanford Encyclopedia of Philosophy*, https://plato.stanford.edu/entries/freewill/.

Olson, E. (2019), 'Personal Identity', in E. Zalta (ed.), *Stanford Encyclopedia of Philosophy*, https://plato.stanford.edu/entries/identity-personal/.

Osborne, M. (2009), *An Introduction to Game Theory*, Oxford: Oxford University Press.

Our World in Data (2020), 'Extreme Poverty', https://ourworldindata.org/extreme-poverty.

Owen, D., and Davidson, J. (2009), 'Hubris Syndrome: An Acquired Personality Dis-order? A Study of US Presidents and UK Prime Ministers over the Last 100 Years', *Brain* 132: 1396–1406.

Oxfam (2017), *An Economy for the 99%*, Oxfam Briefing Paper, https://www.oxfam.org/sites/www.oxfam.org/files/file_attachments/bp-economy-for-99-percent-160117-en.pdf.

Pateman, B. (ed.) (2005), *Chomsky on Anarchism*, Edinburgh: AK Press.

Penz, P., Drydyk, J., and Bose, P. (2011), *Displacement by Development: Ethics, Rights and Responsibilities*, Cambridge: Cambridge University Press.

Perspectives in C (2017), 'A Quick Mathematical Debunking of Trickle-Down Eco-nomics', *Medium Corporation*, 13/7/2017, https://medium.com/@PerspectivesInC/a-quick-mathematical-debunking-of-trickle-down-economics-1d190835066a.

Petersen, W. (1979), *Malthus*, 2nd edn, London: Heinemann.

Petrović, G. (1967), *Marx in the Mid-Twentieth Century*, Garden City, NY: Doubleday & Co.

Piketty, T. (2013), *Le Capital au XXIe Siècle*, Paris: Seuil; translated into English as *Capital in the Twenty-First Century*, Cambridge, MA: Belknap Press, 2014.

Poverty USA (2020), 'The Population of Poverty in the USA', Pew Research Institute, https://www.povertyusa.org/facts.

Priest, G. (1987), *In Contradiction*, Dordrecht: Martinus Nijhoff; 2nd edn, Oxford: Oxford University Press, 2006.

Priest, G. (2006), 'Zen and the Art of Harley Riding', pp. 2–12 of B. E. Rollin, C. M. Gray, K. Mommer, and C. Pineo (eds.), *Harley Davidson and Philosophy (Popular Culture and Philosophy*, Vol. 18), Chicago: Open Court.

Priest, G. (2012), 'A Prolegomenon to Any Planning for the Future', *Ormond Papers* 29: 136–43.

Priest, G. (2013), 'The Martial Arts and Buddhist Philosophy', *Royal Institute of Philosophy*, 73: 17–28; reprinted as ch. 11 of Priest and Young (2014).

Priest, G. (2014) *One*, Oxford: Oxford University Press.

Priest, G. (2017), 'Buddhist Ethics: A Perspective', ch. 5 of J. Davis (ed.), *A Mirror Is for Reflection: Understanding Buddhist Ethics*, New York, NY: Oxford University Press.

Priest, G. (2018a), 'Marxism and Buddhism:—Not Such Strange Bed-Fellows', *Journal of the American Philosophical Association* 4: 2–13.

Priest, G. (2018b), *The Fifth Corner of Four*, Oxford: Oxford University Press.

Priest, G. (2019), 'Fictional Objects Fictional Subjects', ch. 7 of D. Rudrum, R. Askin, and F. Beckman (eds.), *New Directions in Philosophy and Literature*, Edinburgh: Edinburgh University Press.

Priest, G., and Young, D. (eds.) (2014), *Philosophy and the Martial Arts: Engagement*, London: Routledge.

Priestland, D. (ed.) (2015), *Peter Kropotkin: The Conquest of Bread*, London: Penguin Books.

Queen, C. (ed.) (1995), *Engaged Buddhism in the West*, Somerville, MA: Wisdom Publications.

Ray, R. A. (2006), 'The Buddha's Politics', pp. 65–75 of McLeod (2006).

Redding, P. (2015), 'Georg Wilhelm Friedrich Hegel', in E. Zalta (ed.), *Stanford Encyclopedia of Philosophy*, https://plato.stanford.edu/entries/hegel/.

Refugee Council of Australia (2020), 'Australia's Offshore Processing Regime: The Facts', 20/5/2020, https://www.refugeecouncil.org.au/offshore-processing-facts/.

Repetti, R. (ed.) (2017), *Buddhist Perspectives on Free Will: Agentless Agency?*, Milton Park: Routledge.

Riezler, K. (1942), 'Will to Power: An Enquiry by Trial and Error', *Social Research* 9: 123–40.

Robinson, E. (2017), 'Trickle-Down Economics Is a Nightmare: Kansas Proved it', *Washington Post*, 12/6/2017, https://www.washingtonpost.com/opinions/trickle-down-economics-is-a-nightmare-kansas-proved-it/2017/06/12/c2d7aae0–4fa6–11e7–91eb–9611861a988f_story.html?utm_term=.0063715580ea.

Robinson, J. (1942), *An Essay on Marxian Economics*, London: Macmillan.

Rocker, R. (1989), *Anarcho-Syndicalism*, London: Pluto Press.

Rocker, R. (1998), *Nationalism and Culture*, Montreal, QC: Black Horse Books.

Rohlf, M. (2015), 'Immanuel Kant', in E. Zalta (ed.), *Stanford Encyclopedia of Philosophy*, https://plato.stanford.edu/entries/kant/.

Rothpearl, A. (1980), 'Personality Traits in Martial Artists: A Descriptive Approach', *Perceptual and Motor Skills* 50: 91–401.

Rubin, G. (2008), 'The Traffic in Women: Notes on the "Political Economy" of Sex', ch. 2 of A. Bailey and C. Cuomo (eds.), *The Feminist Philosophy Reader*, New York, NY: McGraw-Hill.

Saul, J. (2018), 'Dogwhistles, Political Manipulation, and Philosophy of Language', ch. 13 of D. Fogal, D. Harris, and M. Moss (eds.), *New Work on Speech Acts*, New York, NY: Oxford University Press.

Sayers, S. (1998), *Marxism and Human Nature*, London: Routledge.

Schapiro, L. (1965), *The Origin of the Communist Autocracy: Political Opposition in the Soviet State, First Phase, 1917–1922*, New York, NY: Frederick A. Praeger.

Schumacher, E. F. (1973), *Small Is Beautiful: Economics as If People Mattered*, New York, NY: Harper and Row Inc.

Schweickart, D. (2011), *After Capitalism*, 2nd edn, New York, NY: Rowman and Littlefield.

Sedlmeier, P., Ebert, J., Schwarz, M., Zimmermann, D., Haarig, F., Jaeger, S., and Kunze, S. (2012), 'The Psychological Effects of Meditation', *Psychological Bulletin* 138: 1139–71.

Selby-Bigge, L. A. (ed.) (1902), *An Enquiry Concerning Human Understanding and Concerning the Principles of Morals*, 2nd edn, Oxford: Oxford University Press.

Selby-Bigge, L. A. (ed.) (1978), *David Hume: A Treatise on Human Nature*, 2nd edn, Oxford: Oxford University Press.

Sharp, G. (1973), *The Politics of Non-Violent Action*, Vol. 1: *Power and Struggle*, Vol. 2: *Methods of Non-Violent Action*, Vol. 3: *The Dynamics of Non-Violent Action*, Boston, MA: Porter Sargent Publishers.

Shields, J. M. (2013), 'Liberation as Revolutionary Praxis: Rethinking Buddhist Materialism', *Journal of Buddhist Ethics* 20: 461–499.

Shiva, V. (2005), 'New Emperors, Old Clothes', *The Ecologist*, 1/7/2005, https://theecologist.org/2005/jul/01/new-emperors-old-clothes.

Siderits, M. (2007), *Buddhism as Philosophy*, Aldershot: Ashgate.

Siderits, M. (2019), 'Buddha', in E. Zalta (ed.), *Stanford Encyclopedia of Philosophy*, https://plato.stanford.edu/entries/buddha/.

Siderits, M., and Goodman, C. (trs.) (2015), '*Bodhicaryāvatāra-pañjikā* VIII: 90–103 by Prajñākaramati, Commenting on Śāntideva', pp. 241–260 of Cowherds (2015).

Singer, P. (1998), *Ethics into Action*, London: Rowman and Littlefield.

Singer, P. (2015), *Animal Liberation*, 4th edn, New York, NY: HarperCollins.

Sivaraksa, S. (1992), *Seeds of Peace: A Buddhist Vision for Renewing Society*, Berkeley, CA: Parallax Press.

Sivaraksa, S. (2006), 'A Buddhist Response to Globalization', pp. 285–90 of McLeod (2006).

Slott, M. (2011), 'Can You Be a Buddhist and a Marxist?', *Contemporary Buddhism* 12: 347–63.

Smith, M. (2006), *I Am Just Going Outside: Captain Oates-Antarctic Tragedy*, New York, NY: Collins Press.

Solnit, R. (2019), *Whose Story Is This? Old Conflicts, New Chapters*, London: Granta Publications.

Spiro, M. (1963), *Kibbutz: Venture into Utopia*, Cambridge, MA: Harvard University Press.

Stiglitz, J. (2019), *People, Power, and Profits: Progressive Capitalism for an Age of Discontent*, New York, NY: Norton and Company.

Struhl, K. (2016), 'Marx and Human Nature: The Historical, Trans-Historical, and Human Flourishing', *Science and Society* 80: 78–104.

Struhl, K. (2017), 'Buddhism and Marxism: Points of Intersection', *International Communication of Chinese Culture* 4: 103–16.

Sustainable Development Solutions Network (2019), *World Happiness Report 2019*, https://worldhappiness.report/ed/2019/.

Suttacentral (2011), *Vāseṭṭha Sutta*, https://suttacentral.net/en/snp3.9.

Sylvan, R. (2007), 'Anarchism', ch. 10, vol. 1, of R. Goodwin, P. Petit, and T. Pogge (eds.), *A Companion to Contemporary Political Philosophy*, 2nd edn, Oxford: Blackwell.

Sztompka, P. (1991), *Society in Action: The Theory of Social Becoming*, Chicago: University of Chicago Press.

Tatz, M. (tr.) (1994) *The Skill in Means* (Upāyakausalya) *Sūtra*, New Delhi: Tibet House and Motilal Barnasidass.

Tenzin Gyatso (Dalai Lama 14) (2006), 'A New Approach to Global Problems', pp. 17–27 of McLeod (2006).

Thompson, E. P. (1991), *The Making of the English Working Class*, London: Penguin Books.

Tye, L. (2002), *The Father of Spin: Edward L. Bernays and the Birth of Public Relations*, New York, NY: Henry Holt and Company.

UNICEF (2004), *The State of the World's Children 2005: Childhood under Threat*, New York, NY: United Nations.

United Nations (2020), 'Peace, Dignity and Equality on a Healthy Planet', https://www.un.org/en/sections/issues-depth/poverty/.

Useem, J. (2017), 'Power Causes Brain Damage', *The Atlantic*, 7/2017, https://www.theatlantic.com/magazine/archive/2017/07/power-causes-brain-damage/528711/?single_page=true.

Van Dam, N., Van Vught, M., Vago, D., Schmalzl, L., Saron, C., Olendzki, A., Meissner, T., Lazar, S., Kerr, C., Gorchov, J., Fox, K., Field, B., Britton, W., Brefczynsk-Lewis, J., and Meyer, D. (2018), 'Mind the Hype: A Critical Evaluation and Prescriptive Agenda for Research on Mindfulness Meditation', *Perspectives on Psychological Science* 13: 36–61.

Victoria, B. (2006), *Zen at War*, Lanham, MD: Rowman and Littlefield.

Waistell, J. (2014), 'Marx and Buddha: A Buddhist-Communist Manifesto', pp. 195–217 of T. N. Tu and T. D. Thien (eds.), *Buddhism for Sustainable Development and Social Change*, Hanoi: Religious Publishing House.

Ward, C. (1996), *Anarchy in Action*, London: Freedom Press.

Ward, C. (2004), *Anarchism: A Very Short Introduction*, Oxford: Oxford University Press.

Watson, B. (tr.) (1993), *The Lotus Sutra*, New York, NY: Columbia University Press.

Westerhoff, J. (2014), 'Nāgārjuna', in E. Zalta (ed.), *Stanford Encyclopedia of Philosophy*, https://plato.stanford.edu/entries/nagarjuna/.

Wheeler, M. (2011), 'Martin Heidegger', in E. Zalta (ed.), *Stanford Encyclopedia of Philosophy*, https://plato.stanford.edu/entries/heidegger/.

Whyte, W. F., and Whyte, K. K. (1988), *Making Mondragon: The Growth and Development of the Worker Cooperative Complex*, Ithaca, NY: Cornell University Press.

Williams, P. (2009), *Mahāyāna Buddhism: The Doctrinal Foundations*, 2nd edn, London: Routledge.

Winter, D. (2018), *Roots of War: Wanting Power, Seeing Threat, Justifying Force*, New York, NY: Oxford University Press.

Wolff, J. (2017), 'Karl Marx', in E. Zalta (ed.), *Stanford Encyclopedia of Philosophy*, https://plato.stanford.edu/entries/marx/.

Wood, A. (2004), *Karl Marx*, 2nd edn, London: Routledge.

Wright, E. O. (2018), *How to Be an Anti-Capitalist for the 21st Century*, London: Verso.

Wright, R. (2017), *Why Buddhism Is True: The Science and Philosophy of Meditation and Enlightenment*, New York: Simon and Schuster.

Wright, T. (tr.) (2005), *How to Cook Your Life: From the Zen Kitchen to Enlightenment*, Boulder, CO: Shambhala.

Yates, M. (2019), 'Why Capitalism Needs to Be Attacked with Equal Force on Every Front', *Canadian Dimension*, 2/1/2019, https://canadiandimension.com/articles/view/exploitation-andexpropriation-or-why-capitalism-must-be-attacked-with-equa.

Young, D. (2009), 'Bowing to Your Enemies: Courtesy, Budo and Japan', *Philosophy East and West* 59: 188–215; reprinted as ch. 12 of Priest and Young (2014).

Zidar, O. (2018), 'Tax Cuts for Whom? Heterogeneous Effects of Income Tax Changes on Growth and Employment', *Journal of Political Economy* 127: 1437–72.

Zuboff, S. (2019), *The Age of Surveillance Capitalism: The Fight for a Human Future at the New Frontier of Power*, New York, NY: Public Affairs.

INDEX

Printed in the United States
by Baker & Taylor Publisher Services